# DEVASTATION
# SPAWN

# TODD McFARLANE
## with CHANCE WOLF and DANI MIKI

# TITAN BOOKS
## in association with IMAGE COMICS

# THE STORY SO FAR...

The story I am about to tell you is beyond belief. For a start, I don't believe it, but that notwithstanding I ask that you listen with an open mind. It is a tale of life and death, damnation and rebirth, hope... and devastation.

It is a story of a man betrayed, by those he trusted and loved, by those he would have willingly died for. And did. His name was Al Simmons, and I, his best-friend, was one of those who betrayed him.

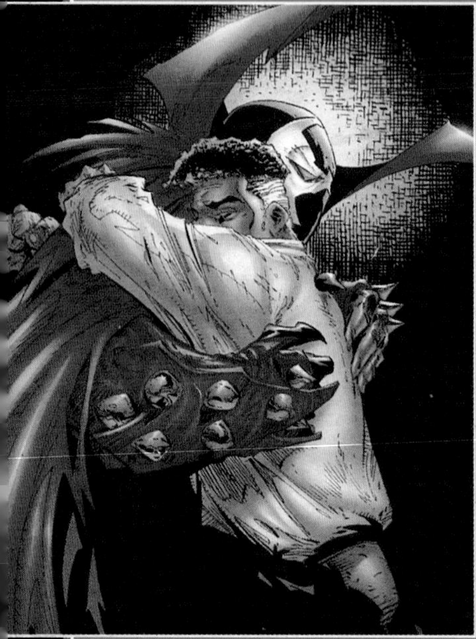

Let me tell you about Al. He was a man of integrity, who believed fervently in the ideals of God and Country. But Al's square-jawed patriotism became corrupted, tainted by the ways and wiles of the covert government agency for which he — and I, for that matter — worked. In fighting for the American dream, he became a part of the American nightmare. Black ops, wetwork, counter insurgency, euphemisms that draped murder and terrorism in the Stars & Stripes. The work exhumed a heart of darkness in Al, and ultimately damned him.

But at home he was everything a husband could be. Wanda was his life, the star around which he orbited, bathed in her love.

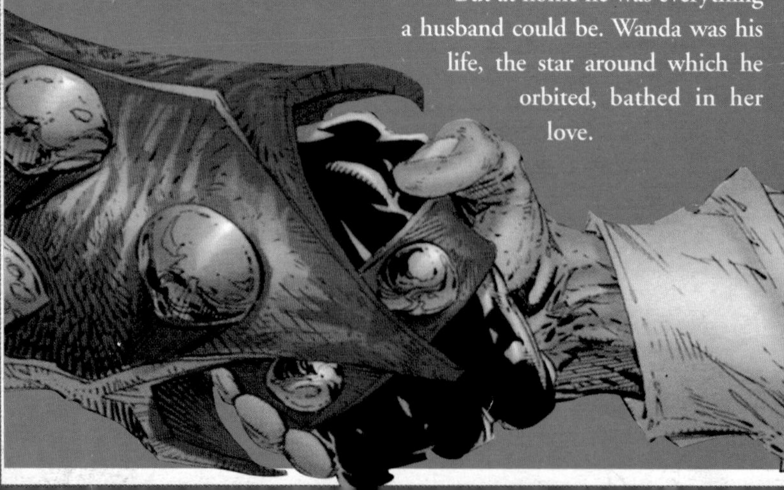

He gave her everything her heart desired... except a child.

Then, one day — and I admit, much of this has yet to be proven — Al's boss, a black, soulless pit of a human being called Jason Wynn, looked long and hard at his trained killer, deemed him a liability, judged his efficacy wanting, and issued the termination order. An assassin, we still don't know for sure who — it may or not have been Chapel, Wynn has many options where murder's concerned — struck, and Al was dead.

But the story doesn't end there. If anything, and I struggle to accept much of this myself, that's where it begins.

Five years passed, a span of time in which both Wanda and I grieved for Al, and in that mutual grief found comfort, companionship and ultimately love. We married, and had a child, Cyan. We were content, complete, and then everything went to Hell... literally.

A creature of the night appeared, haunting the periphery of our lives, a grim spectre both chillingly alien and uncomfortably familiar.

The creature was a Hellspawn, or Spawn, and in its wake came terror and death.

Much of what I now recount comes from the Spawn itself, and again — I stress — I believe only so much.

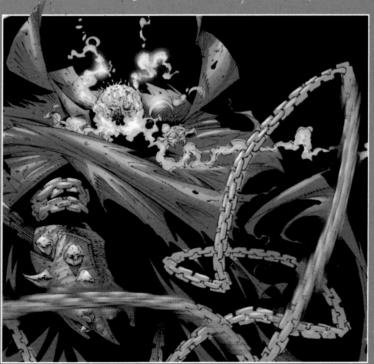

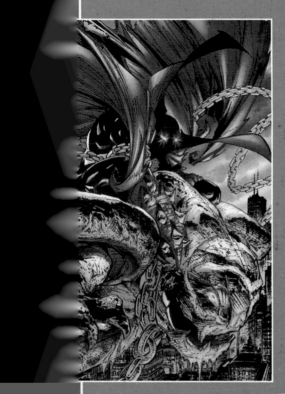

To accept it all is to court madness. The Spawn, you see, is Al Simmons, back from the dead, recreated by some unspeakable demon as a General in its army of damned souls. Al had struck a deal with the demon, Malebolgia he called it, and in return for his servitude was allowed to see Wanda again. Naturally, the demon failed to mention Al's horrifically altered appearance, his living symbiotic costume, or that Wanda and I were now married. It was hardly the teary reunion Al had likely anticipated.

And with Spawn came other demons — a vile clown with a predatory alter-ego, the Violator — Cyborgs, hunter Angels, genetically altered giant apes and all manner of unspeakable abominations. Chaos reigned, and Al's already shattered hopes were dragged deeper into the mire of despair. He felt betrayed at all turns; by Wynn, by Malebolgia and by me.

Helped by an enigmatic tutor named Cogliostro, Al/Spawn fashioned if not order, at least purpose, a focus for all his frustrations and anger. He dedicated himself to exposing and destroying Jason Wynn, the original author of his downfall. Wynn was involved in all manner of illegal and plainly immoral pursuits; arms trafficking, the funding of dictators, the toppling of governments, murder, extortion. You name it, Wynn had a concession.

Strangely, it transpired that both Al and I were working at the same goal from different angles. I'd come to realise myself that Wynn's hands were hardly clean, and manoeuvred myself into a position of trust that allowed me access to damning evidence of Wynn's malfeasance.

But Wynn is a canny opponent; certainly not one to be trifled with, and I fear that backed into a corner as he is, he is at his most dangerous. How long, I wonder, before it all comes home to roost, how long before I — and perhaps my family as well — must pay the Devil his due?

# 1

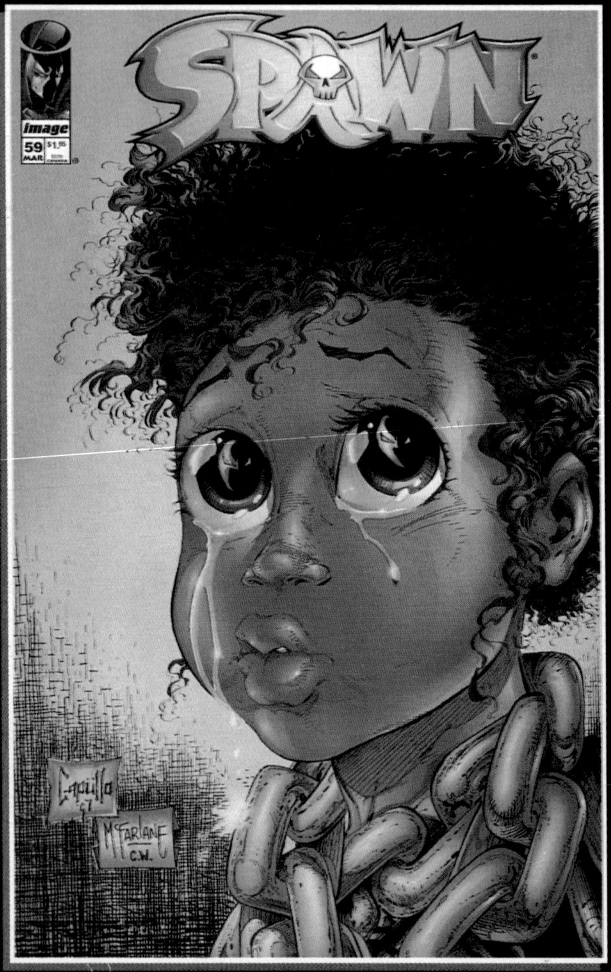

SPAWN
image
59
MAR
$1.95
Capullo
McFarlane
C.W.


# V A N I S H E D

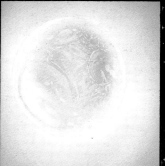

IT'S BEEN SAID THAT WE SHALL EACH REAP WHAT WE SOW. EVENTUALLY, THERE WILL OCCUR *A BALANCE* BASED ON THE CHOICES AND ACTIONS WE MAKE IN LIFE.

WHATEVER IS THEN CARRIED OUT UPON US AT DEATH IS NOT JUDGMENT, BUT *SENTENCING*,...

...FOR GOD IS MERELY FACILITATING OUR *SELF-DETERMINED FATE*...

...HAVING ALLOWED EACH OF US TO BE OUR OWN MASTERS.

TO BE IN CONTROL OF OUR DESTINIES.

WITH A MILLION PATHS TO CHOOSE FROM, ONLY **ONE** THING GUIDES US:

**GUILT.** THE INNER VOICE WE IGNORE AT OUR **PERIL**...

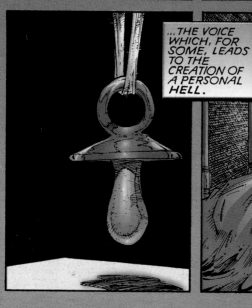

...THE VOICE WHICH, FOR SOME, LEADS TO THE CREATION OF A PERSONAL HELL.

SLEEP TIGHT, ANGEL.

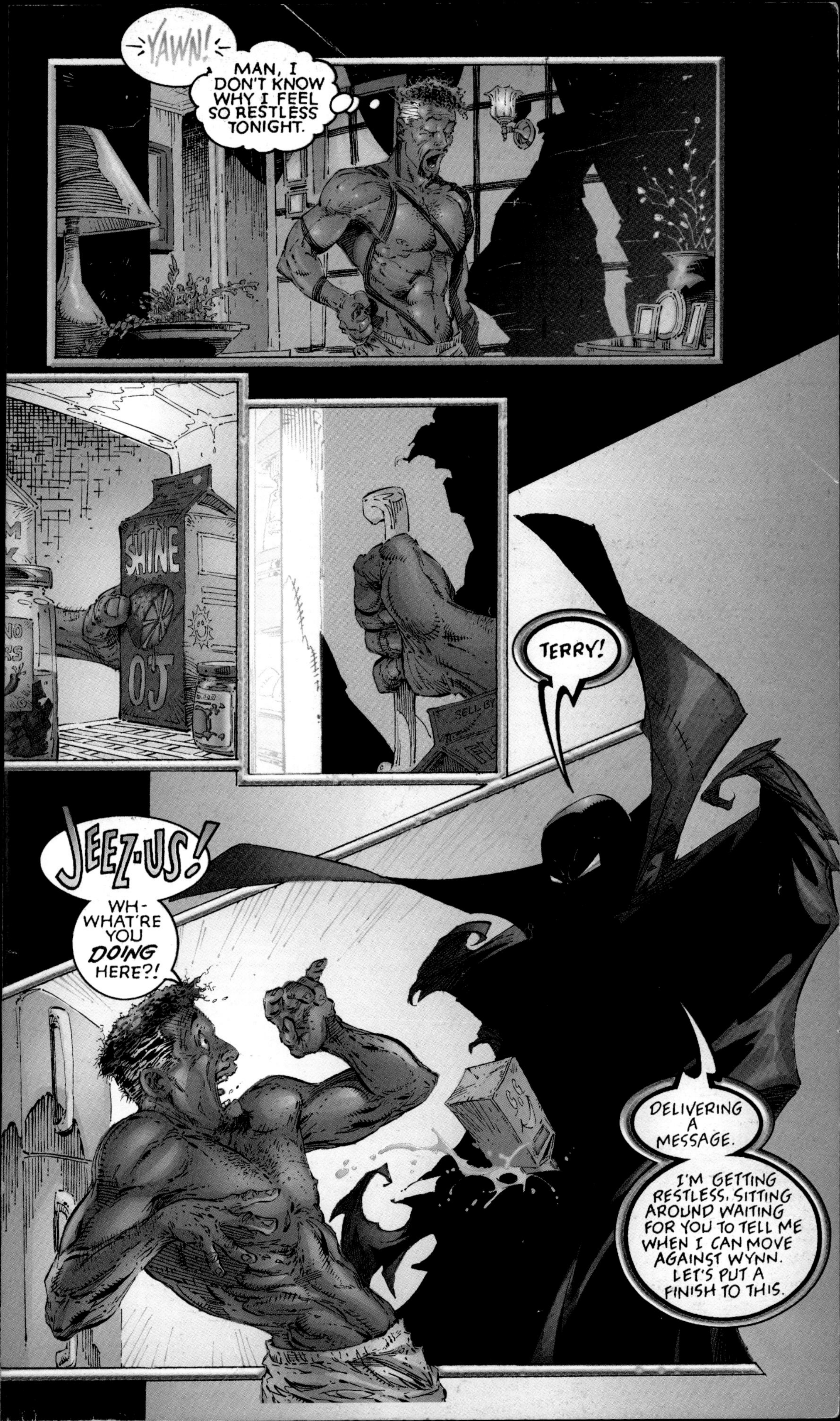
YAWN!
MAN, I DON'T KNOW WHY I FEEL SO RESTLESS TONIGHT.
SHINE OJ
SELL BY
TERRY!
JEEZ-US!
WH- WHAT'RE YOU DOING HERE?!
DELIVERING A MESSAGE.
I'M GETTING RESTLESS, SITTING AROUND WAITING FOR YOU TO TELL ME WHEN I CAN MOVE AGAINST WYNN. LET'S PUT A FINISH TO THIS.

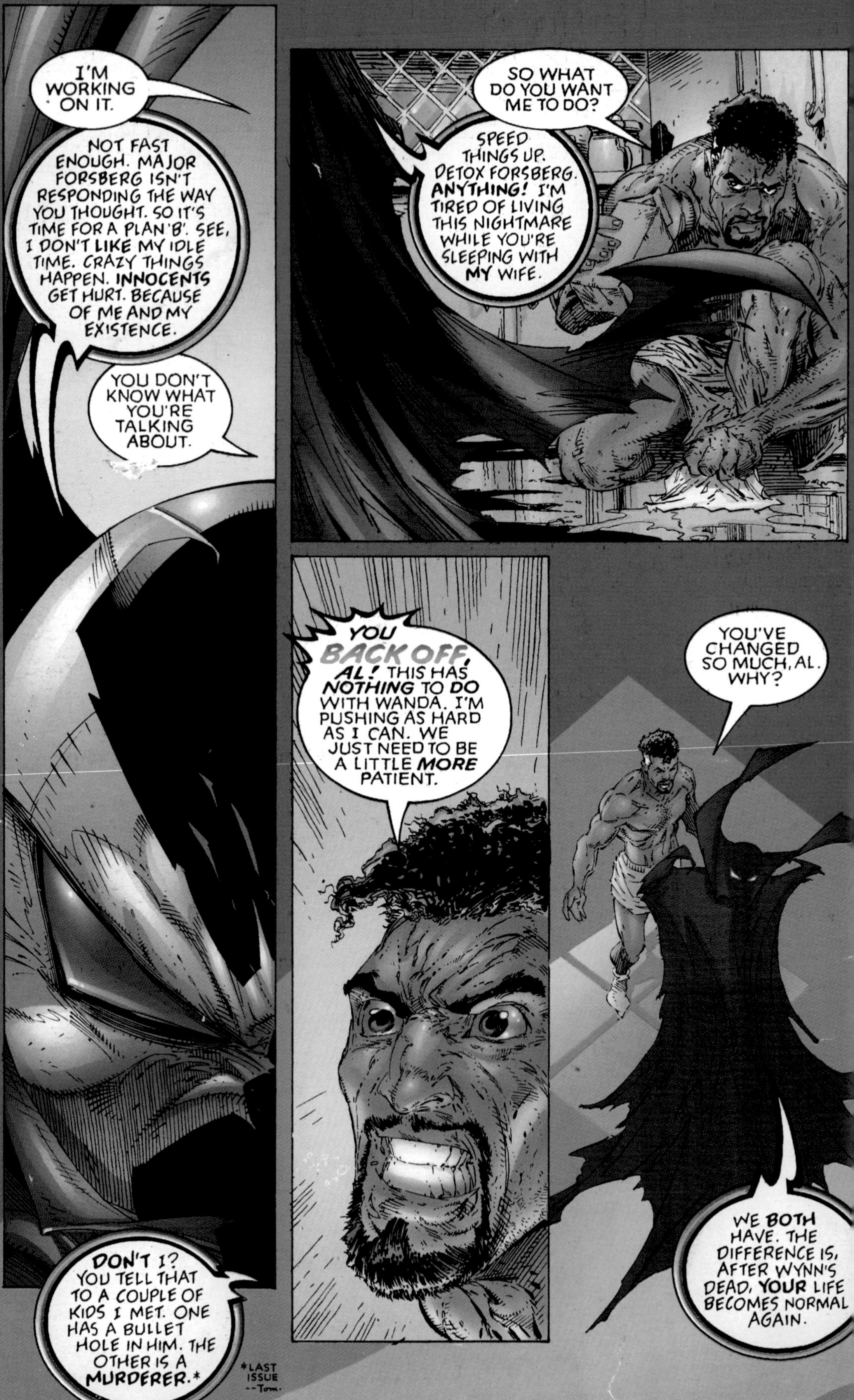
I'M WORKING ON IT.
NOT FAST ENOUGH. MAJOR FORSBERG ISN'T RESPONDING THE WAY YOU THOUGHT. SO IT'S TIME FOR A PLAN 'B'. SEE, I DON'T LIKE MY IDLE TIME. CRAZY THINGS HAPPEN. INNOCENTS GET HURT. BECAUSE OF ME AND MY EXISTENCE.
YOU DON'T KNOW WHAT YOU'RE TALKING ABOUT.
DON'T I? YOU TELL THAT TO A COUPLE OF KIDS I MET. ONE HAS A BULLET HOLE IN HIM. THE OTHER IS A MURDERER.*
*LAST ISSUE --Tom.
SO WHAT DO YOU WANT ME TO DO?
SPEED THINGS UP. DETOX FORSBERG. ANYTHING! I'M TIRED OF LIVING THIS NIGHTMARE WHILE YOU'RE SLEEPING WITH MY WIFE.
YOU BACK OFF, AL! THIS HAS NOTHING TO DO WITH WANDA. I'M PUSHING AS HARD AS I CAN. WE JUST NEED TO BE A LITTLE MORE PATIENT.
YOU'VE CHANGED SO MUCH, AL. WHY?
WE BOTH HAVE. THE DIFFERENCE IS, AFTER WYNN'S DEAD, YOUR LIFE BECOMES NORMAL AGAIN.

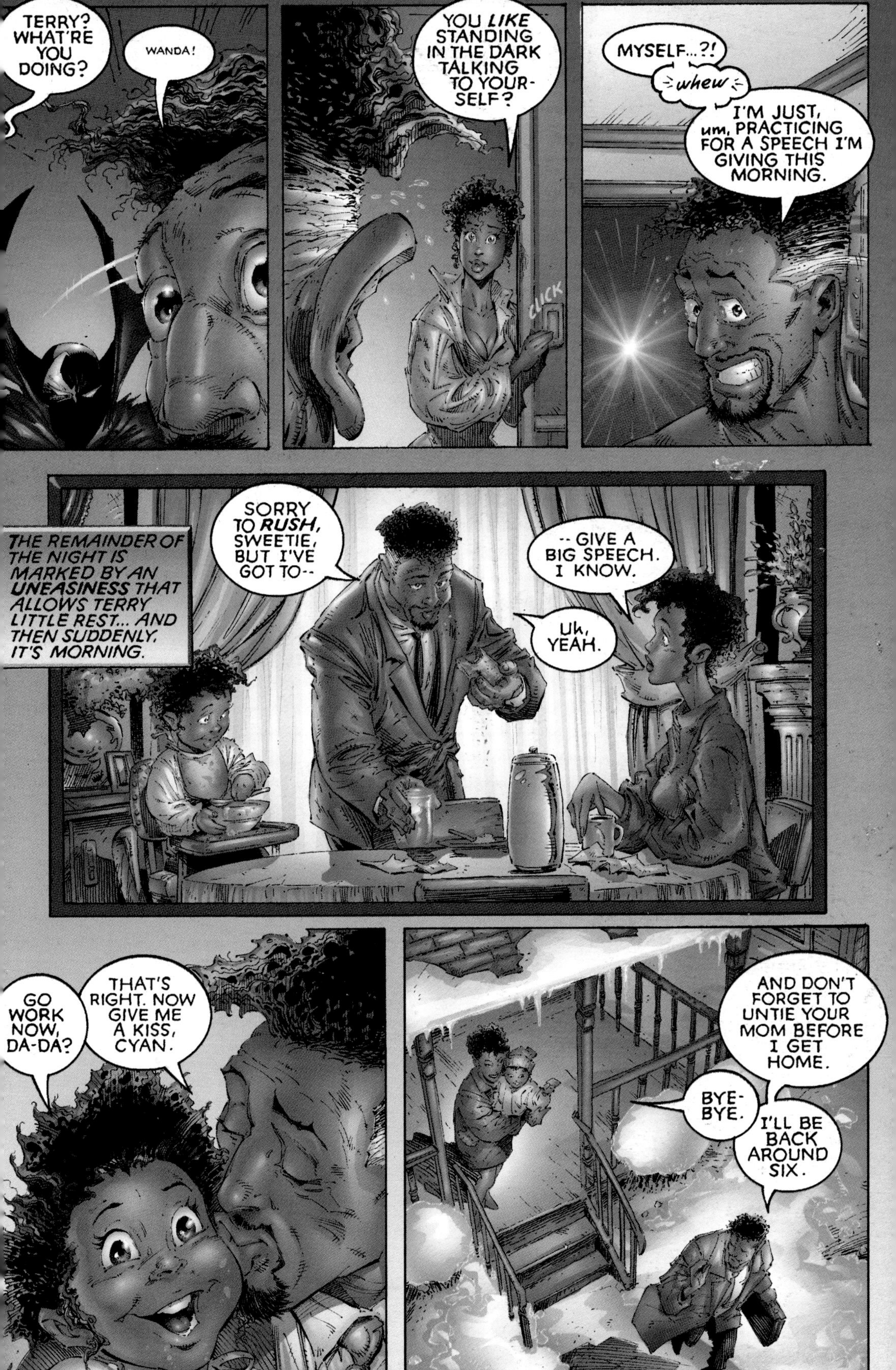
TERRY? WHAT'RE YOU DOING?
WANDA!
YOU LIKE STANDING IN THE DARK TALKING TO YOURSELF?
CLICK
MYSELF...?!
whew
I'M JUST, um, PRACTICING FOR A SPEECH I'M GIVING THIS MORNING.
THE REMAINDER OF THE NIGHT IS MARKED BY AN UNEASINESS THAT ALLOWS TERRY LITTLE REST... AND THEN SUDDENLY, IT'S MORNING.
SORRY TO RUSH, SWEETIE, BUT I'VE GOT TO--
-- GIVE A BIG SPEECH. I KNOW.
Uh, YEAH.
GO WORK NOW, DA-DA?
THAT'S RIGHT. NOW GIVE ME A KISS, CYAN.
AND DON'T FORGET TO UNTIE YOUR MOM BEFORE I GET HOME.
BYE-BYE.
I'LL BE BACK AROUND SIX.

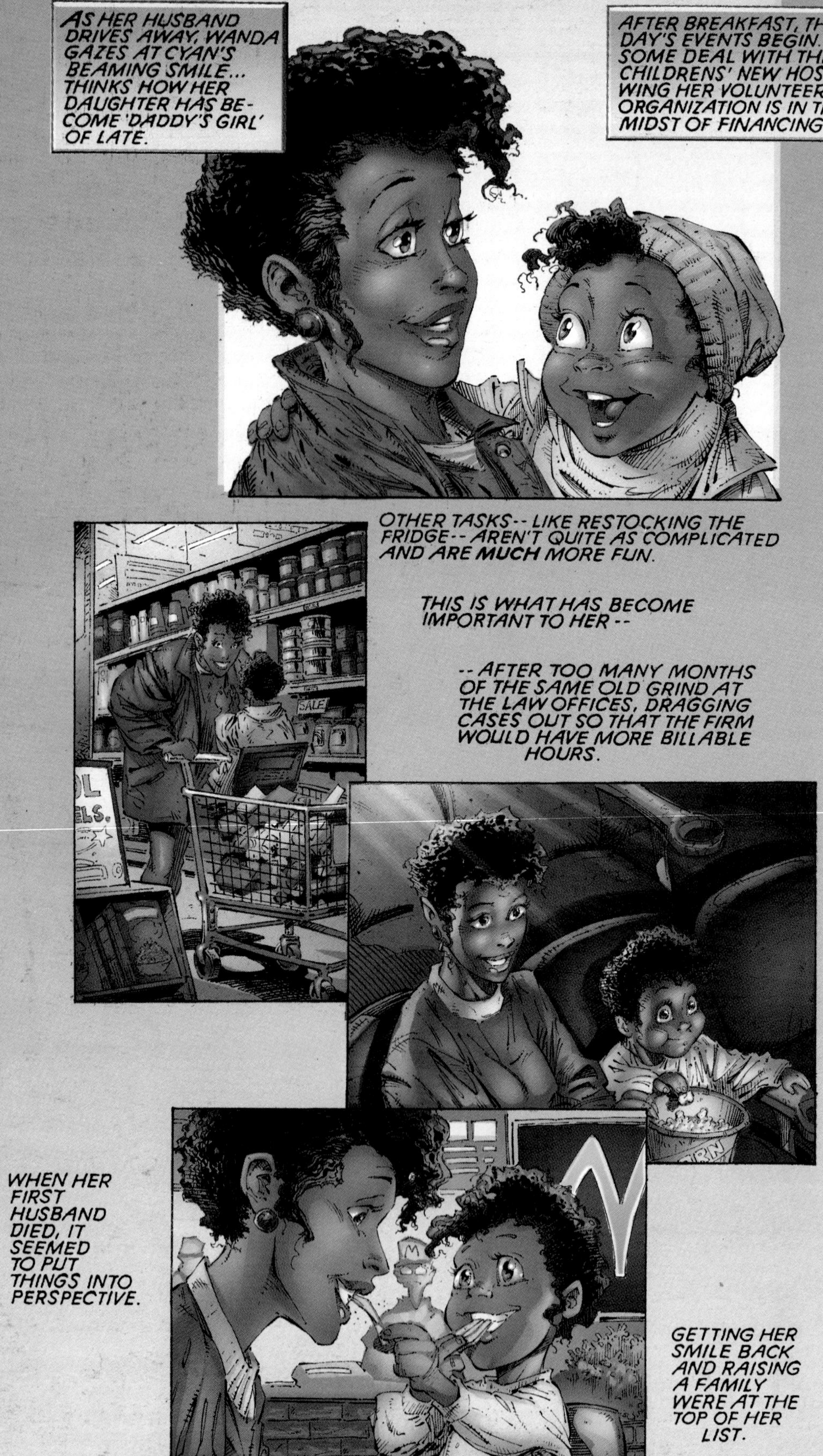

AS HER HUSBAND DRIVES AWAY, WANDA GAZES AT CYAN'S BEAMING SMILE... THINKS HOW HER DAUGHTER HAS BE-COME 'DADDY'S GIRL' OF LATE.
AFTER BREAKFAST, THE DAY'S EVENTS BEGIN. SOME DEAL WITH THE CHILDRENS' NEW HOSPITAL WING HER VOLUNTEER ORGANIZATION IS IN THE MIDST OF FINANCING.
OTHER TASKS-- LIKE RESTOCKING THE FRIDGE-- AREN'T QUITE AS COMPLICATED AND ARE **MUCH** MORE FUN.
SALE
THIS IS WHAT HAS BECOME IMPORTANT TO HER --
-- AFTER TOO MANY MONTHS OF THE SAME OLD GRIND AT THE LAW OFFICES, DRAGGING CASES OUT SO THAT THE FIRM WOULD HAVE MORE BILLABLE HOURS.
WHEN HER FIRST HUSBAND DIED, IT SEEMED TO PUT THINGS INTO PERSPECTIVE.
GETTING HER SMILE BACK AND RAISING A FAMILY WERE AT THE TOP OF HER LIST.

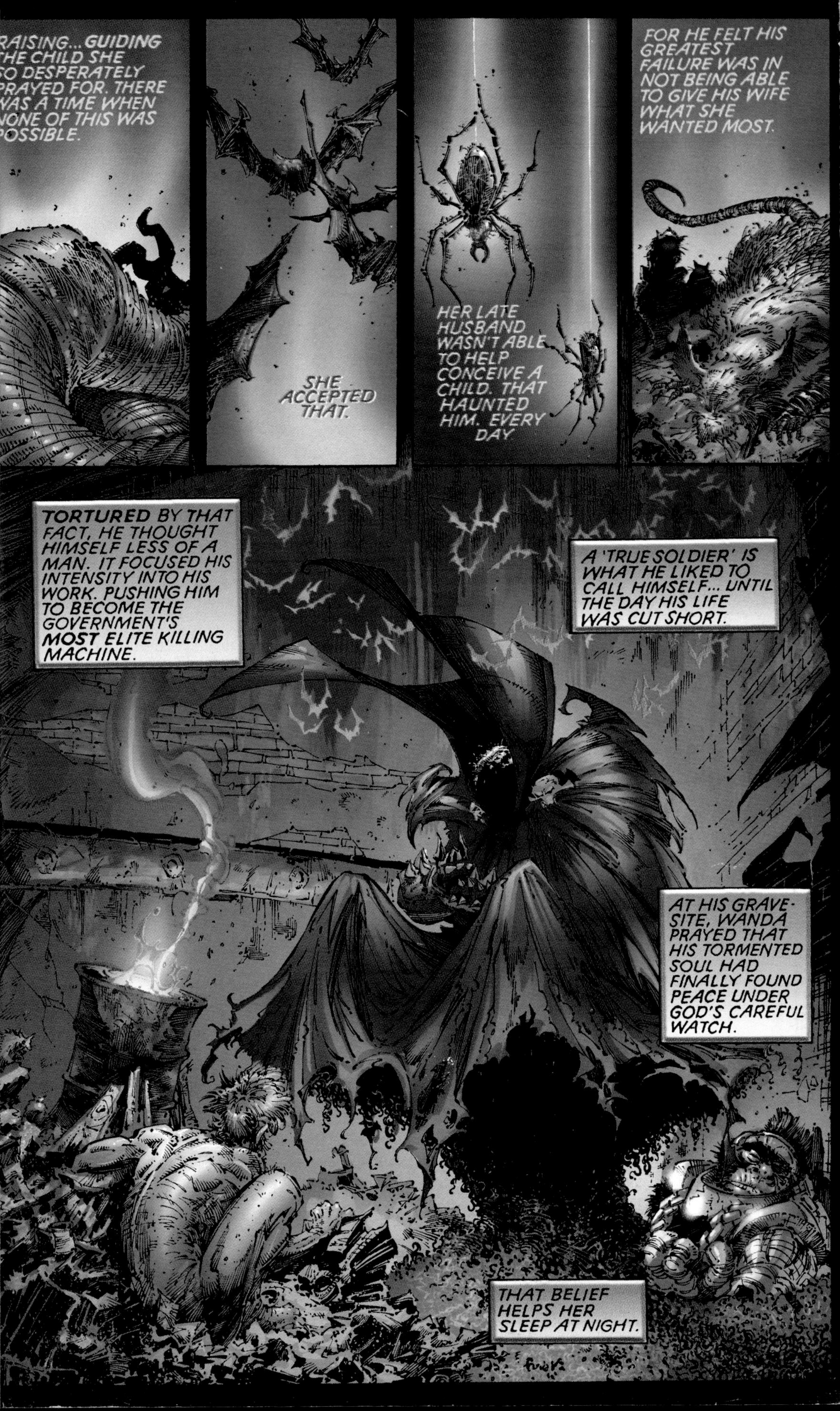

RAISING... GUIDING THE CHILD SHE SO DESPERATELY PRAYED FOR. THERE WAS A TIME WHEN NONE OF THIS WAS POSSIBLE.
SHE ACCEPTED THAT.
HER LATE HUSBAND WASN'T ABLE TO HELP CONCEIVE A CHILD. THAT HAUNTED HIM. EVERY DAY.
FOR HE FELT HIS GREATEST FAILURE WAS IN NOT BEING ABLE TO GIVE HIS WIFE WHAT SHE WANTED MOST.
TORTURED BY THAT FACT, HE THOUGHT HIMSELF LESS OF A MAN. IT FOCUSED HIS INTENSITY INTO HIS WORK. PUSHING HIM TO BECOME THE GOVERNMENT'S MOST ELITE KILLING MACHINE.
A 'TRUE SOLDIER' IS WHAT HE LIKED TO CALL HIMSELF... UNTIL THE DAY HIS LIFE WAS CUT SHORT.
AT HIS GRAVESITE, WANDA PRAYED THAT HIS TORMENTED SOUL HAD FINALLY FOUND PEACE UNDER GOD'S CAREFUL WATCH.
THAT BELIEF HELPS HER SLEEP AT NIGHT.

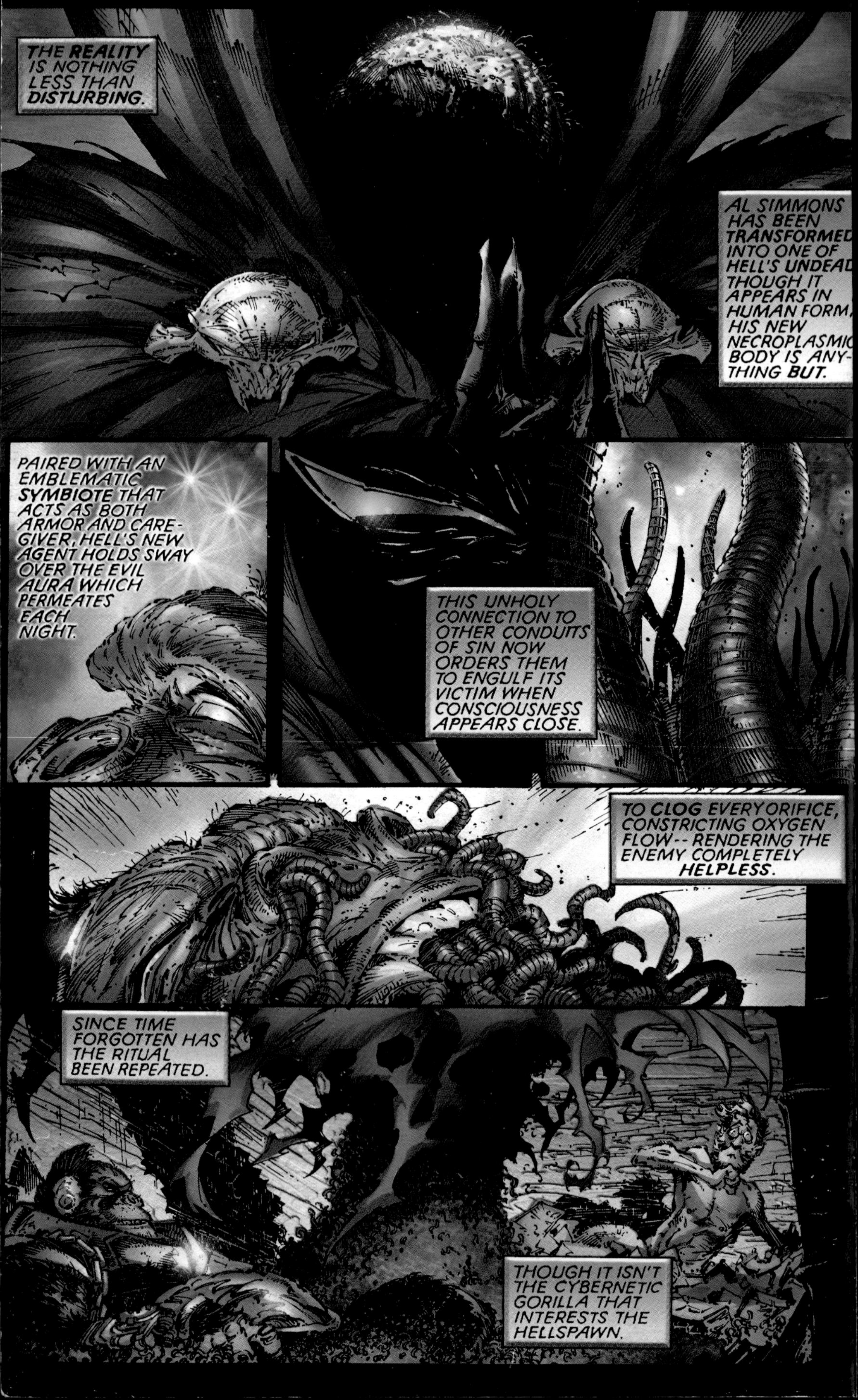
THE REALITY IS NOTHING LESS THAN DISTURBING.
AL SIMMONS HAS BEEN TRANSFORMED INTO ONE OF HELL'S UNDEAD. THOUGH IT APPEARS IN HUMAN FORM, HIS NEW NECROPLASMIC BODY IS ANYTHING BUT.
PAIRED WITH AN EMBLEMATIC SYMBIOTE THAT ACTS AS BOTH ARMOR AND CARE-GIVER, HELL'S NEW AGENT HOLDS SWAY OVER THE EVIL AURA WHICH PERMEATES EACH NIGHT.
THIS UNHOLY CONNECTION TO OTHER CONDUITS OF SIN NOW ORDERS THEM TO ENGULF ITS VICTIM WHEN CONSCIOUSNESS APPEARS CLOSE.
TO CLOG EVERY ORIFICE, CONSTRICTING OXYGEN FLOW-- RENDERING THE ENEMY COMPLETELY HELPLESS.
SINCE TIME FORGOTTEN HAS THE RITUAL BEEN REPEATED.
THOUGH IT ISN'T THE CYBERNETIC GORILLA THAT INTERESTS THE HELLSPAWN.

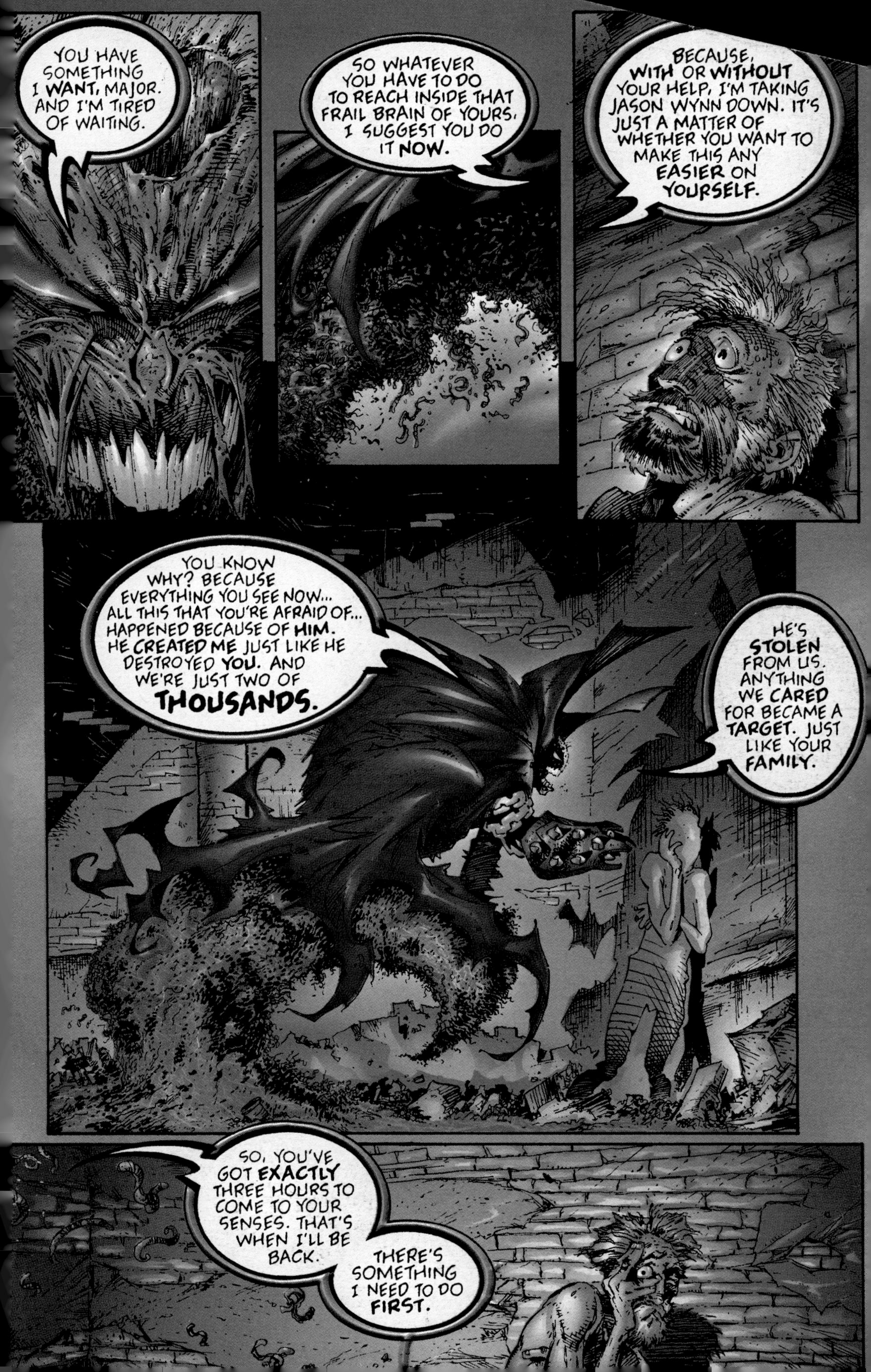
YOU HAVE SOMETHING I WANT, MAJOR. AND I'M TIRED OF WAITING.
SO WHATEVER YOU HAVE TO DO TO REACH INSIDE THAT FRAIL BRAIN OF YOURS, I SUGGEST YOU DO IT NOW.
BECAUSE, WITH OR WITHOUT YOUR HELP, I'M TAKING JASON WYNN DOWN. IT'S JUST A MATTER OF WHETHER YOU WANT TO MAKE THIS ANY EASIER ON YOURSELF.
YOU KNOW WHY? BECAUSE EVERYTHING YOU SEE NOW... ALL THIS THAT YOU'RE AFRAID OF... HAPPENED BECAUSE OF HIM. HE CREATED ME JUST LIKE HE DESTROYED YOU. AND WE'RE JUST TWO OF THOUSANDS.
HE'S STOLEN FROM US. ANYTHING WE CARED FOR BECAME A TARGET. JUST LIKE YOUR FAMILY.
SO, YOU'VE GOT EXACTLY THREE HOURS TO COME TO YOUR SENSES. THAT'S WHEN I'LL BE BACK.
THERE'S SOMETHING I NEED TO DO FIRST.

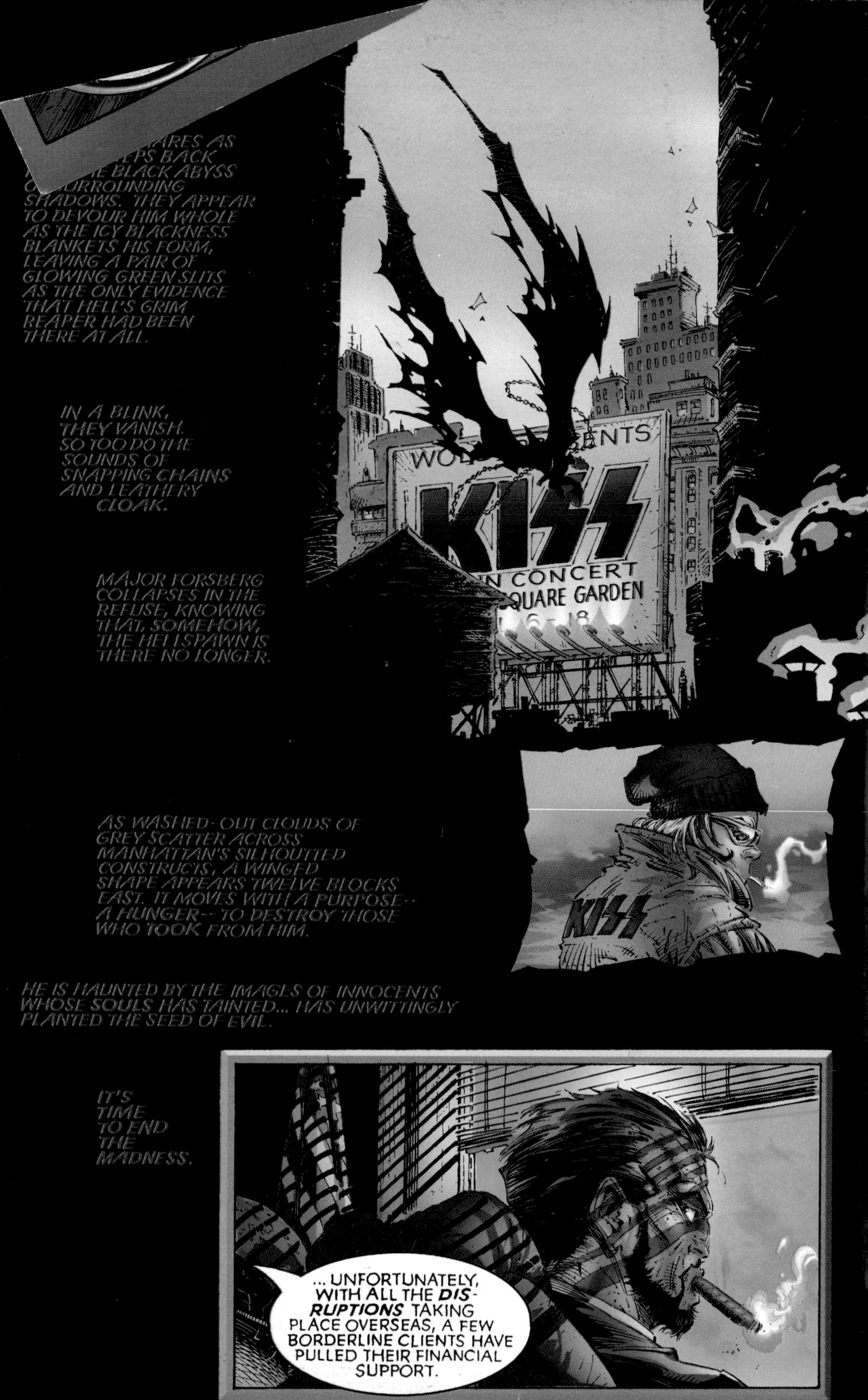

...RES AS
...EPS BACK
...E BLACK ABYSS
...URROUNDING
SHADOWS. THEY APPEAR
TO DEVOUR HIM WHOLE
AS THE ICY BLACKNESS
BLANKETS HIS FORM,
LEAVING A PAIR OF
GLOWING GREEN SLITS
AS THE ONLY EVIDENCE
THAT HELL'S GRIM
REAPER HAD BEEN
THERE AT ALL.
IN A BLINK, THEY VANISH. SO TOO DO THE SOUNDS OF SNAPPING CHAINS AND LEATHERY CLOAK.
KISS
IN CONCERT
SQUARE GARDEN
MAJOR FORSBERG COLLAPSES IN THE REFUSE, KNOWING THAT, SOMEHOW, THE HELLSPAWN IS THERE NO LONGER.
AS WASHED-OUT CLOUDS OF GREY SCATTER ACROSS MANHATTAN'S SILHOUTTED CONSTRUCTS, A WINGED SHAPE APPEARS TWELVE BLOCKS EAST. IT MOVES WITH A PURPOSE-- A HUNGER-- TO DESTROY THOSE WHO TOOK FROM HIM.
KISS
HE IS HAUNTED BY THE IMAGES OF INNOCENTS WHOSE SOULS HAS TAINTED... HAS UNWITTINGLY PLANTED THE SEED OF EVIL.
IT'S TIME TO END THE MADNESS.
...UNFORTUNATELY, WITH ALL THE DISRUPTIONS TAKING PLACE OVERSEAS, A FEW BORDERLINE CLIENTS HAVE PULLED THEIR FINANCIAL SUPPORT.

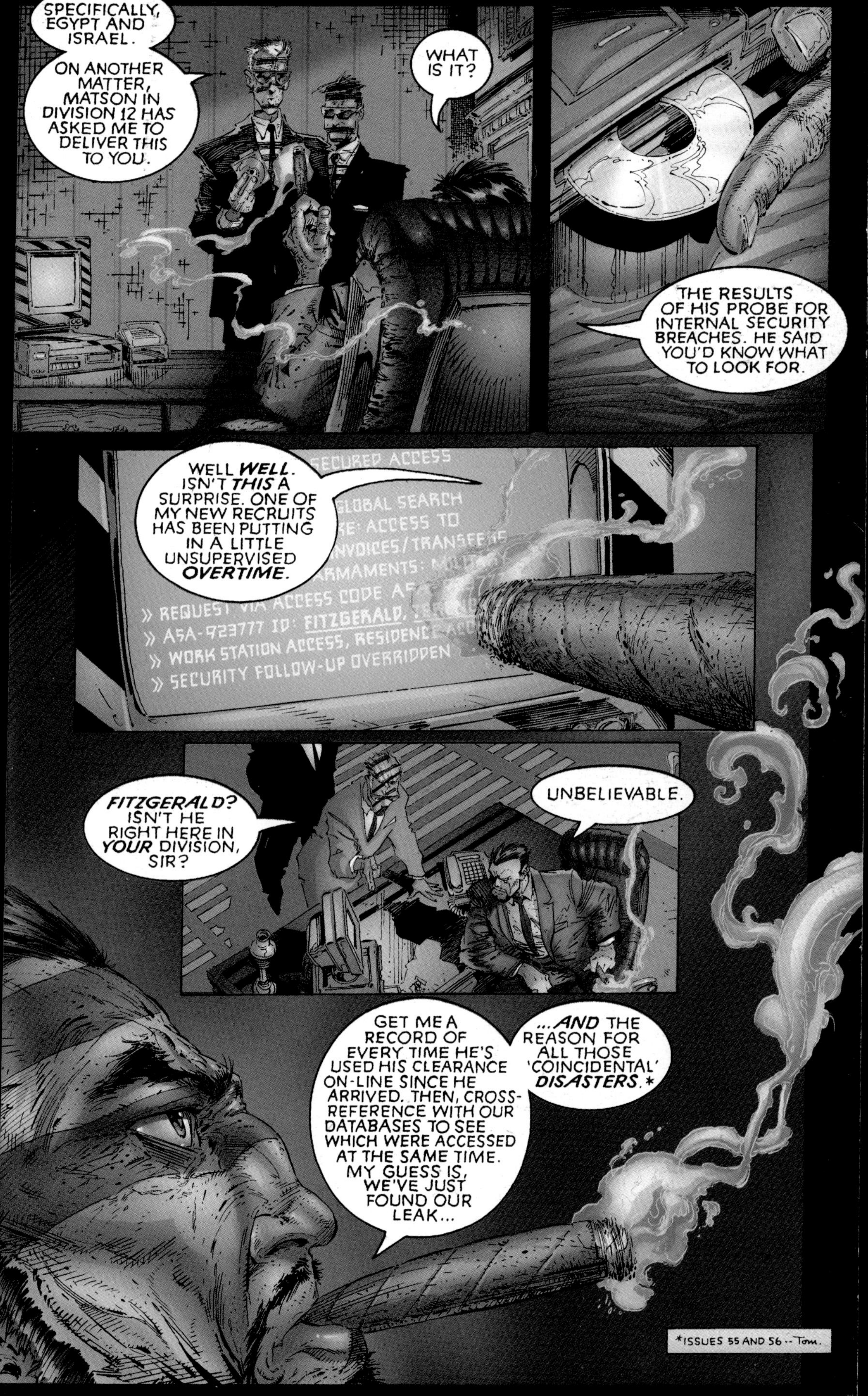
SPECIFICALLY, EGYPT AND ISRAEL.
ON ANOTHER MATTER, MATSON IN DIVISION 12 HAS ASKED ME TO DELIVER THIS TO YOU.
WHAT IS IT?
THE RESULTS OF HIS PROBE FOR INTERNAL SECURITY BREACHES. HE SAID YOU'D KNOW WHAT TO LOOK FOR.
WELL *WELL*. ISN'T *THIS* A SURPRISE. ONE OF MY NEW RECRUITS HAS BEEN PUTTING IN A LITTLE UNSUPERVISED *OVERTIME*.
SECURED ACCESS
GLOBAL SEARCH
» A5A-923777 ID: FITZGERALD,
» SECURITY FOLLOW-UP OVERRIDDEN
*FITZGERALD?* ISN'T HE RIGHT HERE IN *YOUR* DIVISION, SIR?
UNBELIEVABLE.
GET ME A RECORD OF EVERY TIME HE'S USED HIS CLEARANCE ON-LINE SINCE HE ARRIVED. THEN, CROSS-REFERENCE WITH OUR DATABASES TO SEE WHICH WERE ACCESSED AT THE SAME TIME. MY GUESS IS, WE'VE JUST FOUND OUR LEAK...
...*AND* THE REASON FOR ALL THOSE 'COINCIDENTAL' *DISASTERS*.*
*ISSUES 55 AND 56 -- Tom.

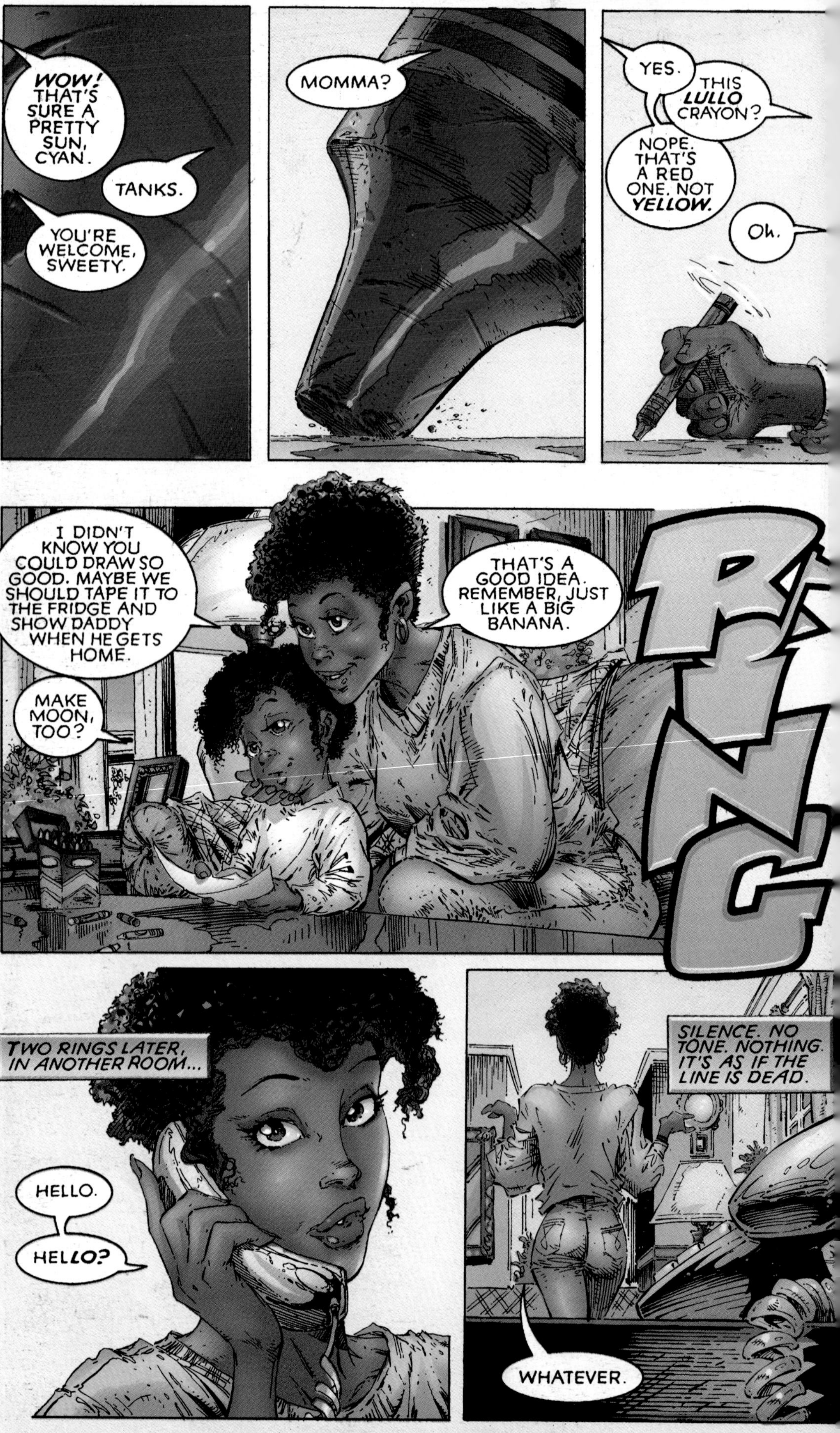

WOW! THAT'S SURE A PRETTY SUN, CYAN.
TANKS.
YOU'RE WELCOME, SWEETY.
MOMMA?
YES.
THIS LULLO CRAYON?
NOPE. THAT'S A RED ONE, NOT YELLOW.
Oh.
I DIDN'T KNOW YOU COULD DRAW SO GOOD. MAYBE WE SHOULD TAPE IT TO THE FRIDGE AND SHOW DADDY WHEN HE GETS HOME.
MAKE MOON, TOO?
THAT'S A GOOD IDEA. REMEMBER, JUST LIKE A BIG BANANA.
RING
TWO RINGS LATER, IN ANOTHER ROOM...
HELLO.
HELLO?
SILENCE. NO TONE. NOTHING. IT'S AS IF THE LINE IS DEAD.
WHATEVER.

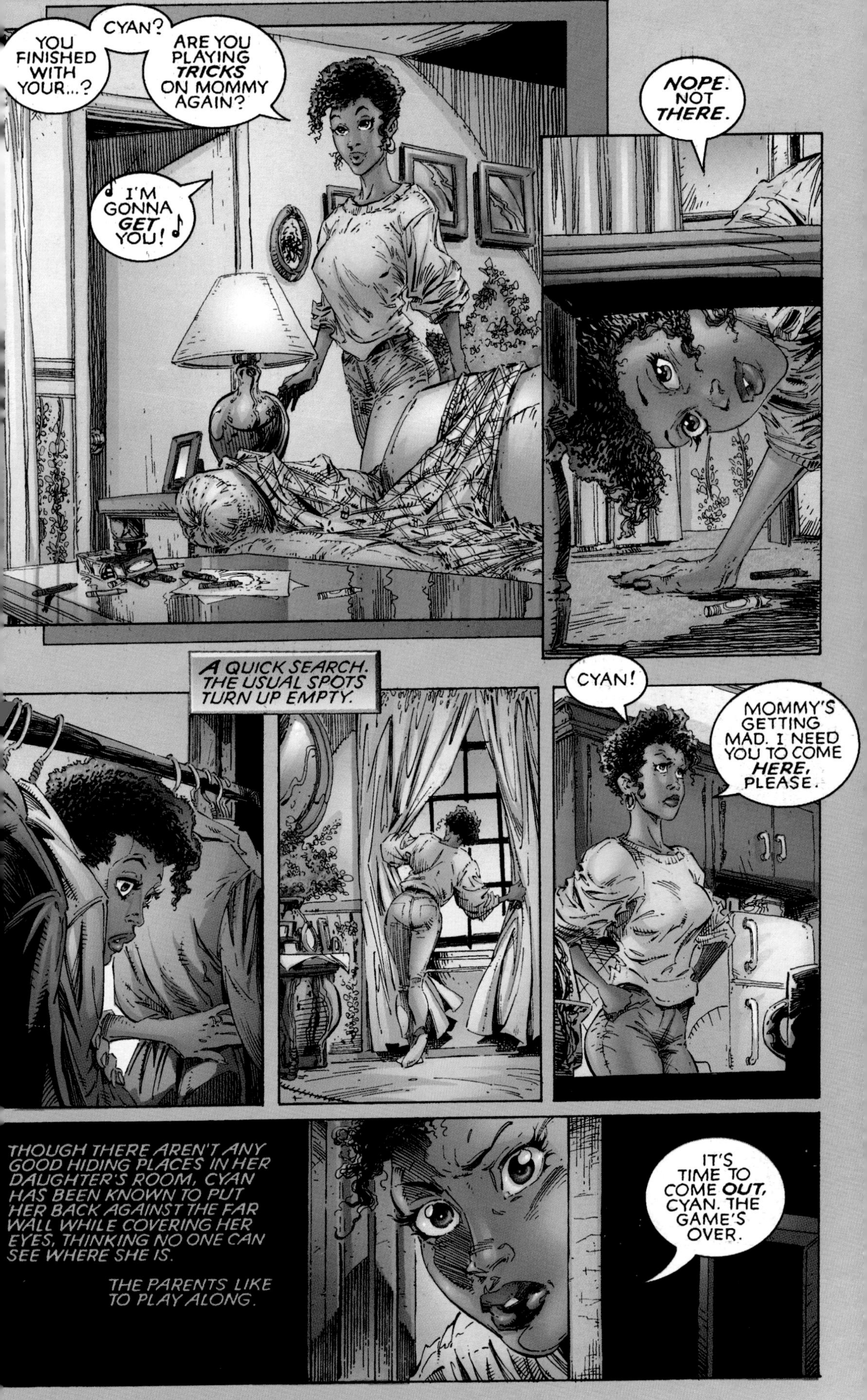
YOU FINISHED WITH YOUR...?
CYAN?
ARE YOU PLAYING TRICKS ON MOMMY AGAIN?
I'M GONNA GET YOU!
NOPE. NOT THERE.
A QUICK SEARCH. THE USUAL SPOTS TURN UP EMPTY.
CYAN!
MOMMY'S GETTING MAD. I NEED YOU TO COME HERE, PLEASE.
THOUGH THERE AREN'T ANY GOOD HIDING PLACES IN HER DAUGHTER'S ROOM, CYAN HAS BEEN KNOWN TO PUT HER BACK AGAINST THE FAR WALL WHILE COVERING HER EYES, THINKING NO ONE CAN SEE WHERE SHE IS.
THE PARENTS LIKE TO PLAY ALONG.
IT'S TIME TO COME OUT, CYAN. THE GAME'S OVER.

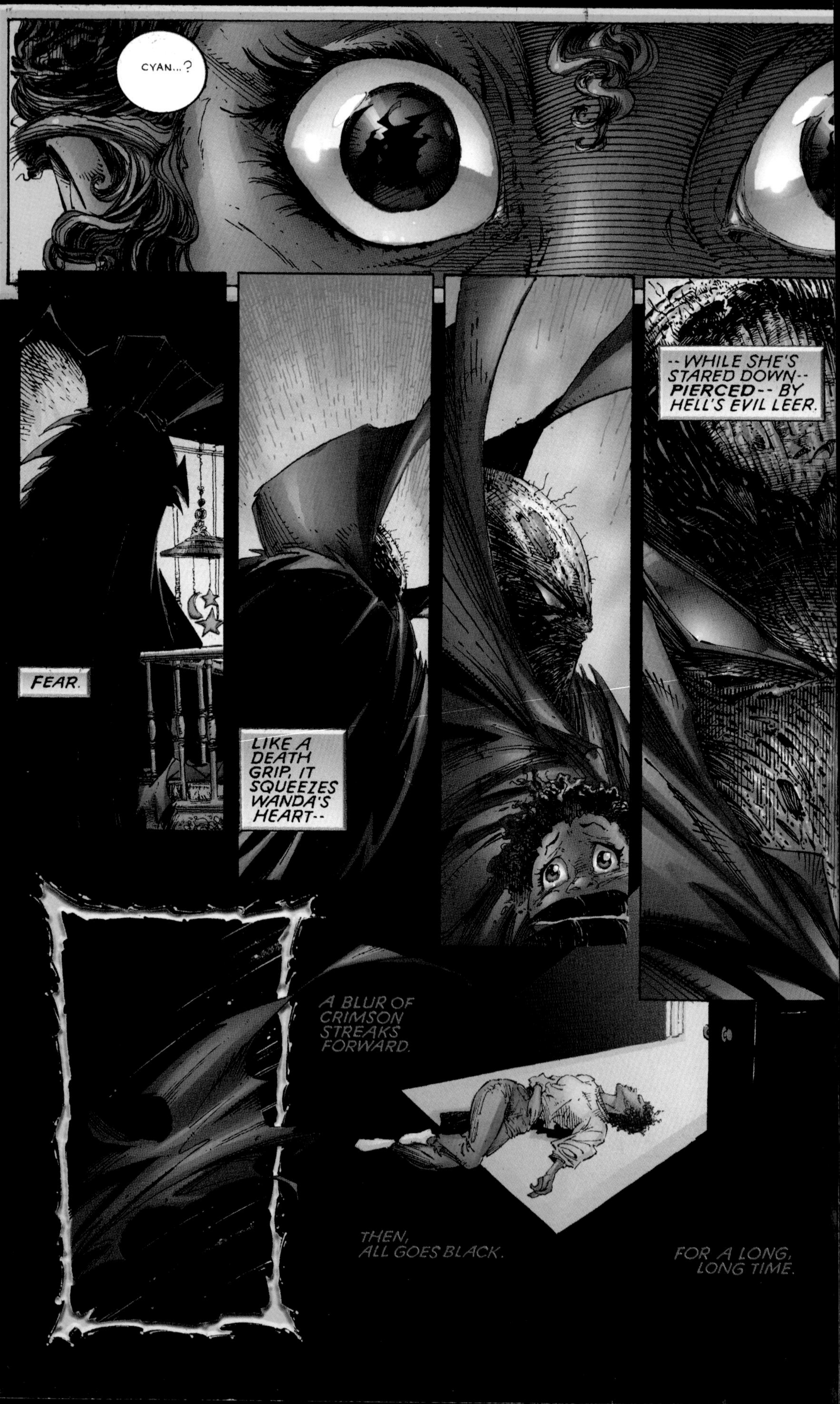
CYAN...?
FEAR.
LIKE A DEATH GRIP, IT SQUEEZES WANDA'S HEART--
--WHILE SHE'S STARED DOWN-- PIERCED-- BY HELL'S EVIL LEER.
A BLUR OF CRIMSON STREAKS FORWARD.
THEN, ALL GOES BLACK.
FOR A LONG, LONG TIME.

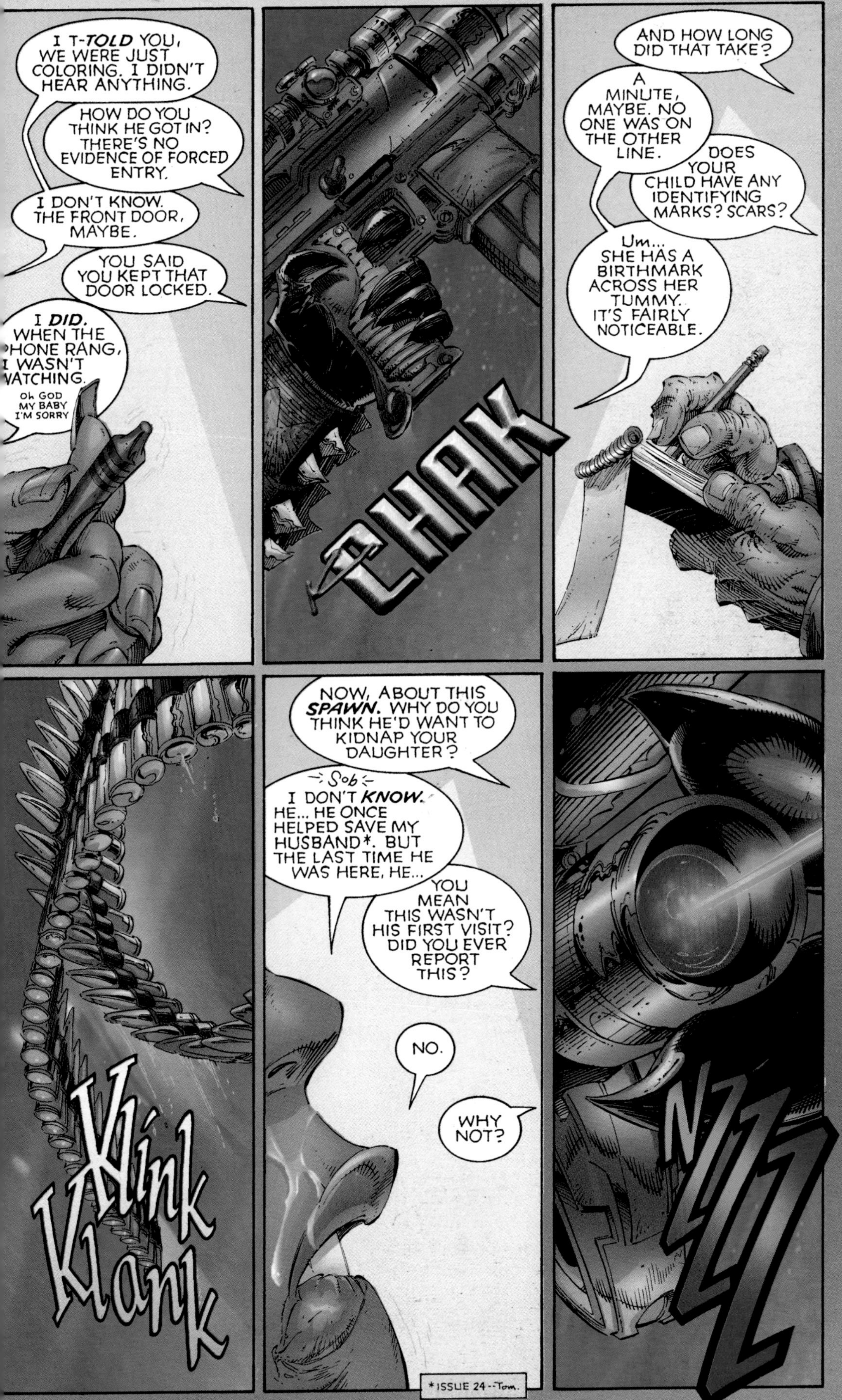

I T-TOLD YOU, WE WERE JUST COLORING. I DIDN'T HEAR ANYTHING.
HOW DO YOU THINK HE GOT IN? THERE'S NO EVIDENCE OF FORCED ENTRY.
I DON'T KNOW. THE FRONT DOOR, MAYBE.
YOU SAID YOU KEPT THAT DOOR LOCKED.
I DID. WHEN THE PHONE RANG, I WASN'T WATCHING.
Oh GOD MY BABY I'M SORRY
CHAK
AND HOW LONG DID THAT TAKE?
A MINUTE, MAYBE. NO ONE WAS ON THE OTHER LINE.
DOES YOUR CHILD HAVE ANY IDENTIFYING MARKS? SCARS?
Um... SHE HAS A BIRTHMARK ACROSS HER TUMMY. IT'S FAIRLY NOTICEABLE.
Klink Klank
NOW, ABOUT THIS SPAWN. WHY DO YOU THINK HE'D WANT TO KIDNAP YOUR DAUGHTER?
Sob
I DON'T KNOW. HE... HE ONCE HELPED SAVE MY HUSBAND*. BUT THE LAST TIME HE WAS HERE, HE...
YOU MEAN THIS WASN'T HIS FIRST VISIT? DID YOU EVER REPORT THIS?
NO.
WHY NOT?
*ISSUE 24--Tom.
NZZ

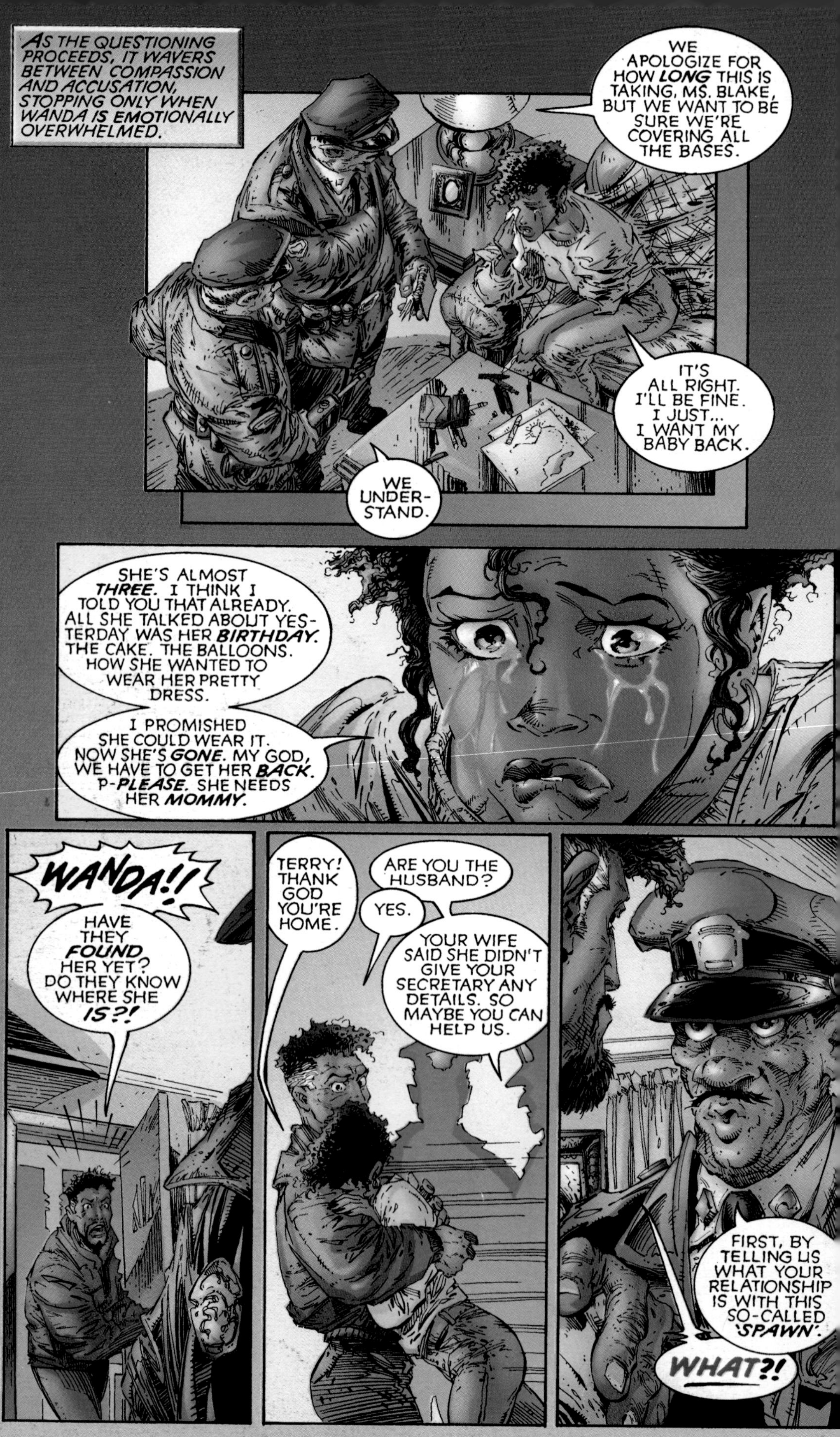

AS THE QUESTIONING PROCEEDS, IT WAVERS BETWEEN COMPASSION AND ACCUSATION, STOPPING ONLY WHEN WANDA IS EMOTIONALLY OVERWHELMED.
WE APOLOGIZE FOR HOW LONG THIS IS TAKING, MS. BLAKE, BUT WE WANT TO BE SURE WE'RE COVERING ALL THE BASES.
IT'S ALL RIGHT. I'LL BE FINE. I JUST... I WANT MY BABY BACK.
WE UNDER-STAND.
SHE'S ALMOST THREE. I THINK I TOLD YOU THAT ALREADY. ALL SHE TALKED ABOUT YES-TERDAY WAS HER BIRTHDAY. THE CAKE. THE BALLOONS. HOW SHE WANTED TO WEAR HER PRETTY DRESS.
I PROMISED SHE COULD WEAR IT. NOW SHE'S GONE. MY GOD, WE HAVE TO GET HER BACK. P-PLEASE. SHE NEEDS HER MOMMY.
WANDA!!
HAVE THEY FOUND HER YET? DO THEY KNOW WHERE SHE IS?!
TERRY! THANK GOD YOU'RE HOME.
ARE YOU THE HUSBAND?
YES.
YOUR WIFE SAID SHE DIDN'T GIVE YOUR SECRETARY ANY DETAILS. SO MAYBE YOU CAN HELP US.
FIRST, BY TELLING US WHAT YOUR RELATIONSHIP IS WITH THIS SO-CALLED 'SPAWN'.
WHAT?!

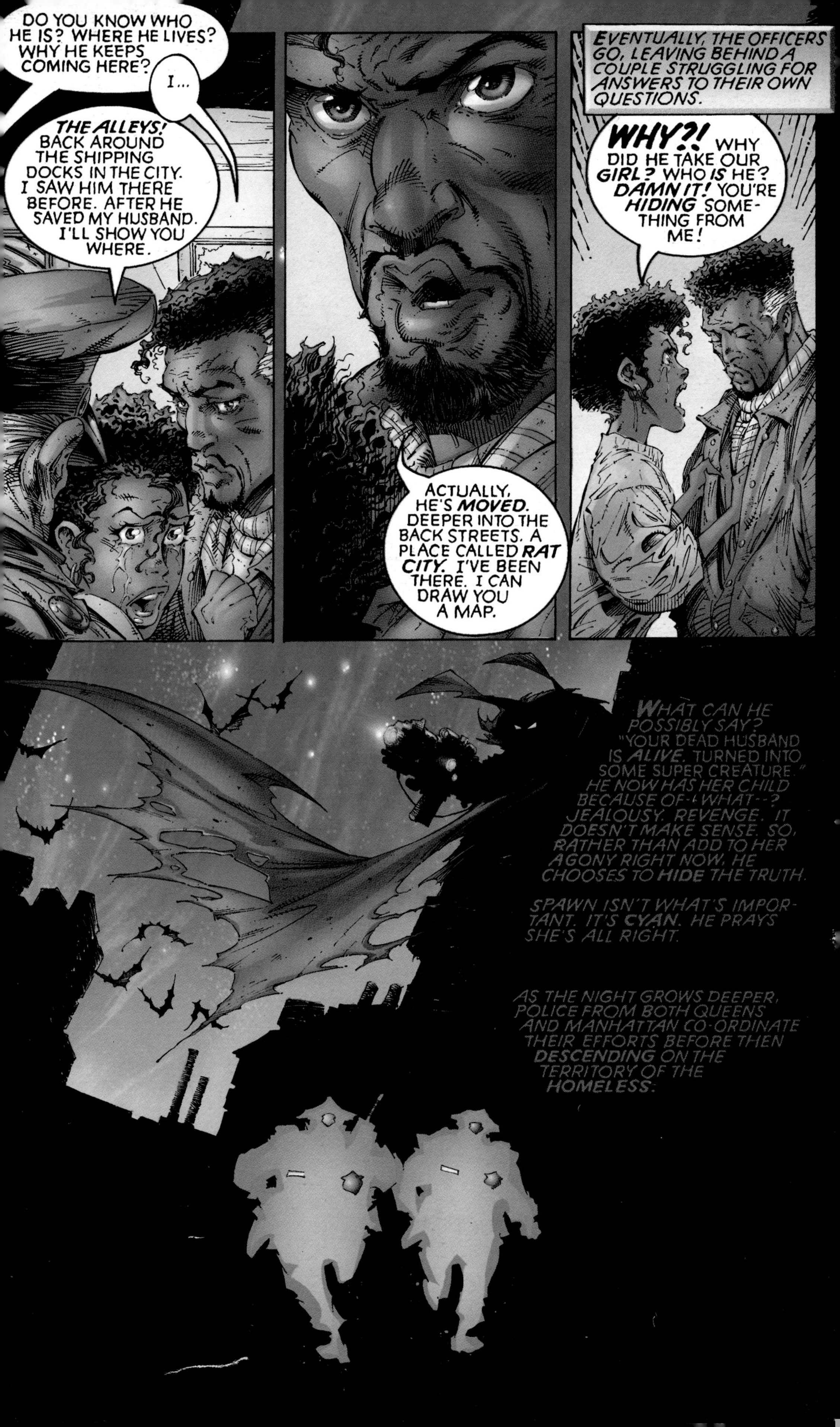
DO YOU KNOW WHO HE IS? WHERE HE LIVES? WHY HE KEEPS COMING HERE?
I...
THE ALLEYS! BACK AROUND THE SHIPPING DOCKS IN THE CITY. I SAW HIM THERE BEFORE. AFTER HE SAVED MY HUSBAND. I'LL SHOW YOU WHERE.
ACTUALLY, HE'S MOVED. DEEPER INTO THE BACK STREETS. A PLACE CALLED RAT CITY. I'VE BEEN THERE. I CAN DRAW YOU A MAP.
EVENTUALLY, THE OFFICERS GO, LEAVING BEHIND A COUPLE STRUGGLING FOR ANSWERS TO THEIR OWN QUESTIONS.
WHY?! WHY DID HE TAKE OUR GIRL? WHO IS HE? DAMN IT! YOU'RE HIDING SOMETHING FROM ME!
WHAT CAN HE POSSIBLY SAY? "YOUR DEAD HUSBAND IS ALIVE. TURNED INTO SOME SUPER CREATURE." HE NOW HAS HER CHILD BECAUSE OF--WHAT--? JEALOUSY. REVENGE. IT DOESN'T MAKE SENSE. SO, RATHER THAN ADD TO HER AGONY RIGHT NOW, HE CHOOSES TO HIDE THE TRUTH.
SPAWN ISN'T WHAT'S IMPORTANT. IT'S CYAN. HE PRAYS SHE'S ALL RIGHT.
AS THE NIGHT GROWS DEEPER, POLICE FROM BOTH QUEENS AND MANHATTAN CO-ORDINATE THEIR EFFORTS BEFORE THEN DESCENDING ON THE TERRITORY OF THE HOMELESS.

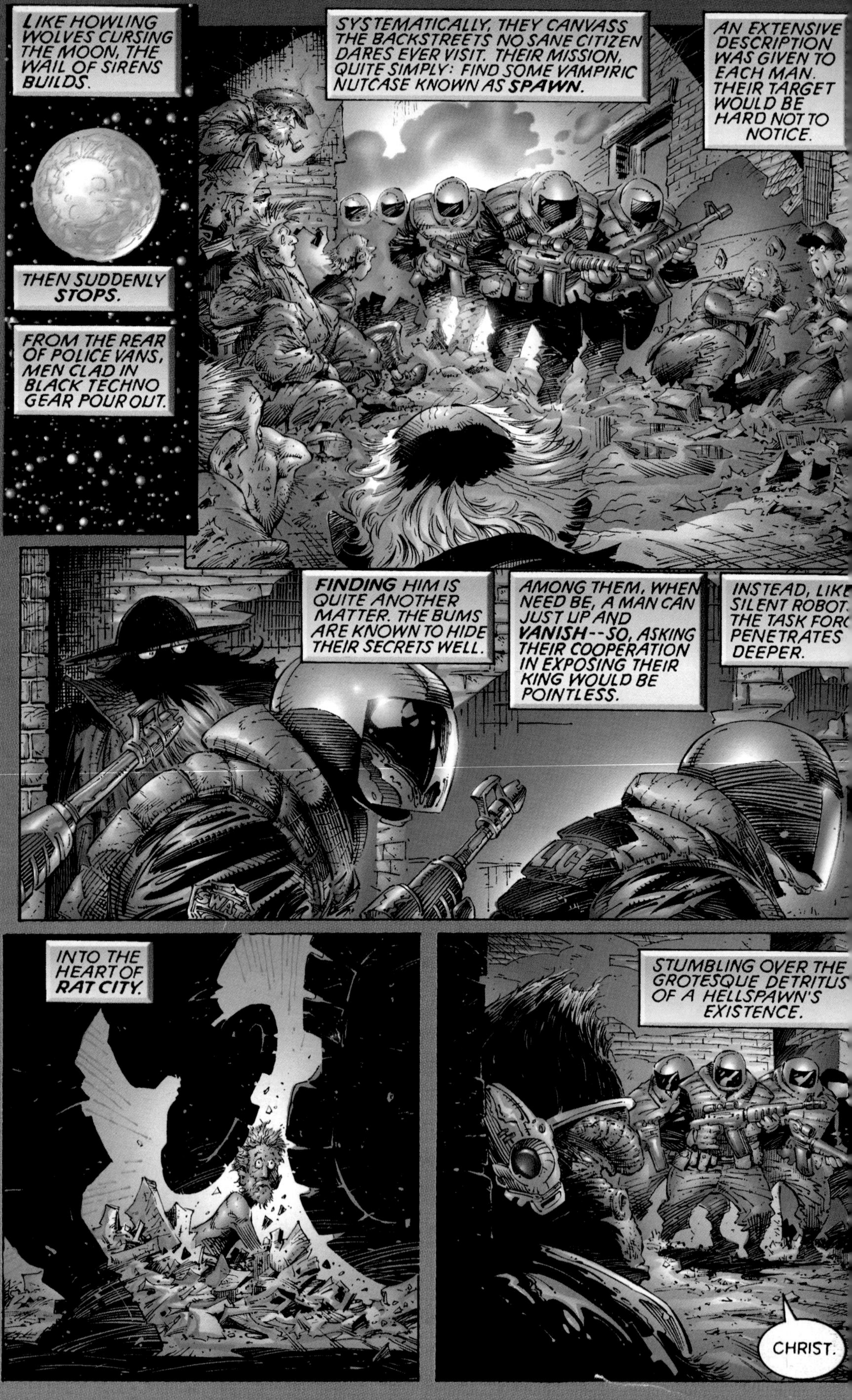

LIKE HOWLING WOLVES CURSING THE MOON, THE WAIL OF SIRENS BUILDS.
THEN SUDDENLY STOPS.
FROM THE REAR OF POLICE VANS, MEN CLAD IN BLACK TECHNO GEAR POUR OUT.
SYSTEMATICALLY, THEY CANVASS THE BACKSTREETS NO SANE CITIZEN DARES EVER VISIT. THEIR MISSION, QUITE SIMPLY: FIND SOME VAMPIRIC NUTCASE KNOWN AS SPAWN.
AN EXTENSIVE DESCRIPTION WAS GIVEN TO EACH MAN. THEIR TARGET WOULD BE HARD NOT TO NOTICE.
FINDING HIM IS QUITE ANOTHER MATTER. THE BUMS ARE KNOWN TO HIDE THEIR SECRETS WELL.
AMONG THEM, WHEN NEED BE, A MAN CAN JUST UP AND VANISH--SO, ASKING THEIR COOPERATION IN EXPOSING THEIR KING WOULD BE POINTLESS.
INSTEAD, LIKE SILENT ROBOT THE TASK FORC PENETRATES DEEPER.
INTO THE HEART OF RAT CITY.
STUMBLING OVER THE GROTESQUE DETRITUS OF A HELLSPAWN'S EXISTENCE.
CHRIST.

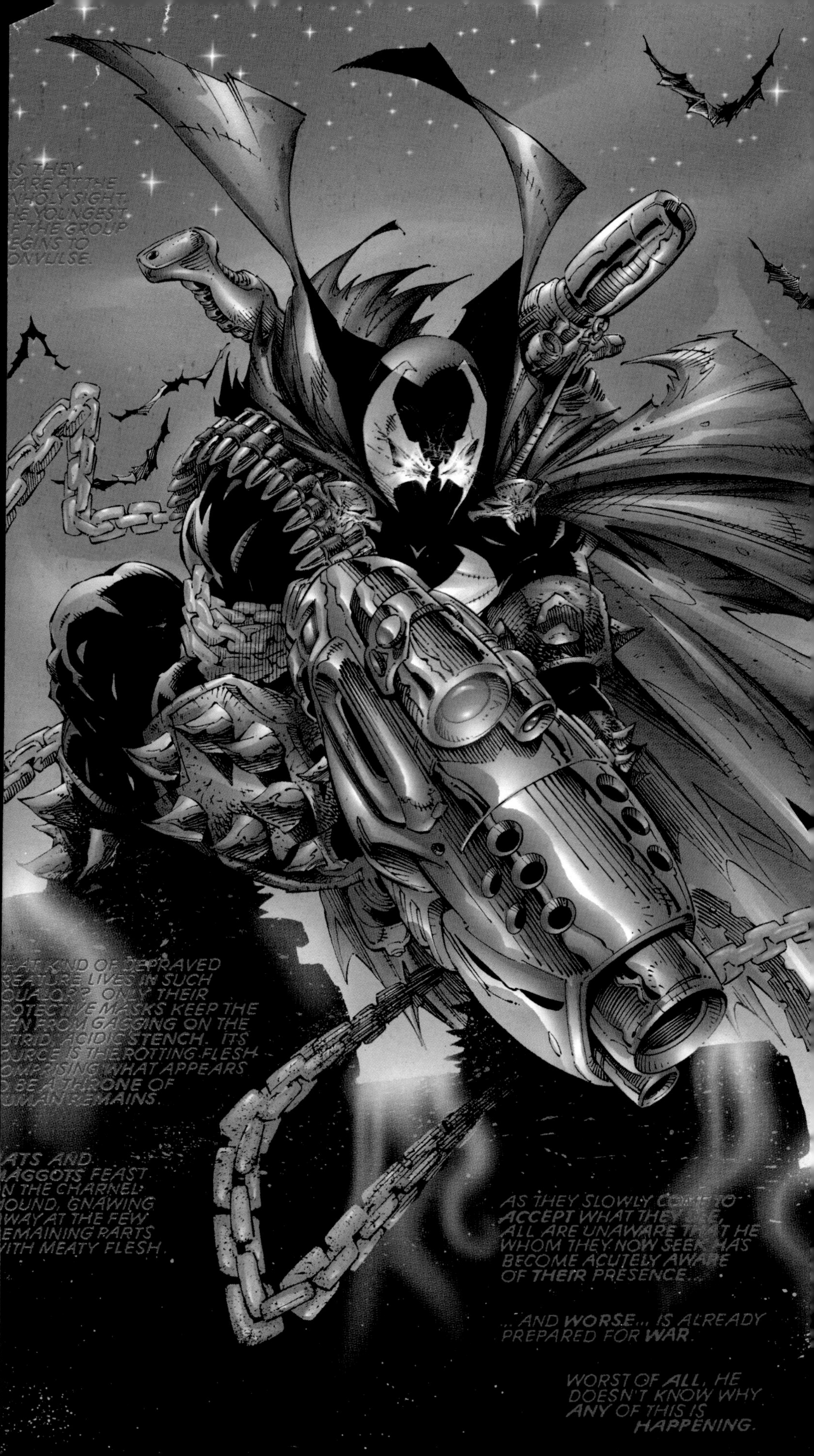

S THEY TARE AT THE NHOLY SIGHT HE YOUNGEST F THE GROUP EGINS TO ONVULSE.
AT KIND OF DEPRAVED REATURE LIVES IN SUCH QUALOR? ONLY THEIR ROTECTIVE MASKS KEEP THE EN FROM GAGGING ON THE UTRID, ACIDIC STENCH. ITS OURCE IS THE ROTTING FLESH OMPRISING WHAT APPEARS O BE A THRONE OF UMAN REMAINS.
ATS AND AGGOTS FEAST N THE CHARNEL OUND, GNAWING WAY AT THE FEW EMAINING PARTS VITH MEATY FLESH.
AS THEY SLOWLY COME TO ACCEPT WHAT THEY SEE, ALL ARE UNAWARE THAT HE WHOM THEY NOW SEEK HAS BECOME ACUTELY AWARE OF THEIR PRESENCE...
...AND WORSE... IS ALREADY PREPARED FOR WAR.
WORST OF ALL, HE DOESN'T KNOW WHY ANY OF THIS IS HAPPENING.

THIS IS ACTUALLY FUN!
JUST DEPENDS ON YOUR INTERPRETATION.
WHAT YOU ARTLESS HUMANS SEE AS A SUN WITH RAYS OF LIGHT JUTTING OUTWARD, I SEE AS A HEAD BEING PIERCED BY A BUNCHA NAILS.
WHA'CHA THINK?
GOOD.
BUT NOT GREAT, hnh? YOU THINK YOU'RE SO DAMN CLEVER, DON'T YOU?

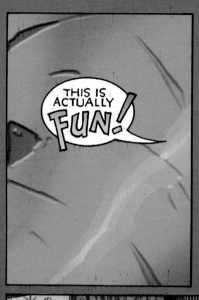

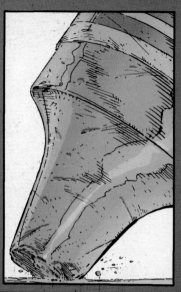

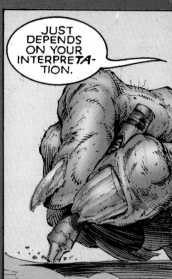

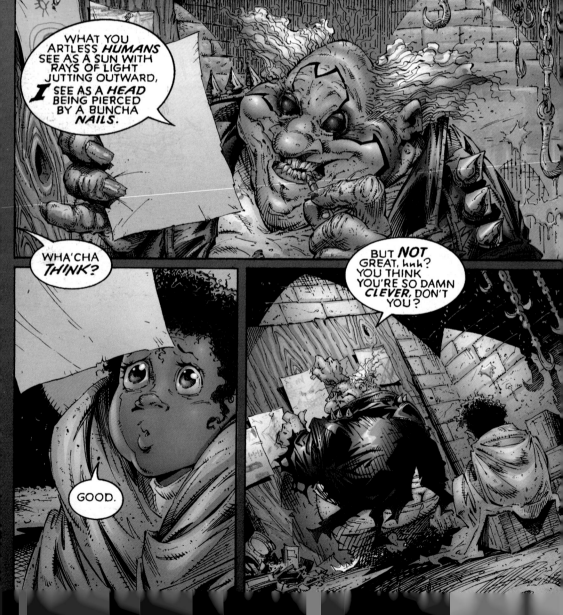

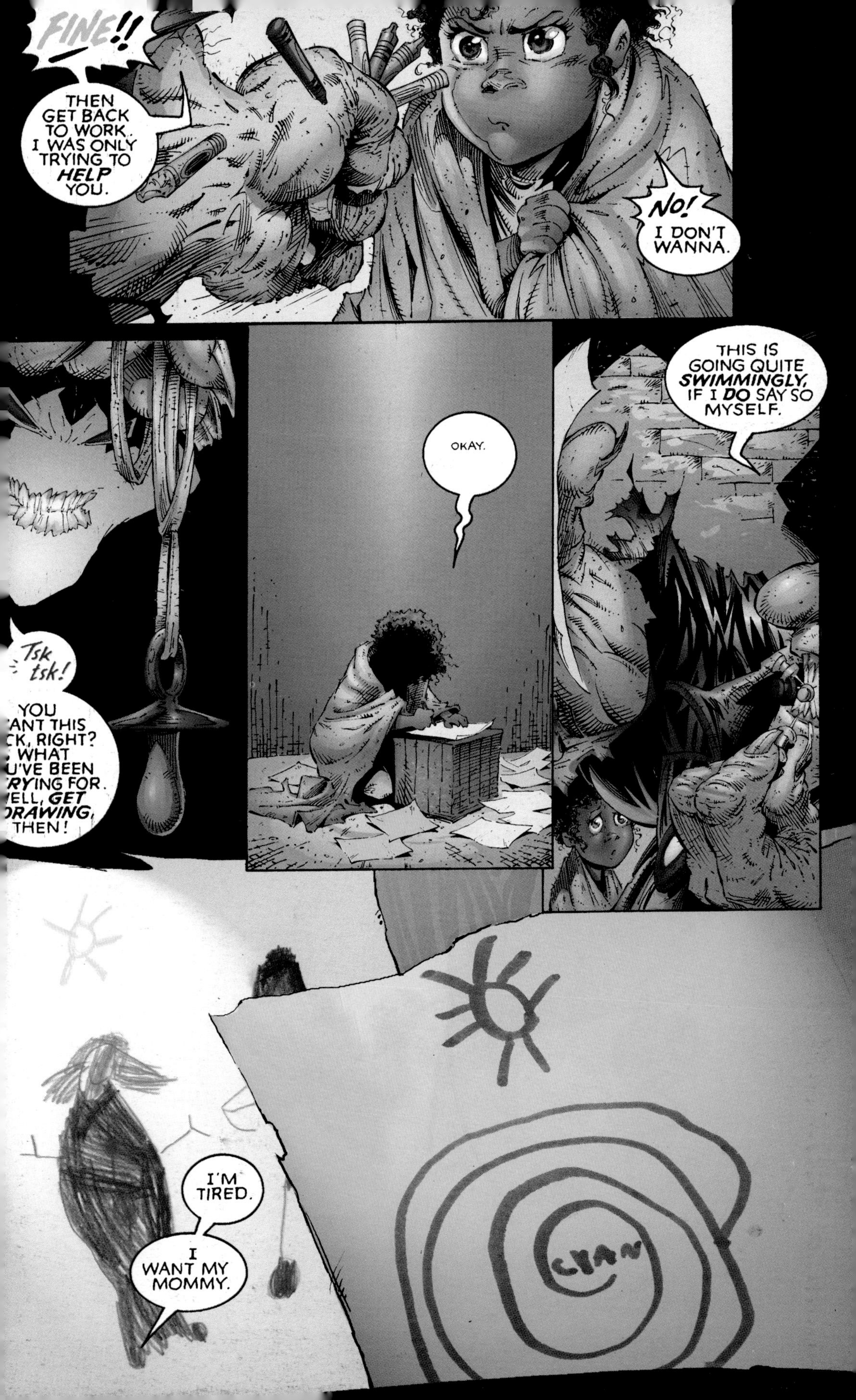
FINE!!
THEN GET BACK TO WORK. I WAS ONLY TRYING TO HELP YOU.
NO! I DON'T WANNA.
Tsk tsk!
YOU
ANT THIS
CK, RIGHT?
WHAT
U'VE BEEN
RYING FOR.
ELL, GET
RAWING,
THEN!
OKAY.
THIS IS GOING QUITE SWIMMINGLY, IF I DO SAY SO MYSELF.
I'M TIRED.
I WANT MY MOMMY.

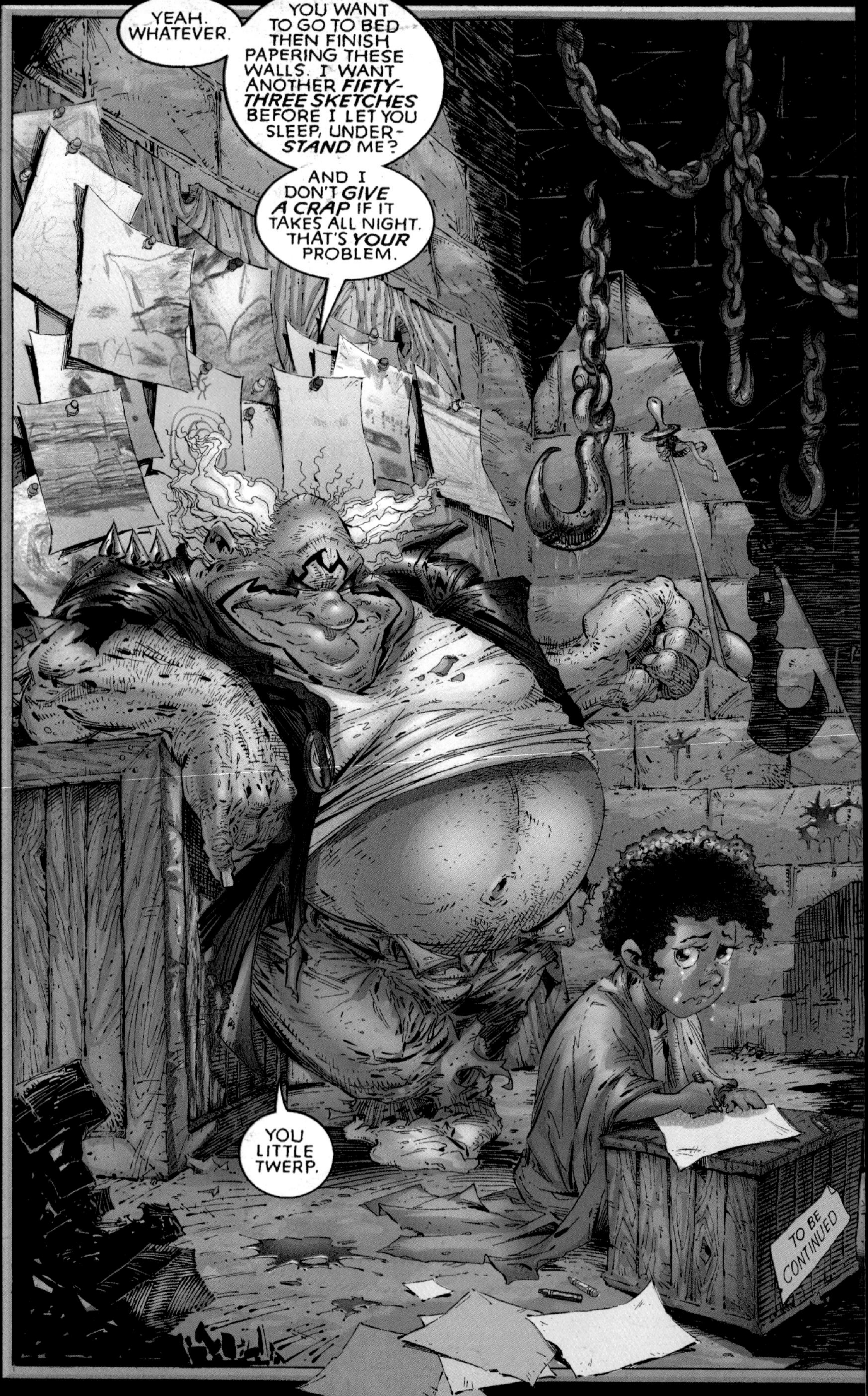

YEAH. WHATEVER.
YOU WANT TO GO TO BED THEN FINISH PAPERING THESE WALLS. I WANT ANOTHER FIFTY-THREE SKETCHES BEFORE I LET YOU SLEEP, UNDER-STAND ME?
AND I DON'T GIVE A CRAP IF IT TAKES ALL NIGHT. THAT'S YOUR PROBLEM.
YOU LITTLE TWERP.
TO BE CONTINUED

SPAWN
image
60
APR
$1.95
SPAWN was HERE

W A R F E D

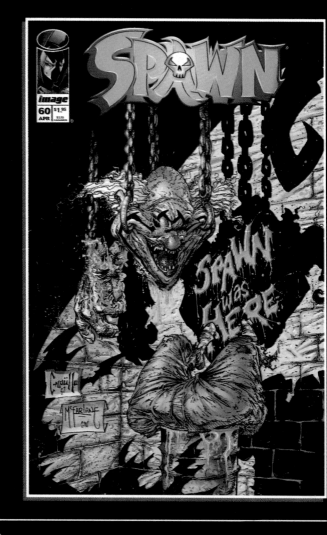

SLEEP.

WANDA HAS, FOR THE
MOMENT, FOUND UNWANTED
RELIEF FROM HER WAKING
*NIGHTMARE*... THE
*ABDUCTION* OF *CYAN,*
HER ONLY DAUGHTER.

WHEN THE POLICE CAME,
SHE TOLD THEM EVERY-
THING SHE COULD
REMEMBER. BUT LONG
AFTER THEIR DEPARTURE,
HER MIND KEPT GNAWING
AT THOSE MEMORIES,
FRANTICALLY SEARCHING
FOR A HIDDEN *CLUE.*
SHE'D FORGOTTEN SOME-
THING. SHE *HAD* TO HAVE.
BECAUSE NONE OF THIS
MAKES ANY SENSE.

AND THOUGH HER FOCUS WAS ON
RETRIEVING EVERY IMPRESSION
OF THOSE MOMENTS, SHE
*STRAYED* FROM THE TASK WITH
THOUGHTS OF HER LITTLE GIRL.

IS SHE *SAFE?*

IS SHE *HUNGRY?*

WHAT'S GOING THROUGH
HER TWO-YEAR-OLD MIND?

WHY IS ANY OF THIS
**HAPPENING?!!**

OVER AND OVER,
WANDA RELIVED
IT ALL, PRAYING
FOR THE RETURN
OF HER BABY.

FINALLY,
EXHAUSTION
*OVERWHELMED*
HER.

LEAVING HER
HUSBAND ALONE
WITH A NAGGING
*FEAR* THAT HE'S
*INVOLVED.*

FEAR THAT THE MAN ONCE
*MARRIED* TO WANDA--
ONCE HIS *BEST FRIEND*--
WHO DIED AND *CAME
BACK TO LIFE*--
COULD ALSO BE THE
*KIDNAPPER.*

*DAMN*
YOU,
AL.

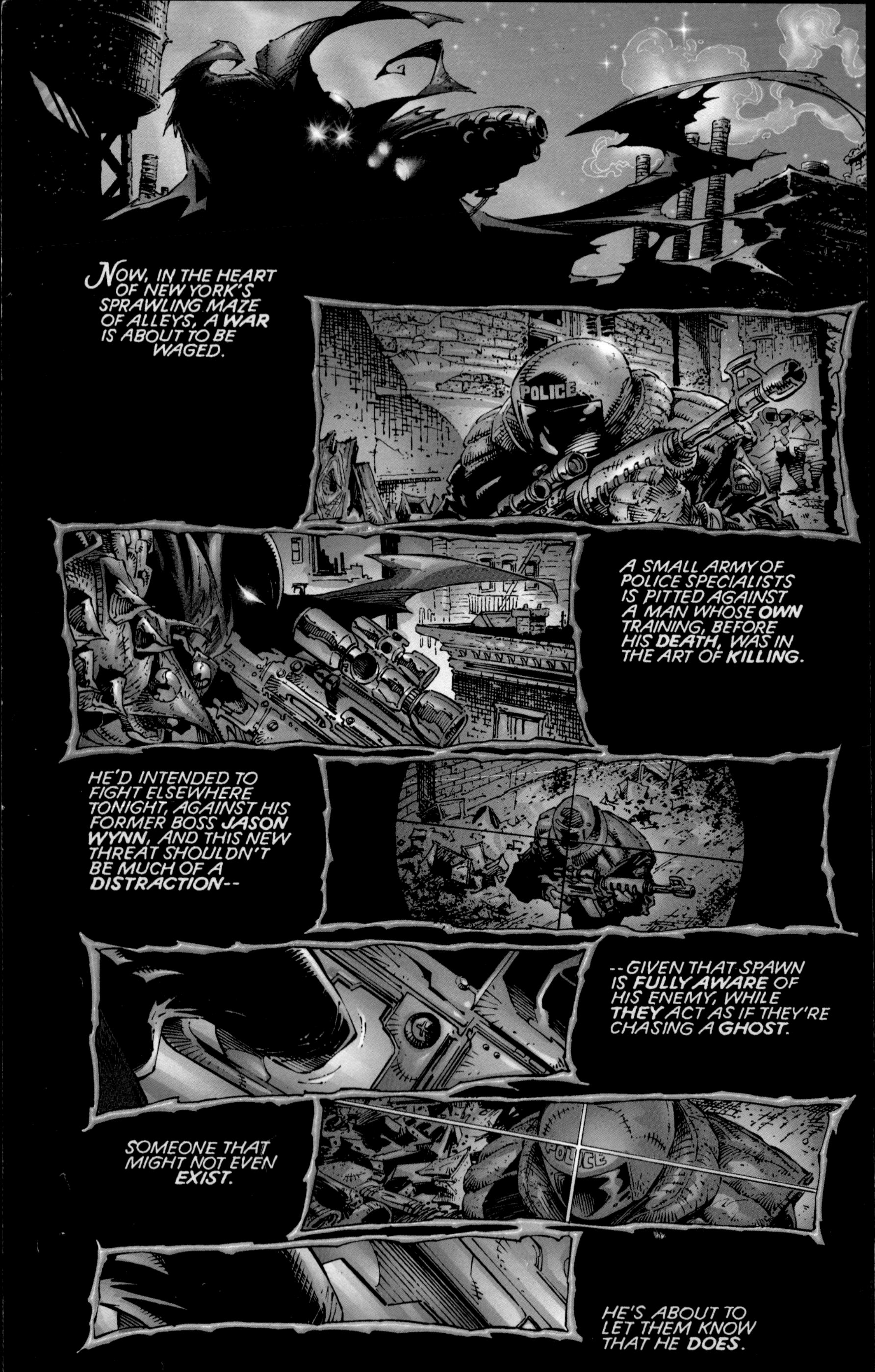
NOW, IN THE HEART OF NEW YORK'S SPRAWLING MAZE OF ALLEYS, A WAR IS ABOUT TO BE WAGED.
POLICE
A SMALL ARMY OF POLICE SPECIALISTS IS PITTED AGAINST A MAN WHOSE OWN TRAINING, BEFORE HIS DEATH, WAS IN THE ART OF KILLING.
HE'D INTENDED TO FIGHT ELSEWHERE TONIGHT, AGAINST HIS FORMER BOSS JASON WYNN, AND THIS NEW THREAT SHOULDN'T BE MUCH OF A DISTRACTION--
--GIVEN THAT SPAWN IS FULLY AWARE OF HIS ENEMY, WHILE THEY ACT AS IF THEY'RE CHASING A GHOST.
SOMEONE THAT MIGHT NOT EVEN EXIST.
HE'S ABOUT TO LET THEM KNOW THAT HE DOES.

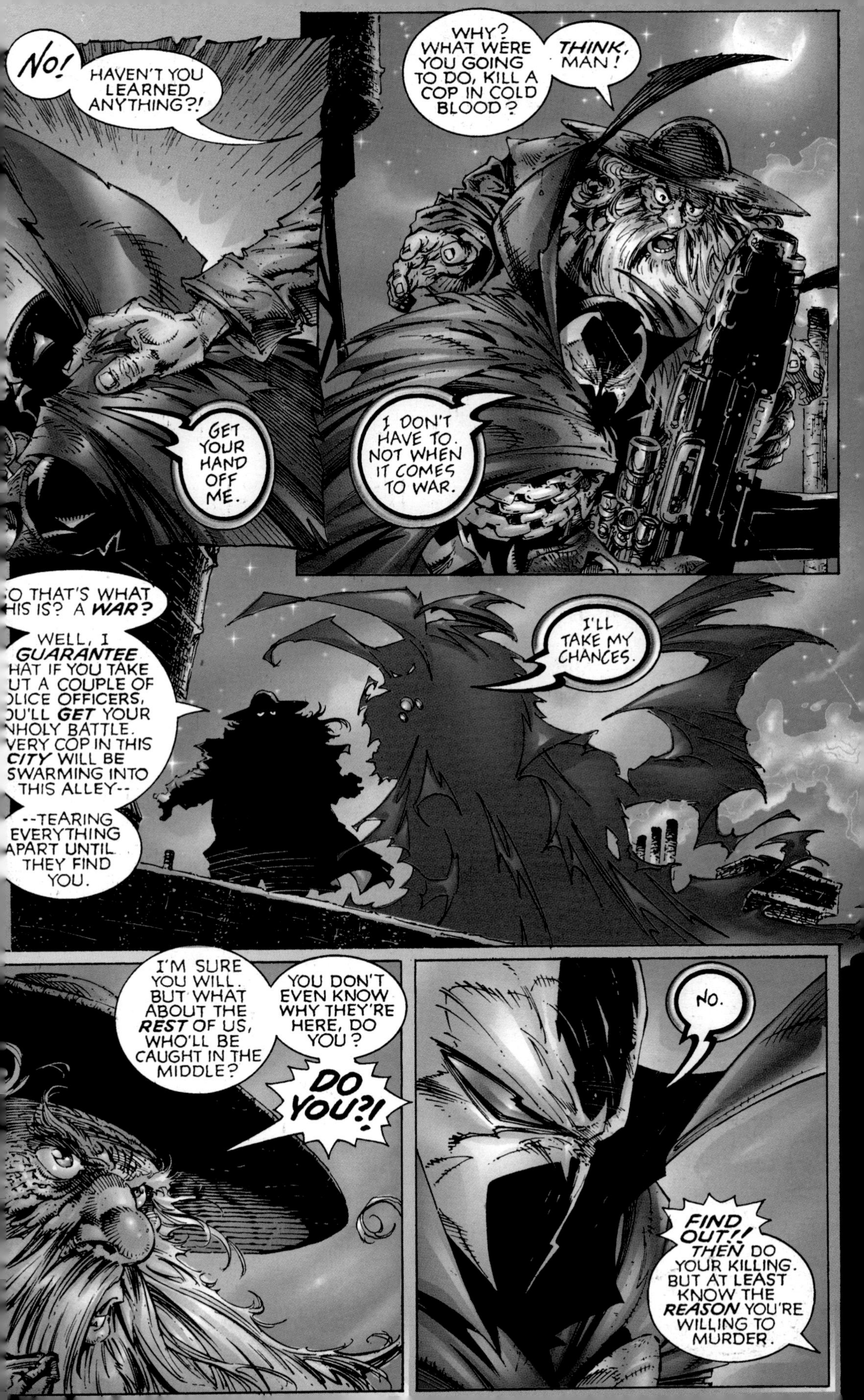
No!
HAVEN'T YOU LEARNED ANYTHING?!
GET YOUR HAND OFF ME.
WHY? WHAT WERE YOU GOING TO DO, KILL A COP IN COLD BLOOD?
THINK, MAN!
I DON'T HAVE TO. NOT WHEN IT COMES TO WAR.
O THAT'S WHAT HIS IS? A WAR?
WELL, I GUARANTEE HAT IF YOU TAKE UT A COUPLE OF OLICE OFFICERS, OU'LL GET YOUR NHOLY BATTLE. VERY COP IN THIS CITY WILL BE SWARMING INTO THIS ALLEY--
--TEARING EVERYTHING APART UNTIL THEY FIND YOU.
I'LL TAKE MY CHANCES.
I'M SURE YOU WILL. BUT WHAT ABOUT THE REST OF US, WHO'LL BE CAUGHT IN THE MIDDLE?
YOU DON'T EVEN KNOW WHY THEY'RE HERE, DO YOU?
DO YOU?!
NO.
FIND OUT!! THEN DO YOUR KILLING. BUT AT LEAST KNOW THE REASON YOU'RE WILLING TO MURDER.

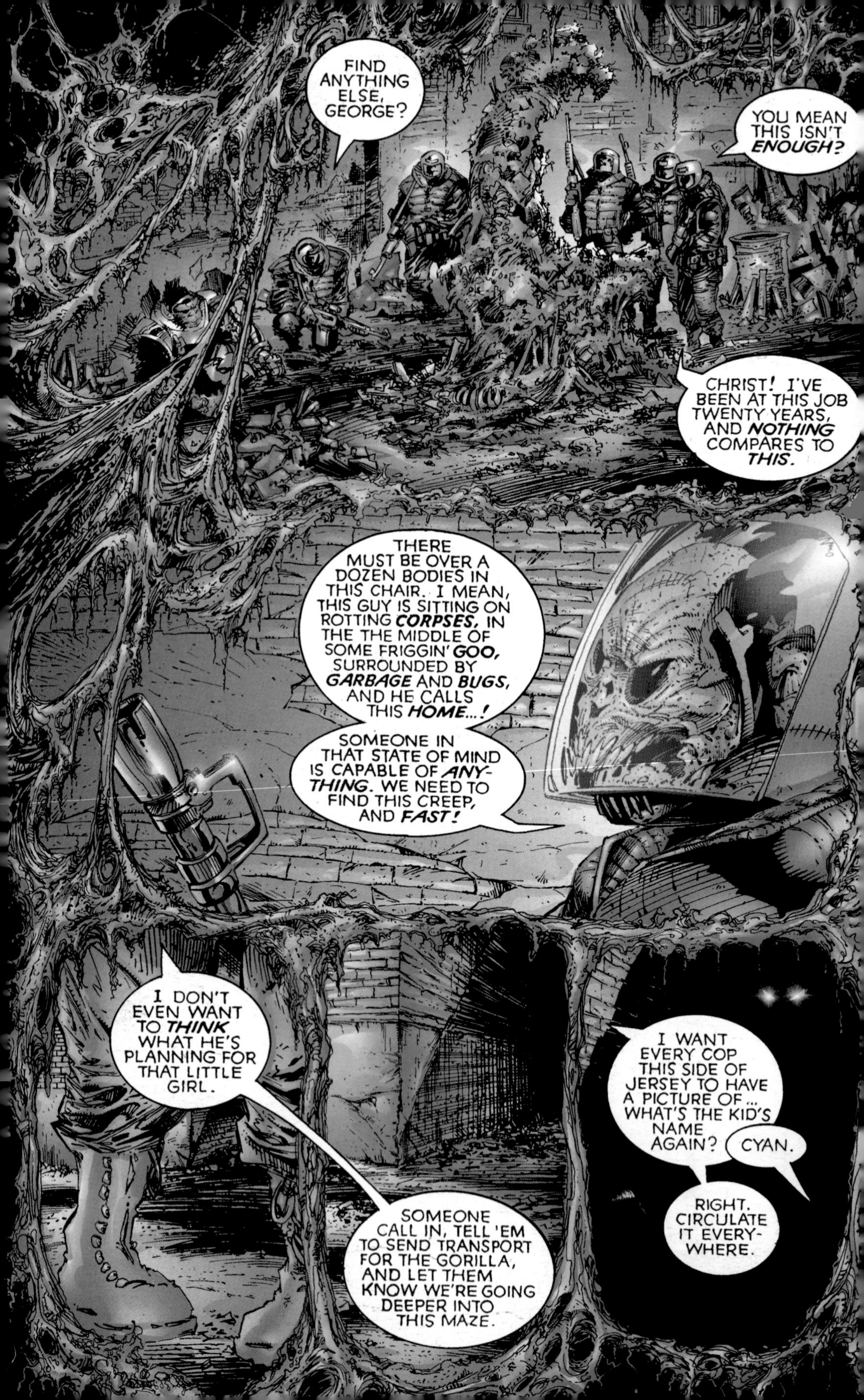
FIND ANYTHING ELSE, GEORGE?
YOU MEAN THIS ISN'T ENOUGH?
CHRIST! I'VE BEEN AT THIS JOB TWENTY YEARS, AND NOTHING COMPARES TO THIS.
THERE MUST BE OVER A DOZEN BODIES IN THIS CHAIR. I MEAN, THIS GUY IS SITTING ON ROTTING CORPSES, IN THE THE MIDDLE OF SOME FRIGGIN' GOO, SURROUNDED BY GARBAGE AND BUGS, AND HE CALLS THIS HOME...!
SOMEONE IN THAT STATE OF MIND IS CAPABLE OF ANY-THING. WE NEED TO FIND THIS CREEP, AND FAST!
I DON'T EVEN WANT TO THINK WHAT HE'S PLANNING FOR THAT LITTLE GIRL.
SOMEONE CALL IN, TELL 'EM TO SEND TRANSPORT FOR THE GORILLA, AND LET THEM KNOW WE'RE GOING DEEPER INTO THIS MAZE.
I WANT EVERY COP THIS SIDE OF JERSEY TO HAVE A PICTURE OF... WHAT'S THE KID'S NAME AGAIN?
CYAN.
RIGHT. CIRCULATE IT EVERY-WHERE.

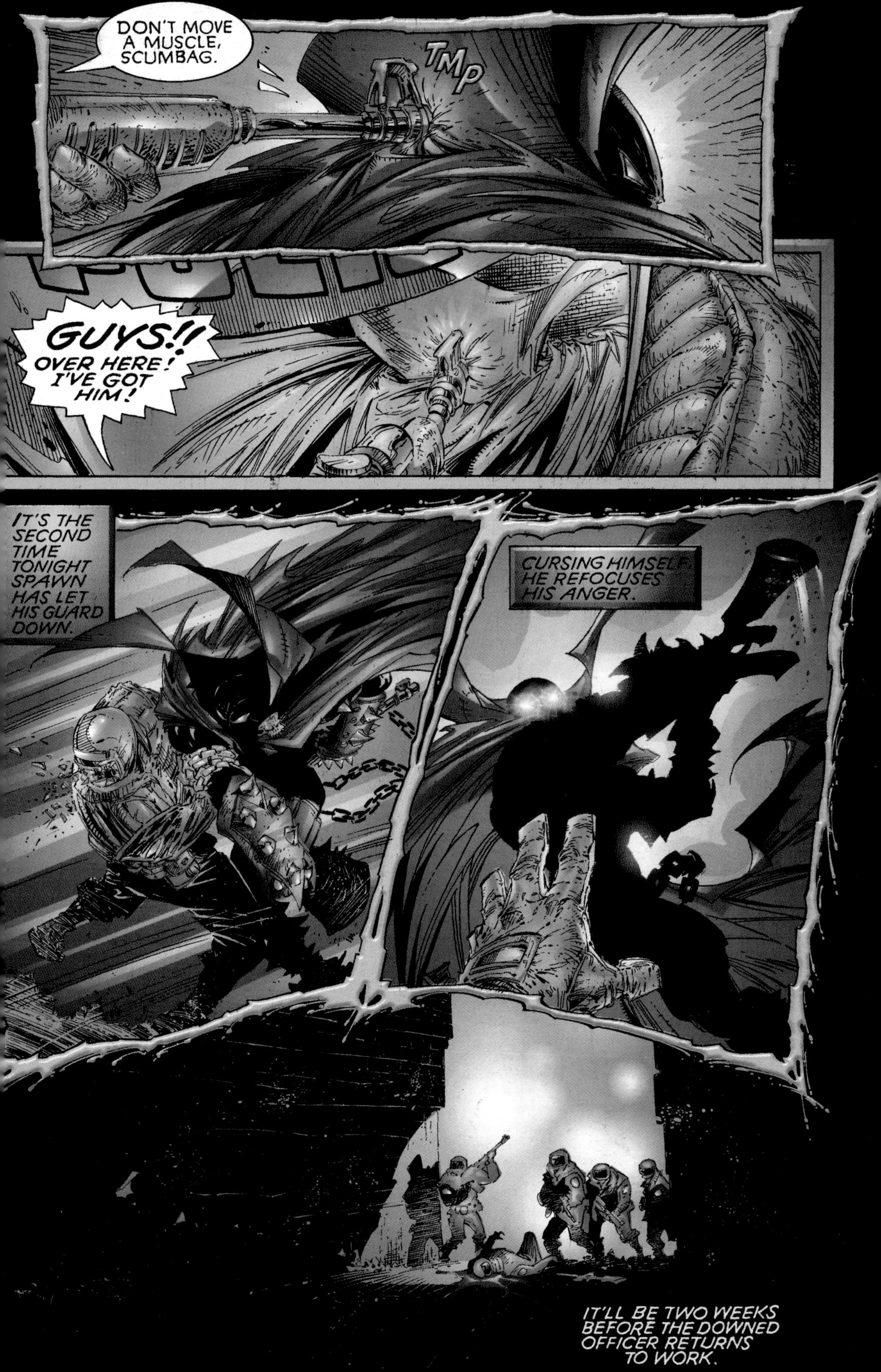
DON'T MOVE A MUSCLE, SCUMBAG.
TMP
GUYS!! OVER HERE! I'VE GOT HIM!
IT'S THE SECOND TIME TONIGHT SPAWN HAS LET HIS GUARD DOWN.
CURSING HIMSELF HE REFOCUSES HIS ANGER.
IT'LL BE TWO WEEKS BEFORE THE DOWNED OFFICER RETURNS TO WORK.

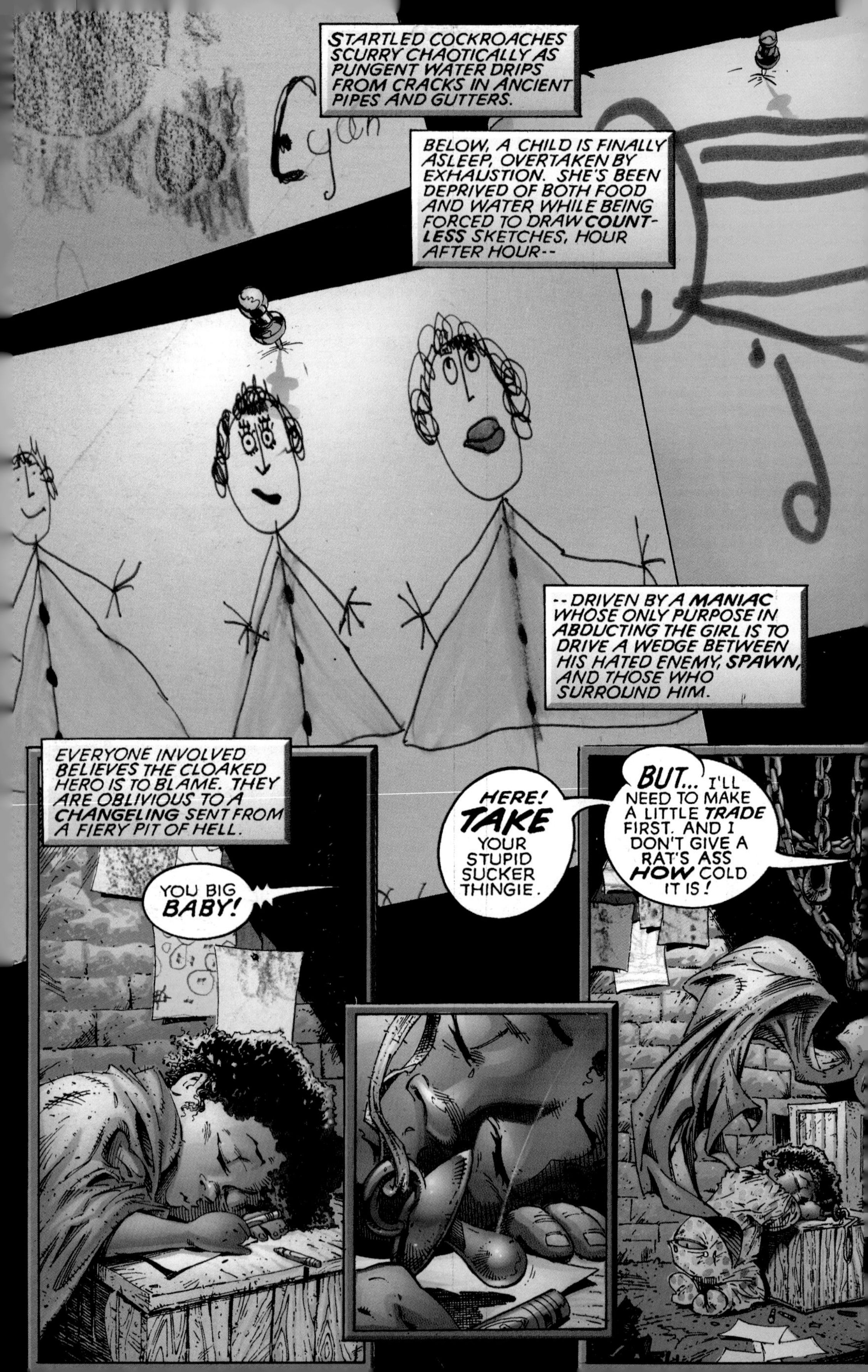
STARTLED COCKROACHES SCURRY CHAOTICALLY AS PUNGENT WATER DRIPS FROM CRACKS IN ANCIENT PIPES AND GUTTERS.
BELOW, A CHILD IS FINALLY ASLEEP, OVERTAKEN BY EXHAUSTION. SHE'S BEEN DEPRIVED OF BOTH FOOD AND WATER WHILE BEING FORCED TO DRAW COUNTLESS SKETCHES, HOUR AFTER HOUR--
--DRIVEN BY A MANIAC WHOSE ONLY PURPOSE IN ABDUCTING THE GIRL IS TO DRIVE A WEDGE BETWEEN HIS HATED ENEMY, SPAWN, AND THOSE WHO SURROUND HIM.
EVERYONE INVOLVED BELIEVES THE CLOAKED HERO IS TO BLAME. THEY ARE OBLIVIOUS TO A CHANGELING SENT FROM A FIERY PIT OF HELL.
YOU BIG BABY!
HERE! TAKE YOUR STUPID SUCKER THINGIE.
BUT... I'LL NEED TO MAKE A LITTLE TRADE FIRST. AND I DON'T GIVE A RAT'S ASS HOW COLD IT IS!

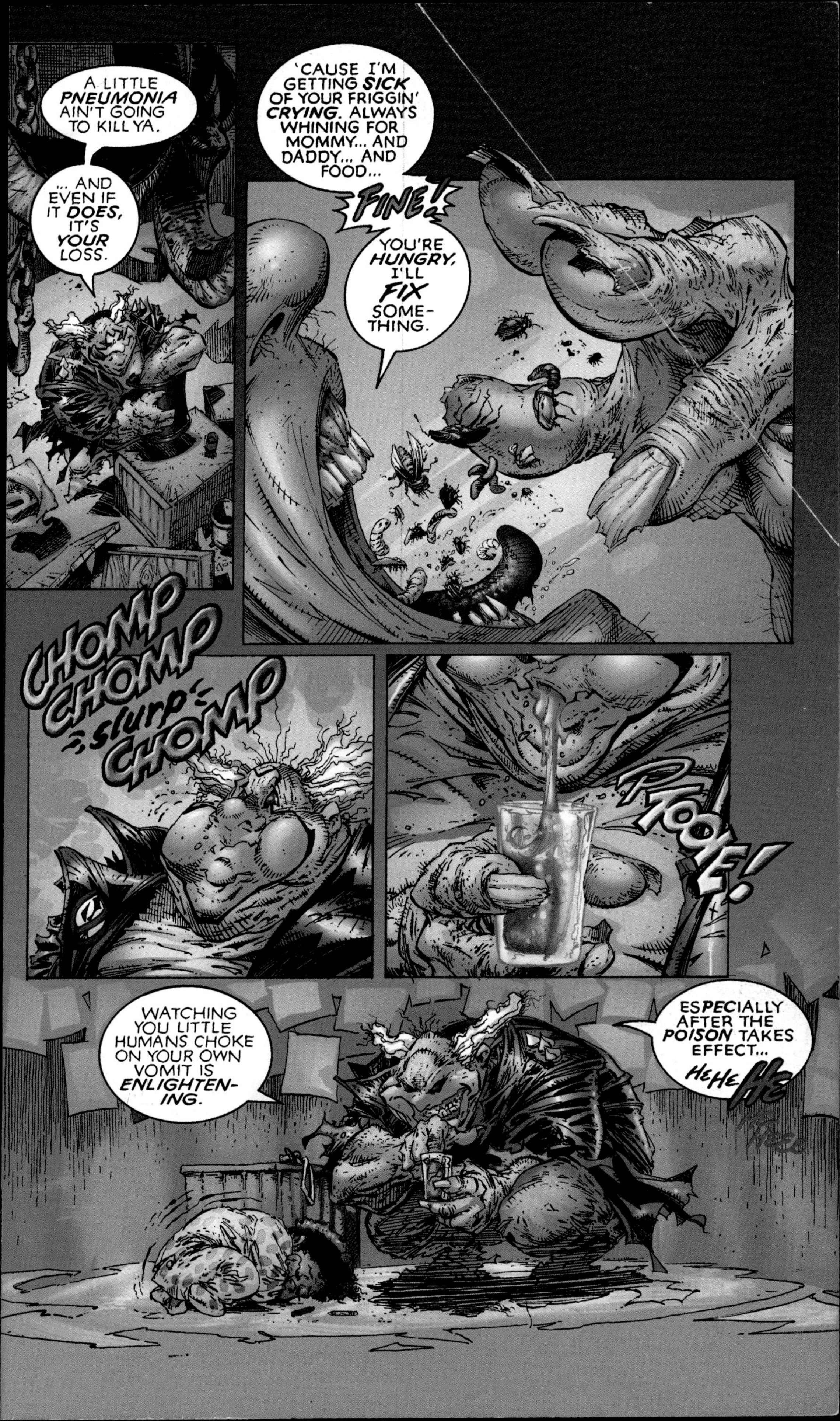
A LITTLE PNEUMONIA AIN'T GOING TO KILL YA.
... AND EVEN IF IT DOES, IT'S YOUR LOSS.
'CAUSE I'M GETTING SICK OF YOUR FRIGGIN' CRYING. ALWAYS WHINING FOR MOMMY... AND DADDY... AND FOOD...
FINE!
YOU'RE HUNGRY, I'LL FIX SOME-THING.
CHOMP CHOMP slurp CHOMP
PTOOIE!
WATCHING YOU LITTLE HUMANS CHOKE ON YOUR OWN VOMIT IS ENLIGHTEN-ING.
ESPECIALLY AFTER THE POISON TAKES EFFECT...
HEHE HE

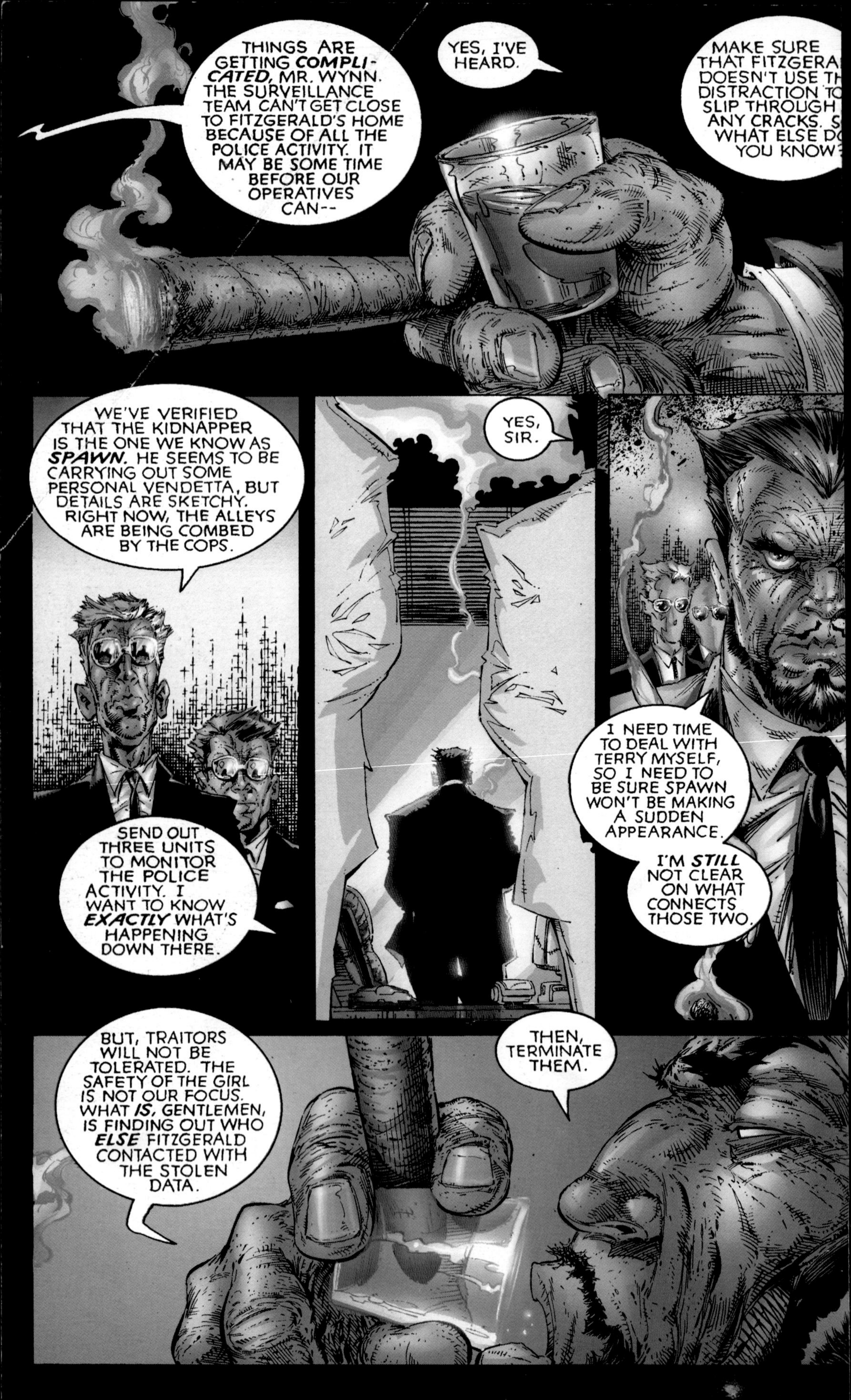
THINGS ARE GETTING COMPLICATED, MR. WYNN. THE SURVEILLANCE TEAM CAN'T GET CLOSE TO FITZGERALD'S HOME BECAUSE OF ALL THE POLICE ACTIVITY. IT MAY BE SOME TIME BEFORE OUR OPERATIVES CAN--
YES, I'VE HEARD.
MAKE SURE THAT FITZGERAL DOESN'T USE TH DISTRACTION TO SLIP THROUGH ANY CRACKS. S WHAT ELSE DO YOU KNOW?
WE'VE VERIFIED THAT THE KIDNAPPER IS THE ONE WE KNOW AS SPAWN. HE SEEMS TO BE CARRYING OUT SOME PERSONAL VENDETTA, BUT DETAILS ARE SKETCHY. RIGHT NOW, THE ALLEYS ARE BEING COMBED BY THE COPS.
SEND OUT THREE UNITS TO MONITOR THE POLICE ACTIVITY. I WANT TO KNOW EXACTLY WHAT'S HAPPENING DOWN THERE.
YES, SIR.
I NEED TIME TO DEAL WITH TERRY MYSELF, SO I NEED TO BE SURE SPAWN WON'T BE MAKING A SUDDEN APPEARANCE.
I'M STILL NOT CLEAR ON WHAT CONNECTS THOSE TWO.
BUT, TRAITORS WILL NOT BE TOLERATED. THE SAFETY OF THE GIRL IS NOT OUR FOCUS. WHAT IS, GENTLEMEN, IS FINDING OUT WHO ELSE FITZGERALD CONTACTED WITH THE STOLEN DATA.
THEN, TERMINATE THEM.

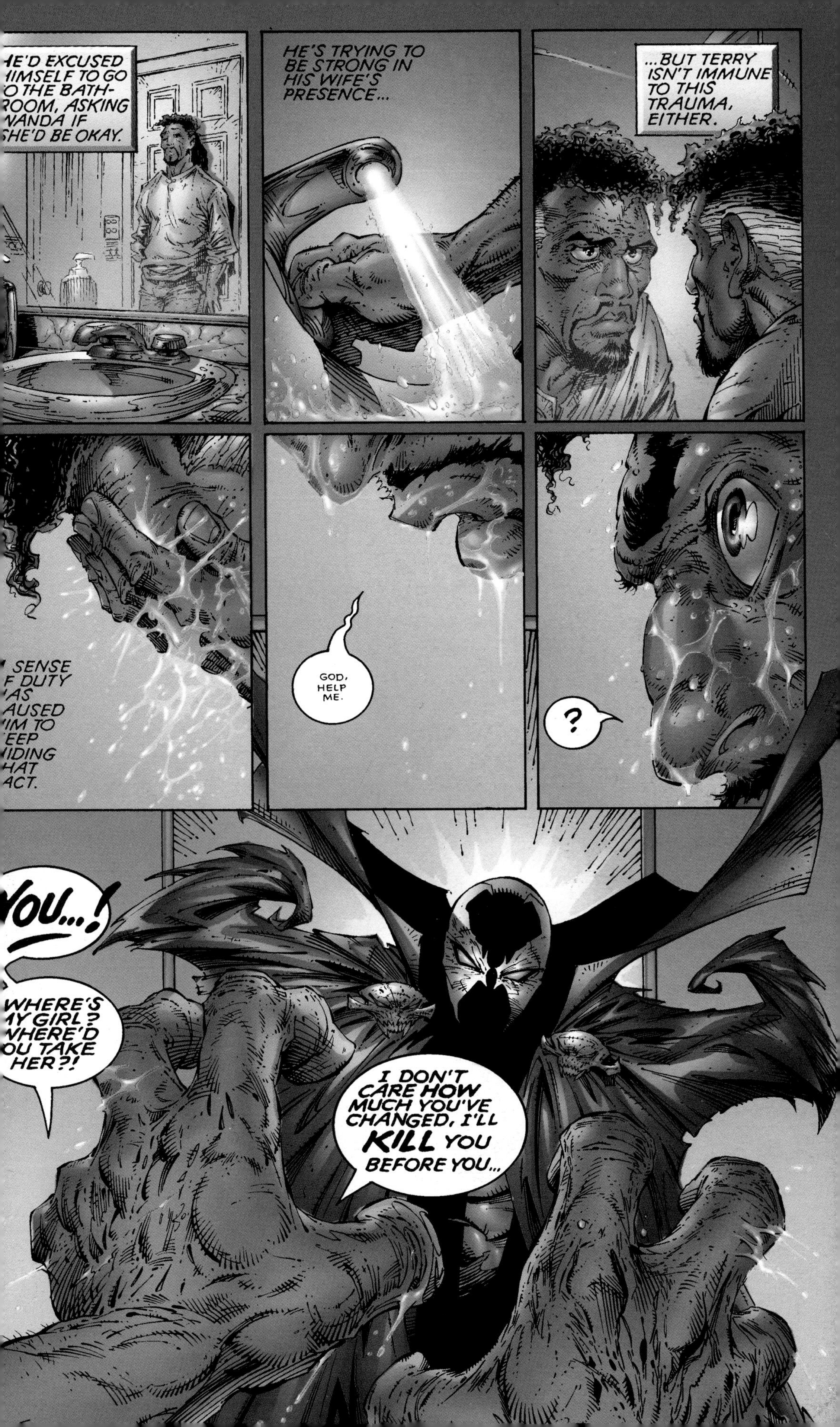
HE'D EXCUSED HIMSELF TO GO TO THE BATH-ROOM, ASKING WANDA IF SHE'D BE OKAY.
HE'S TRYING TO BE STRONG IN HIS WIFE'S PRESENCE...
...BUT TERRY ISN'T IMMUNE TO THIS TRAUMA, EITHER.
SENSE OF DUTY HAS CAUSED HIM TO KEEP HIDING THAT FACT.
GOD, HELP ME.
?
YOU...!
WHERE'S MY GIRL? WHERE'D YOU TAKE HER?!
I DON'T CARE HOW MUCH YOU'VE CHANGED, I'LL KILL YOU BEFORE YOU...

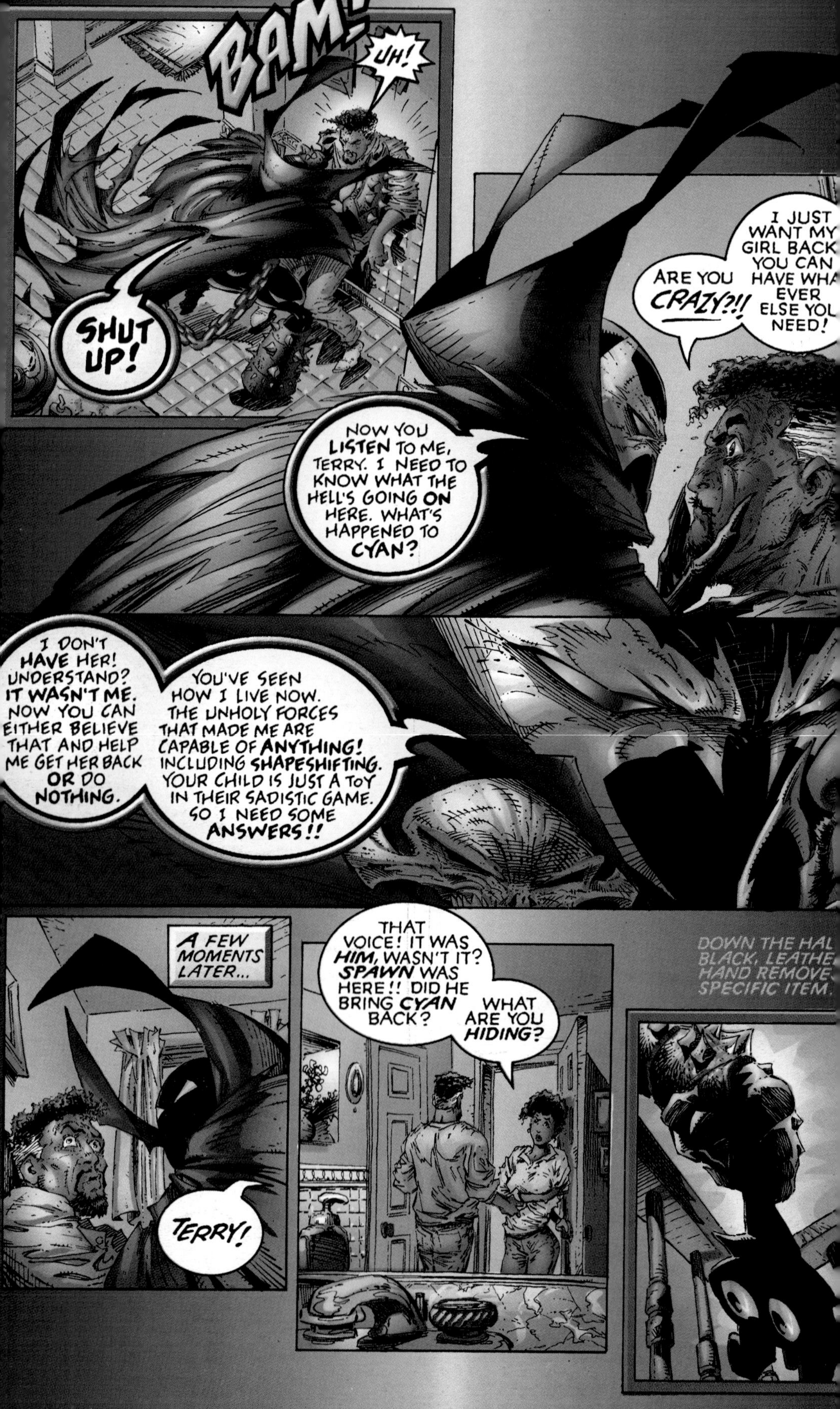
BAM!
UH!
SHUT UP!
ARE YOU CRAZY?!!
I JUST WANT MY GIRL BACK YOU CAN HAVE WHA EVER ELSE YOU NEED!
NOW YOU LISTEN TO ME, TERRY. I NEED TO KNOW WHAT THE HELL'S GOING ON HERE. WHAT'S HAPPENED TO CYAN?
I DON'T HAVE HER! UNDERSTAND? IT WASN'T ME. NOW YOU CAN EITHER BELIEVE THAT AND HELP ME GET HER BACK OR DO NOTHING.
YOU'VE SEEN HOW I LIVE NOW. THE UNHOLY FORCES THAT MADE ME ARE CAPABLE OF ANYTHING! INCLUDING SHAPESHIFTING. YOUR CHILD IS JUST A TOY IN THEIR SADISTIC GAME. SO I NEED SOME ANSWERS!!
A FEW MOMENTS LATER...
TERRY!
THAT VOICE! IT WAS HIM, WASN'T IT? SPAWN WAS HERE!! DID HE BRING CYAN BACK?
WHAT ARE YOU HIDING?
DOWN THE HAL BLACK, LEATHE HAND REMOVE SPECIFIC ITEM.

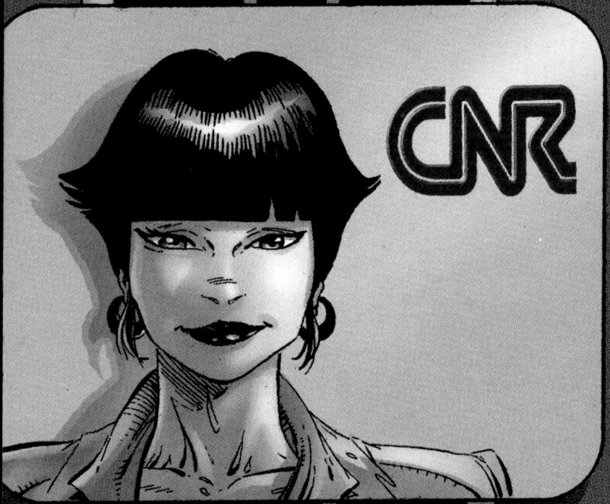
CNR

. . . IN GENEVA AGREED TO INVESTIGATIONS INTO WHAT THEY CALLED "THESE DISRUPTIONS". BOTH SIDES PLEDGED TO WORK TOWARD RESUMPTION OF PEACE NEGOTIATIONS. THE PRESIDENT ISSUED A STATEMENT, CALLING THE TALKS A "PRIORITY OF THE HIGHEST ORDER, AN OPPORTUNITY TO PUT ASIDE SHORT-TERM INTERESTS AND SUSPICIONS IN FAVOR OF LARGER NATIONAL AND INTERNATIONAL IDEALS."

IN THE BACKGROUND TO THE TENSIONS ARE ARMS SALES AGREEMENTS WHICH ARE BEING IGNORED, ACCORDING TO WELL-DOCUMENTED REPORTS. REBEL GROUPS, GENERALLY ARMING THEMSELVES WITH WEAPONS STOLEN FROM THE MILITARY, HAVE BEGUN RAIDING EACH OTHERS' CAMPS FOR INCREASINGLY SCARCE GUNS AND AMMUNITION, WHILE MILITARY BASES ON BOTH SIDES HAVE BEEFED UP SECURITY AROUND THEIR OWN ORDNANCE STOCKPILES.

ARMS MANUFACTURERS IN THE U.S HAVE DENIED KNOWLEDGE OF ANY DISRUPTIONS IN SHIPMENT DELIVERIES.

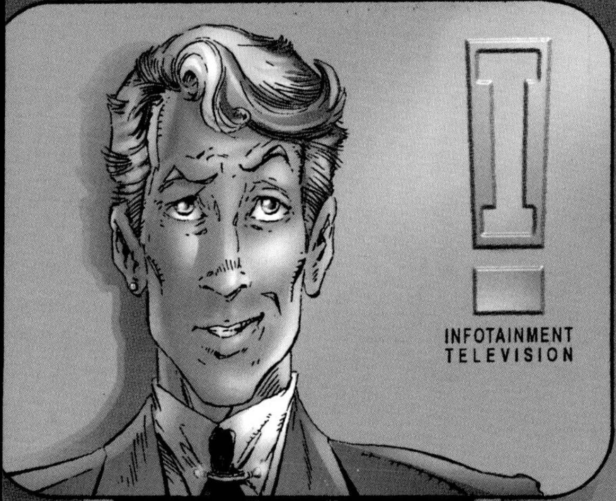
INFOTAINMENT
TELEVISION

THE ***LIES!*** THE SCHEMES AND ***DUPLICITY!*** THERE'S JUST ***NOTHING*** LIKE BEING ON HAND WHEN GREAT NATIONS SIT DOWN TO MAKE NICE WITH ONE ANOTHER.

THE TOPIC ON ***EVERY***ONE'S MIND AT THESE PEACE TALKS IS THE SHORTAGE OF ***GUNS,*** AND THIS REPORTER HAS TO WONDER IF WE'RE ALL IN THE SAME ***REALITY.*** I'VE SEEN ***NO*** SHORTAGE OF ARMED MEN SINCE I ARRIVED AT THE CONFERENCE SITE HERE IN GENEVA. MAYBE IT'S JUST AN AFFECTATION OF THE LANGUAGE OF DIPLOMACY.

***MEAN***WHILE, THE BUZZ BEHIND THE BUZZ HAS TO DO WITH A SHORTAGE OF, NOT GUNS, BUT ***UNIFORMS*** AMONG THE REBELS. IT SEEMS THESE NATIONS' ARMIES HAVE BEEN STORMING THE REBEL CAMPS TO STEAL THEIR WEAPONS ***BACK.*** THEY'VE BEEN HAVING THE ***WORST*** TIME TRYING TO DETERMINE IF THE DOORS THEY'RE BREAKING DOWN BELONG TO REBELS OR JUST BLACK MARKETEERS. ONE ***HATES*** TO APOLOGIZE UNNECESSARILY!

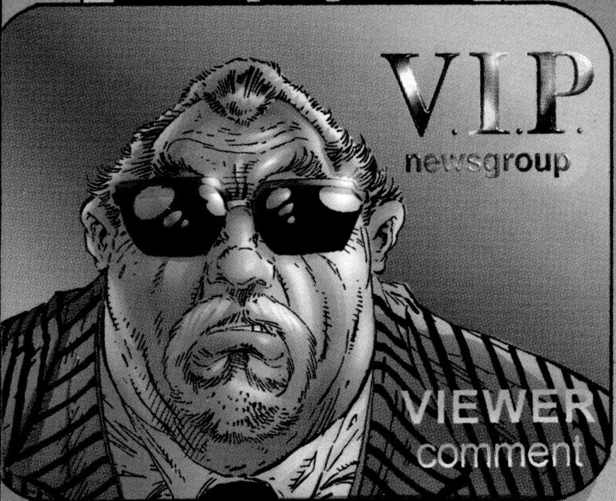
V.I.P.
newsgroup
VIEWER
comment

***NOW HERE'S A GOOD ONE!*** ENTIRE CONTAINER SHIPS FILLED WITH MAYHEM DELIVERY SYSTEMS ARE VANISHING AND NO ONE IS WILLING TO SAY THE WORD ***"THEFT"!*** COULD IT BE THAT THE ADMINISTRATION IS UNAWARE OF THE CABAL OF ROGUE AGENTS ON ITS VERY ***PAYROLL?***

HEL***LO!*** IS ANYONE ***AWAKE?***

ISN'T IT TIME TO ASK SOME ***QUESTIONS*** OF THOSE BADLY-DRESSED GUYS WITH THE PASSPORTS AND THE BLACK BUDGET, THOSE ***CENTRALLY-INTELLIGENT AGENTS?*** THERE'S NO REASON TO ***DOUBT*** THAT IF OUR BUBBA CATCHES ONE OF HIS "BOYS' CLUB" PALS WITH HIS HAND IN THE INTERNATIONAL COOKIE JAR, WHY, HE'LL JUST COME RIGHT OUT AND ***TELL*** US, RIGHT?

WHAT A GREAT SYSTEM!

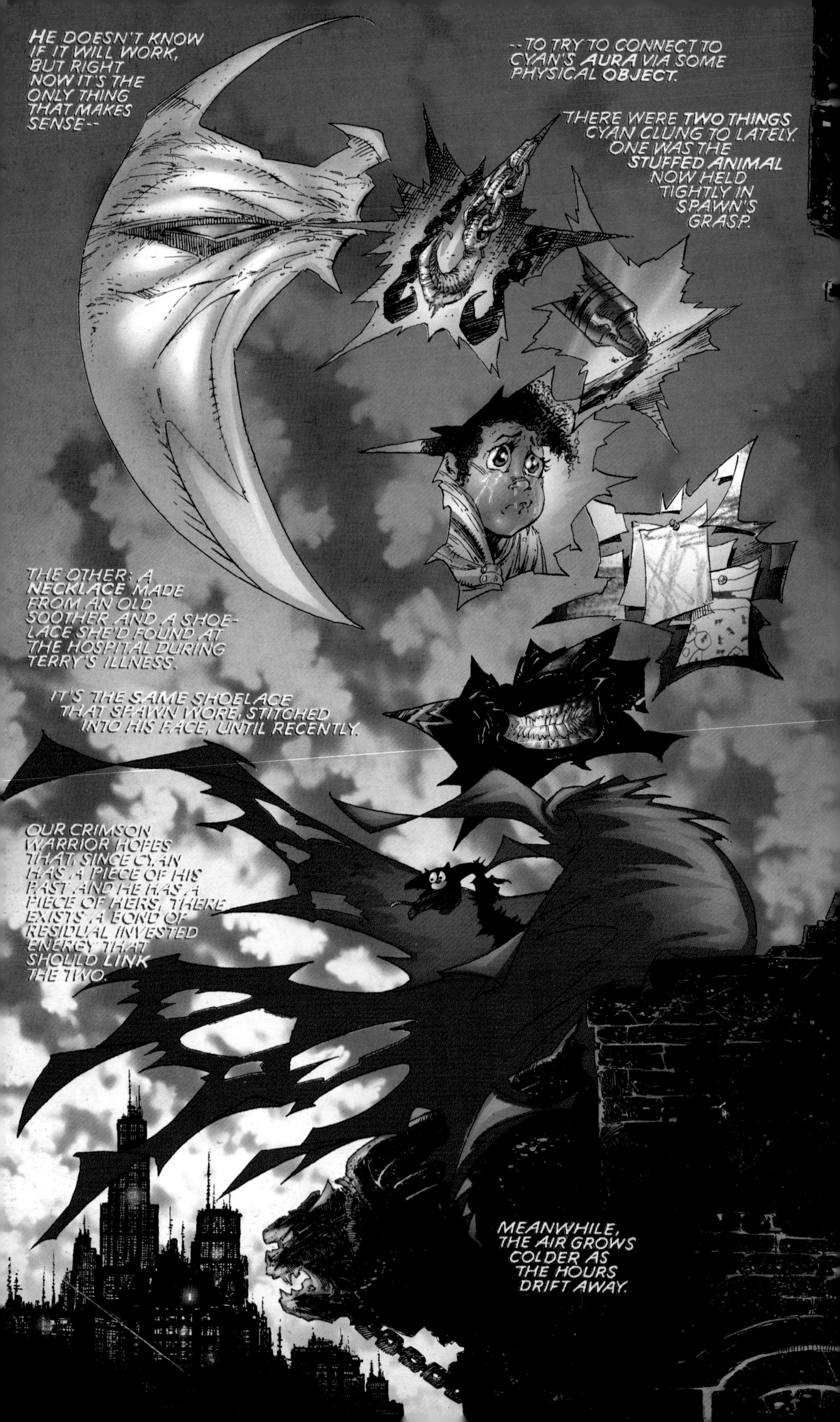
HE DOESN'T KNOW IF IT WILL WORK, BUT RIGHT NOW IT'S THE ONLY THING THAT MAKES SENSE--
--TO TRY TO CONNECT TO CYAN'S AURA VIA SOME PHYSICAL OBJECT.
THERE WERE TWO THINGS CYAN CLUNG TO LATELY. ONE WAS THE STUFFED ANIMAL NOW HELD TIGHTLY IN SPAWN'S GRASP.
THE OTHER: A NECKLACE MADE FROM AN OLD SOOTHER AND A SHOE-LACE SHE'D FOUND AT THE HOSPITAL DURING TERRY'S ILLNESS.
IT'S THE SAME SHOELACE THAT SPAWN WORE, STITCHED INTO HIS FACE, UNTIL RECENTLY.
OUR CRIMSON WARRIOR HOPES THAT, SINCE CYAN HAS A PIECE OF HIS PAST AND HE HAS A PIECE OF HERS, THERE EXISTS A BOND OF RESIDUAL INVESTED ENERGY THAT SHOULD LINK THE TWO.
MEANWHILE, THE AIR GROWS COLDER AS THE HOURS DRIFT AWAY.

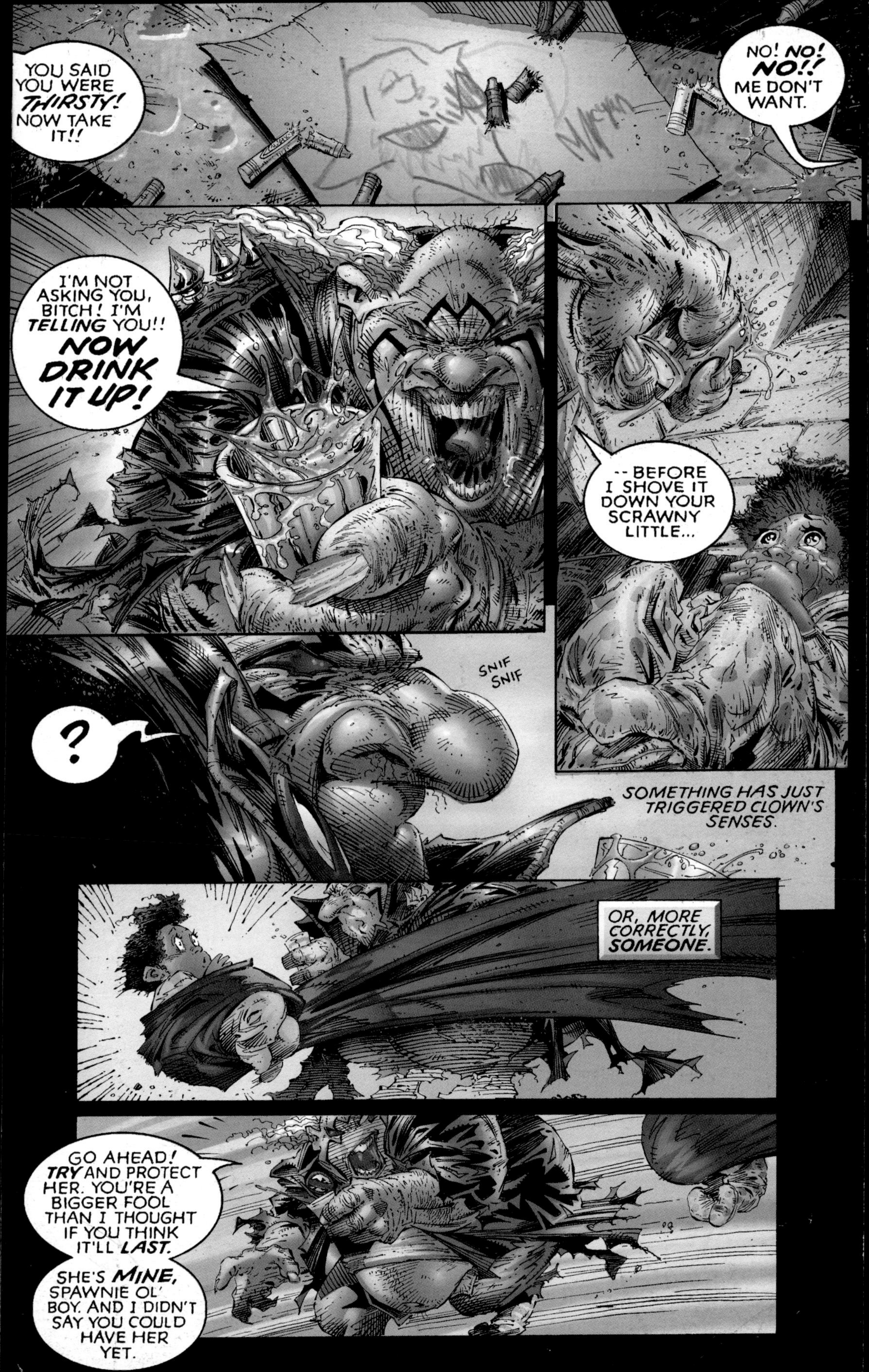
YOU SAID YOU WERE THIRSTY! NOW TAKE IT!!
NO! NO! NO!! ME DON'T WANT.
I'M NOT ASKING YOU, BITCH! I'M TELLING YOU!! NOW DRINK IT UP!
-- BEFORE I SHOVE IT DOWN YOUR SCRAWNY LITTLE...
SNIF SNIF
?
SOMETHING HAS JUST TRIGGERED CLOWN'S SENSES.
OR, MORE CORRECTLY, SOMEONE.
GO AHEAD! TRY AND PROTECT HER. YOU'RE A BIGGER FOOL THAN I THOUGHT IF YOU THINK IT'LL LAST.
SHE'S MINE, SPAWNIE OL' BOY. AND I DIDN'T SAY YOU COULD HAVE HER YET.

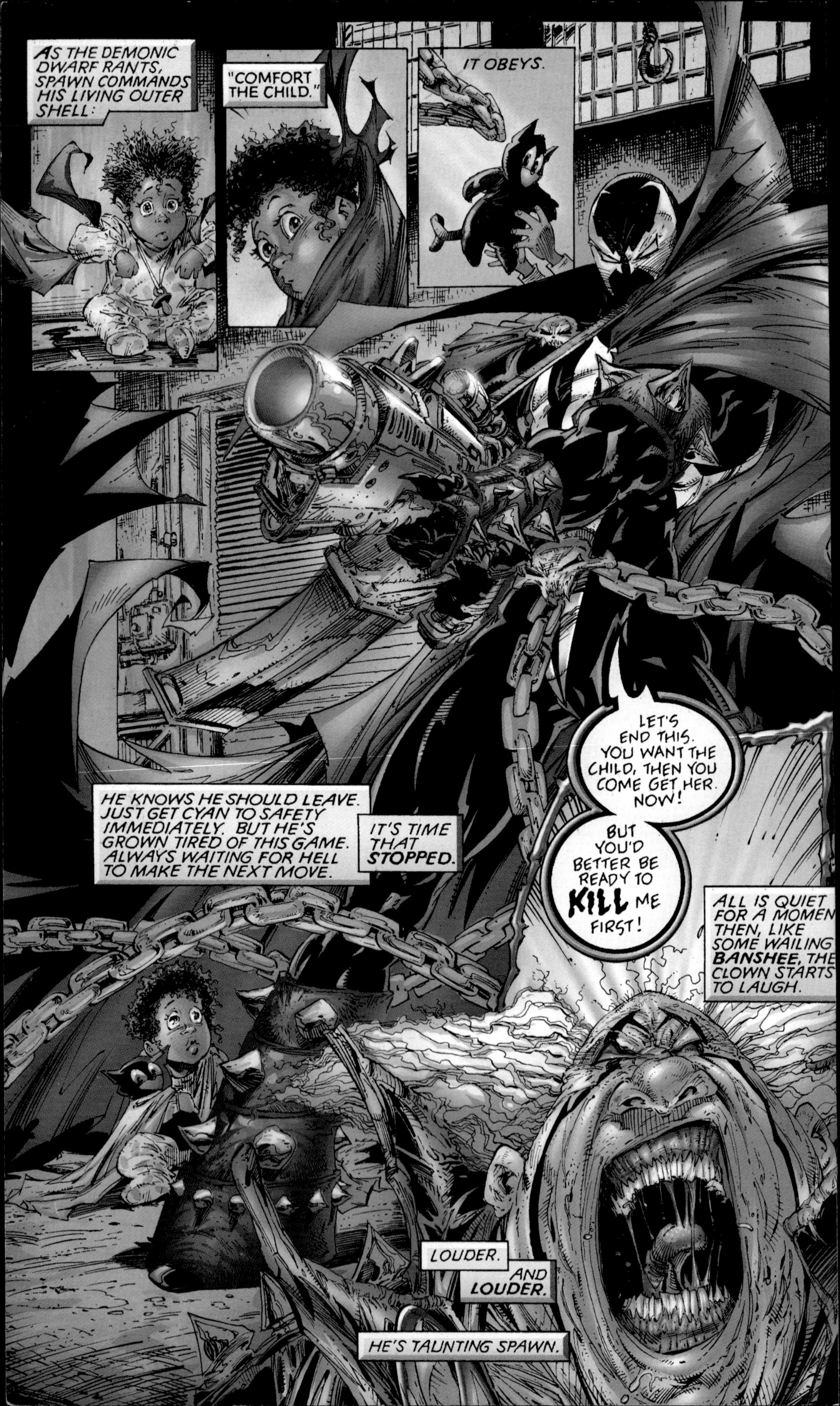

AS THE DEMONIC DWARF RANTS, SPAWN COMMANDS HIS LIVING OUTER SHELL:
"COMFORT THE CHILD."
IT OBEYS.
HE KNOWS HE SHOULD LEAVE. JUST GET CYAN TO SAFETY IMMEDIATELY. BUT HE'S GROWN TIRED OF THIS GAME. ALWAYS WAITING FOR HELL TO MAKE THE NEXT MOVE.
IT'S TIME THAT STOPPED.
LET'S END THIS. YOU WANT THE CHILD, THEN YOU COME GET HER. NOW!
BUT YOU'D BETTER BE READY TO KILL ME FIRST!
ALL IS QUIET FOR A MOMEN THEN, LIKE SOME WAILING BANSHEE, THE CLOWN STARTS TO LAUGH.
LOUDER.
AND LOUDER.
HE'S TAUNTING SPAWN.

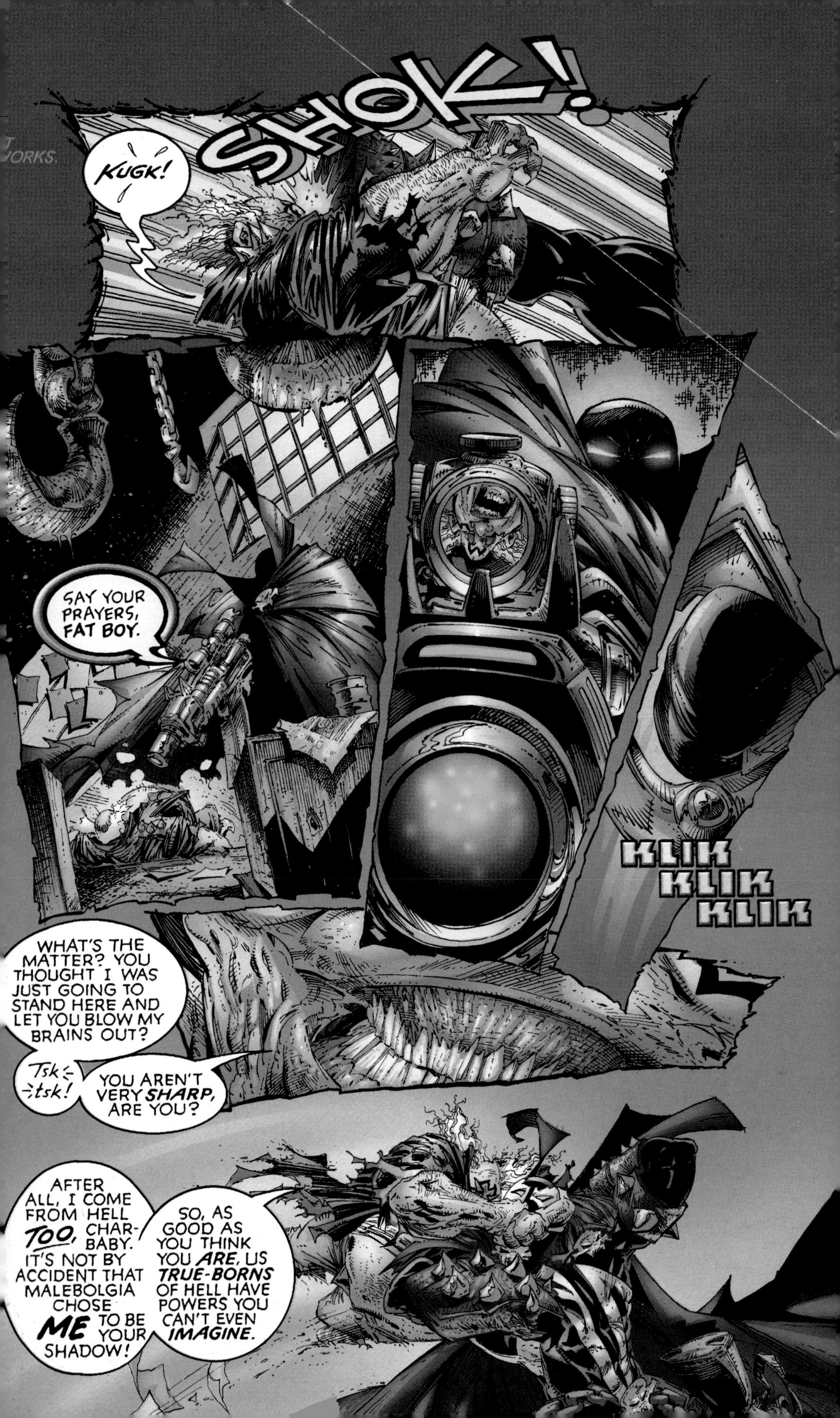

SHOK!
KUGK!
SAY YOUR PRAYERS, FAT BOY.
KLIK KLIK KLIK
WHAT'S THE MATTER? YOU THOUGHT I WAS JUST GOING TO STAND HERE AND LET YOU BLOW MY BRAINS OUT?
Tsk tsk!
YOU AREN'T VERY SHARP, ARE YOU?
AFTER ALL, I COME FROM HELL TOO, CHAR-BABY. IT'S NOT BY ACCIDENT THAT MALEBOLGIA CHOSE ME TO BE YOUR SHADOW!
SO, AS GOOD AS YOU THINK YOU ARE, US TRUE-BORNS OF HELL HAVE POWERS YOU CAN'T EVEN IMAGINE.

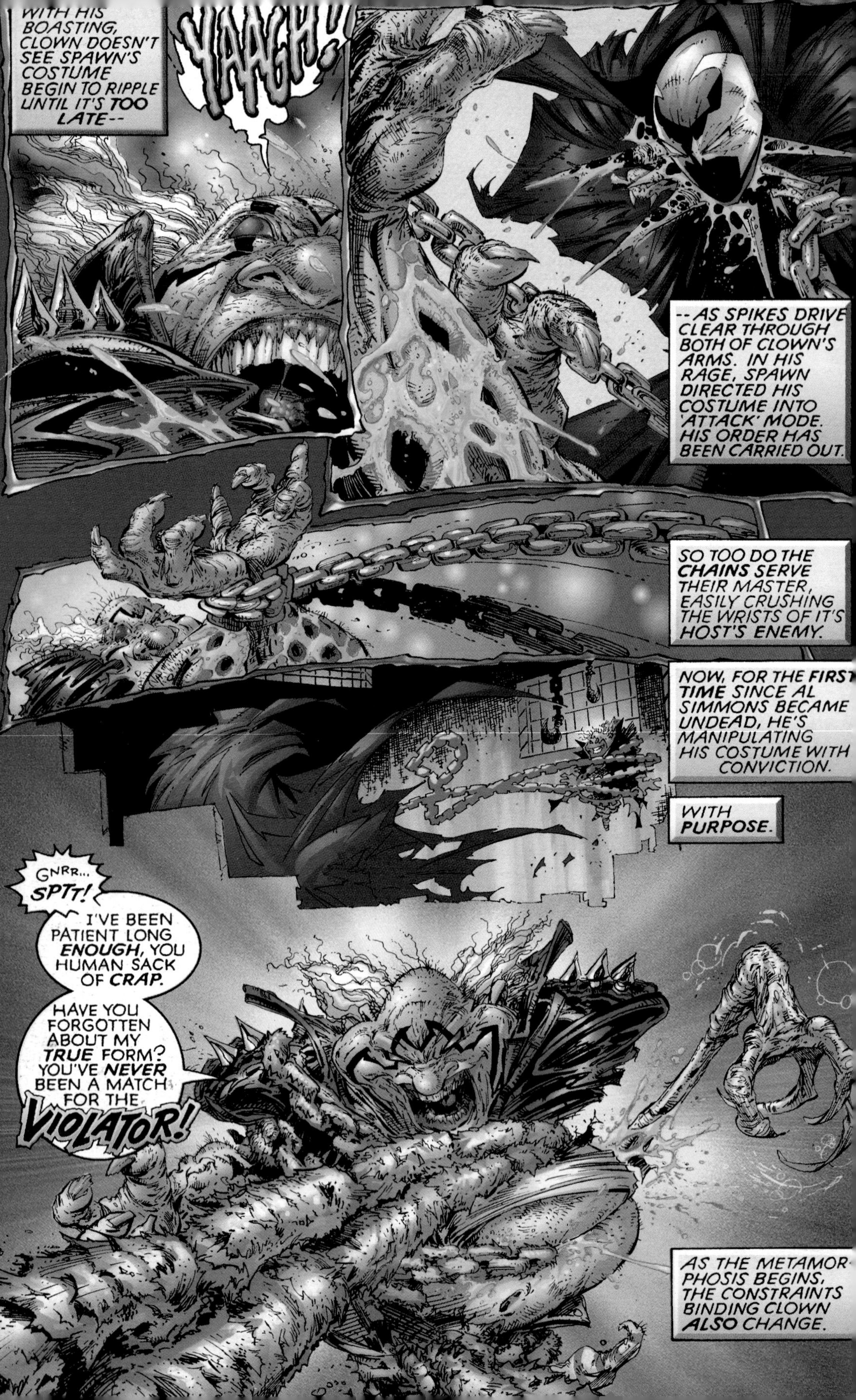
WITH HIS BOASTING, CLOWN DOESN'T SEE SPAWN'S COSTUME BEGIN TO RIPPLE UNTIL IT'S TOO LATE--
YAAGH!!
--AS SPIKES DRIVE CLEAR THROUGH BOTH OF CLOWN'S ARMS. IN HIS RAGE, SPAWN DIRECTED HIS COSTUME INTO 'ATTACK' MODE. HIS ORDER HAS BEEN CARRIED OUT.
SO TOO DO THE CHAINS SERVE THEIR MASTER, EASILY CRUSHING THE WRISTS OF IT'S HOST'S ENEMY.
NOW, FOR THE FIRST TIME SINCE AL SIMMONS BECAME UNDEAD, HE'S MANIPULATING HIS COSTUME WITH CONVICTION.
WITH PURPOSE.
GNRR... SPTT!
I'VE BEEN PATIENT LONG ENOUGH, YOU HUMAN SACK OF CRAP.
HAVE YOU FORGOTTEN ABOUT MY TRUE FORM? YOU'VE NEVER BEEN A MATCH FOR THE VIOLATOR!
AS THE METAMORPHOSIS BEGINS, THE CONSTRAINTS BINDING CLOWN ALSO CHANGE.

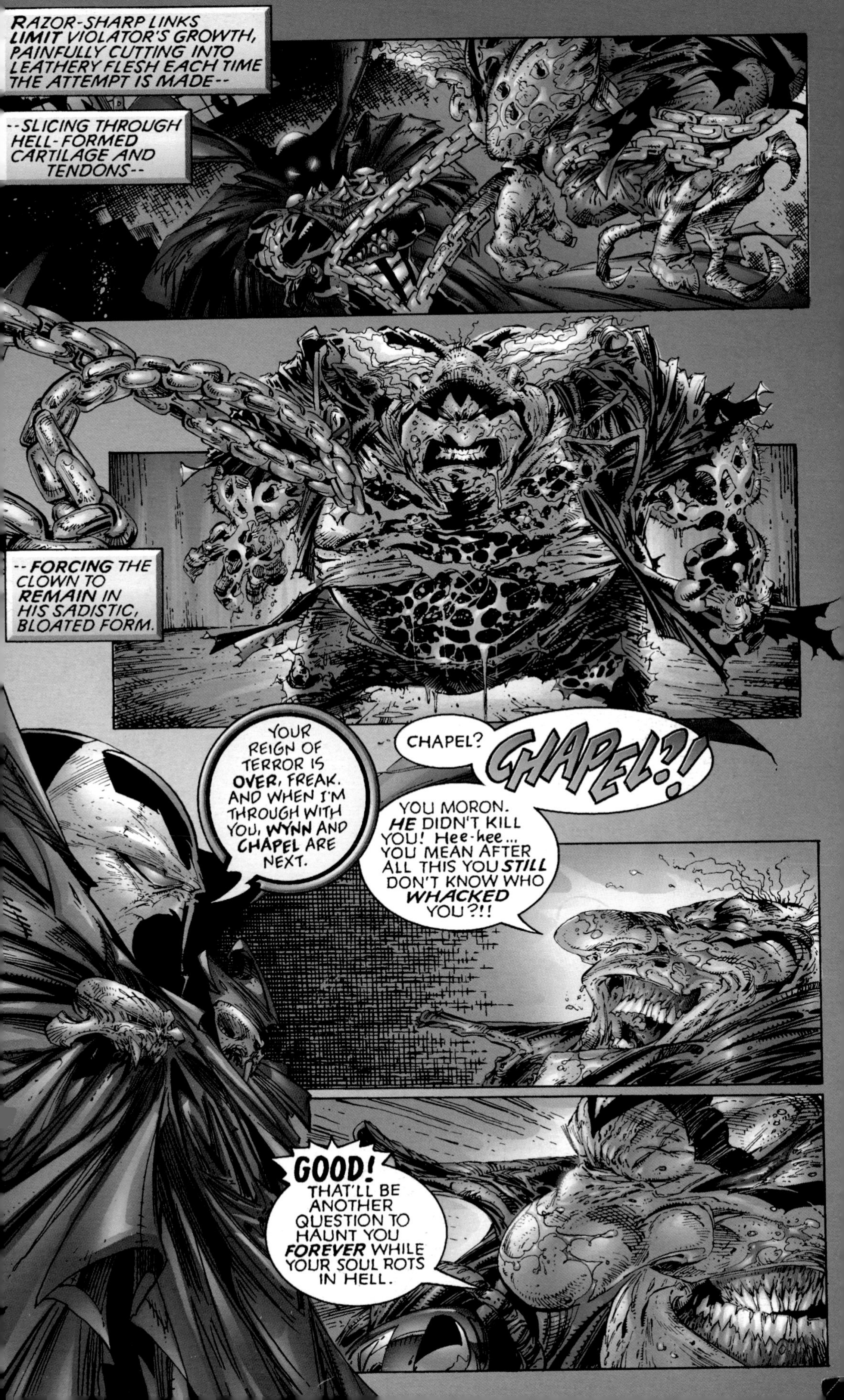
RAZOR-SHARP LINKS LIMIT VIOLATOR'S GROWTH, PAINFULLY CUTTING INTO LEATHERY FLESH EACH TIME THE ATTEMPT IS MADE--
--SLICING THROUGH HELL-FORMED CARTILAGE AND TENDONS--
--FORCING THE CLOWN TO REMAIN IN HIS SADISTIC, BLOATED FORM.
YOUR REIGN OF TERROR IS OVER, FREAK. AND WHEN I'M THROUGH WITH YOU, WYNN AND CHAPEL ARE NEXT.
CHAPEL? CHAPEL?!
YOU MORON. HE DIDN'T KILL YOU! Hee-hee... YOU MEAN AFTER ALL THIS YOU STILL DON'T KNOW WHO WHACKED YOU?!!
GOOD! THAT'LL BE ANOTHER QUESTION TO HAUNT YOU FOREVER WHILE YOUR SOUL ROTS IN HELL.

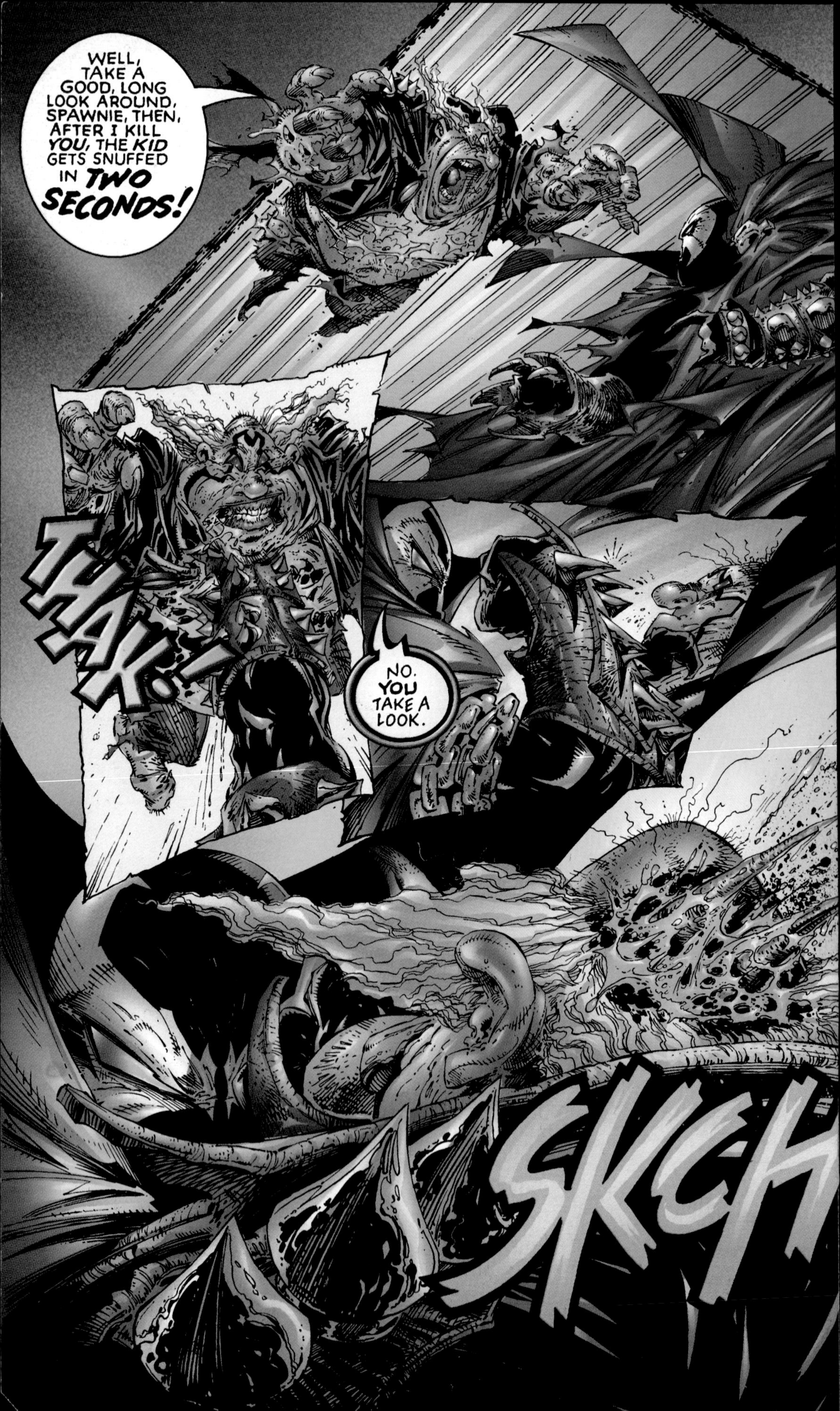
WELL, TAKE A GOOD, LONG LOOK AROUND, SPAWNIE, THEN, AFTER I KILL *YOU*, THE *KID* GETS SNUFFED IN *TWO SECONDS!*
THAK!
NO. **YOU** TAKE A LOOK.
SKCH

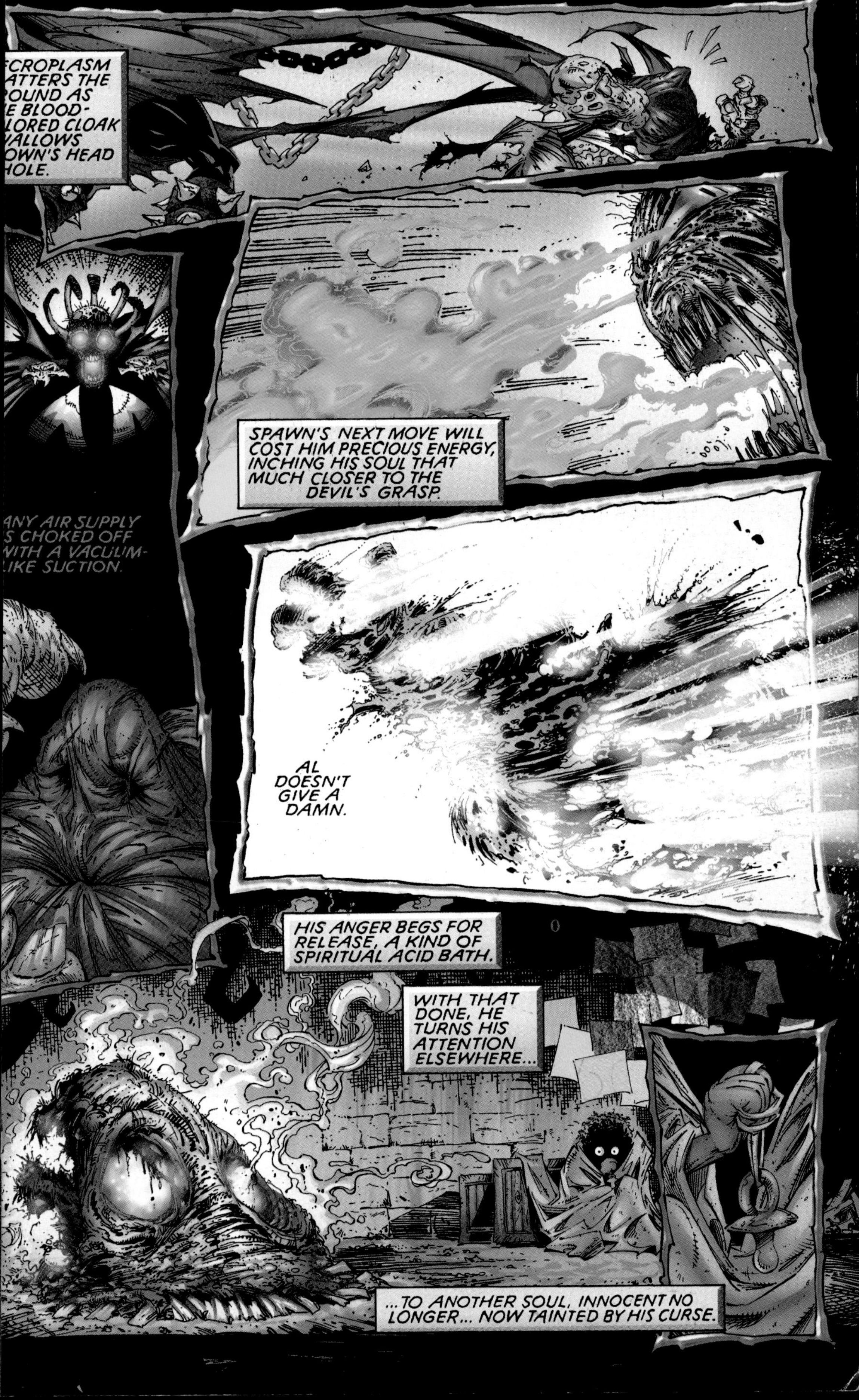

ECROPLASM ATTERS THE ROUND AS E BLOOD-LORED CLOAK WALLOWS OWN'S HEAD HOLE.
SPAWN'S NEXT MOVE WILL COST HIM PRECIOUS ENERGY, INCHING HIS SOUL THAT MUCH CLOSER TO THE DEVIL'S GRASP.
ANY AIR SUPPLY S CHOKED OFF WITH A VACUUM-LIKE SUCTION.
AL DOESN'T GIVE A DAMN.
HIS ANGER BEGS FOR RELEASE, A KIND OF SPIRITUAL ACID BATH.
WITH THAT DONE, HE TURNS HIS ATTENTION ELSEWHERE...
...TO ANOTHER SOUL, INNOCENT NO LONGER... NOW TAINTED BY HIS CURSE.

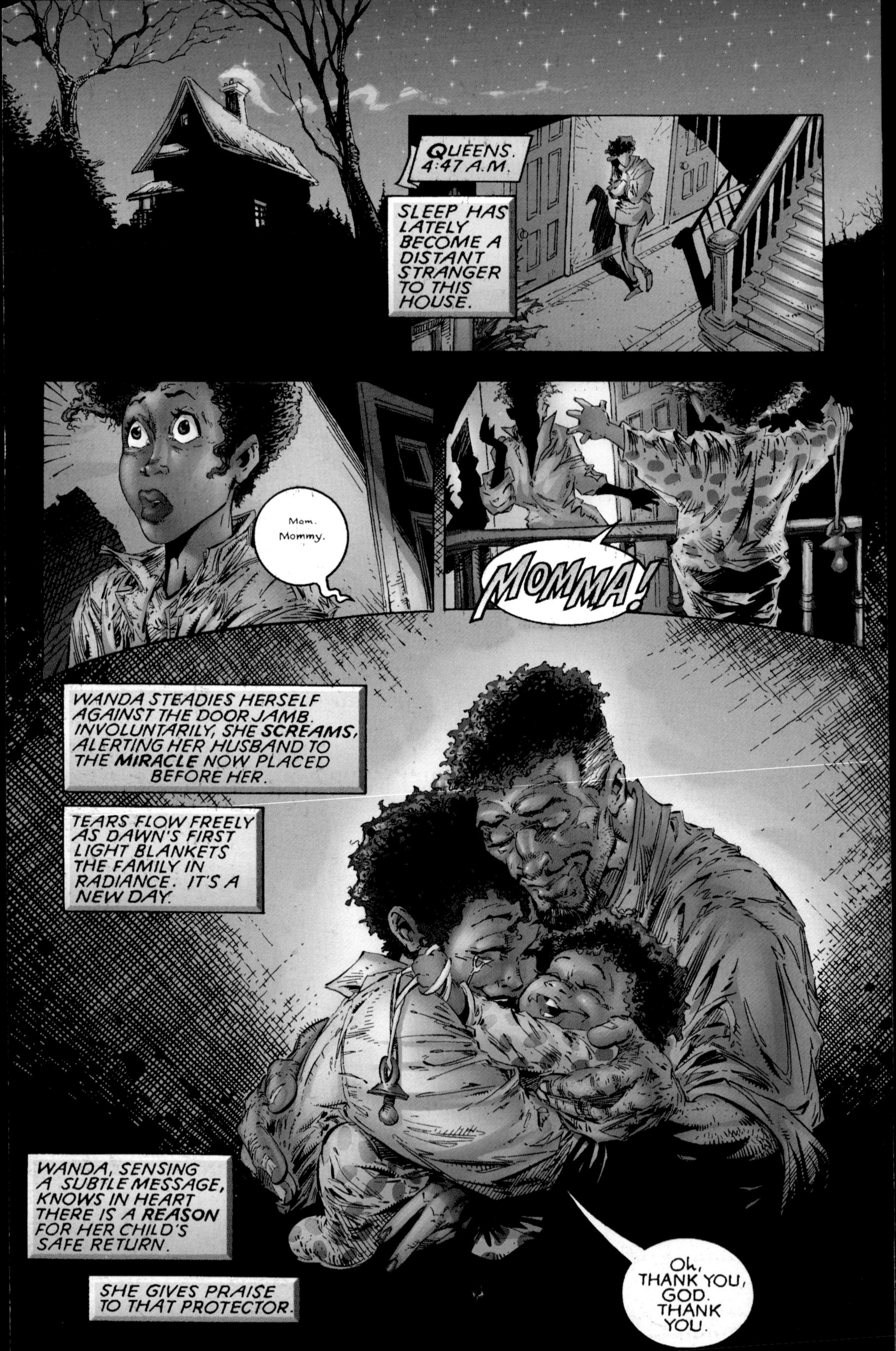
QUEENS. 4:47 A.M.
SLEEP HAS LATELY BECOME A DISTANT STRANGER TO THIS HOUSE.
Mom. Mommy.
MOMMA!
WANDA STEADIES HERSELF AGAINST THE DOOR JAMB. INVOLUNTARILY, SHE SCREAMS, ALERTING HER HUSBAND TO THE MIRACLE NOW PLACED BEFORE HER.
TEARS FLOW FREELY AS DAWN'S FIRST LIGHT BLANKETS THE FAMILY IN RADIANCE. IT'S A NEW DAY.
WANDA, SENSING A SUBTLE MESSAGE, KNOWS IN HEART THERE IS A REASON FOR HER CHILD'S SAFE RETURN.
SHE GIVES PRAISE TO THAT PROTECTOR.
Oh, THANK YOU, GOD. THANK YOU.

SPAWN
image
61
MAY
$1.95

S A N C T U A R Y

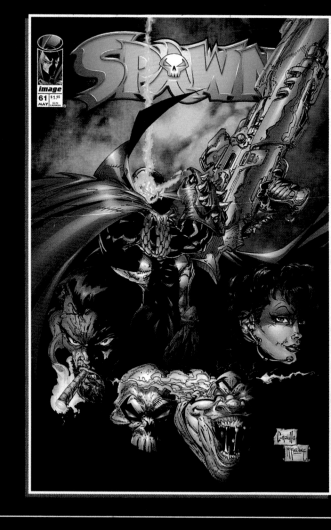

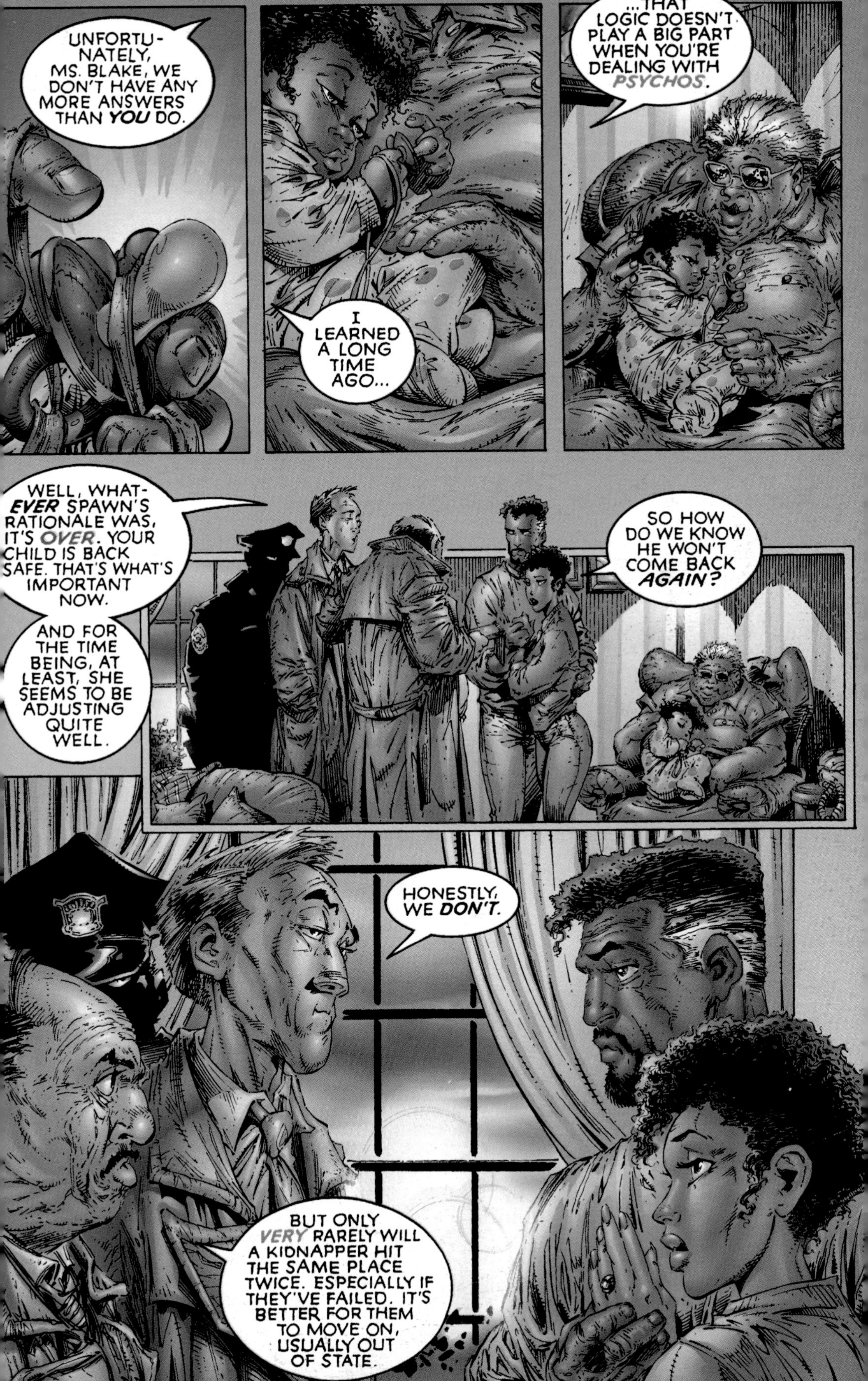
UNFORTU-NATELY, MS. BLAKE, WE DON'T HAVE ANY MORE ANSWERS THAN YOU DO.
I LEARNED A LONG TIME AGO...
...THAT LOGIC DOESN'T PLAY A BIG PART WHEN YOU'RE DEALING WITH PSYCHOS.
WELL, WHAT-EVER SPAWN'S RATIONALE WAS, IT'S OVER. YOUR CHILD IS BACK SAFE. THAT'S WHAT'S IMPORTANT NOW.
AND FOR THE TIME BEING, AT LEAST, SHE SEEMS TO BE ADJUSTING QUITE WELL.
SO HOW DO WE KNOW HE WON'T COME BACK AGAIN?
HONESTLY, WE DON'T.
BUT ONLY VERY RARELY WILL A KIDNAPPER HIT THE SAME PLACE TWICE. ESPECIALLY IF THEY'VE FAILED. IT'S BETTER FOR THEM TO MOVE ON, USUALLY OUT OF STATE.

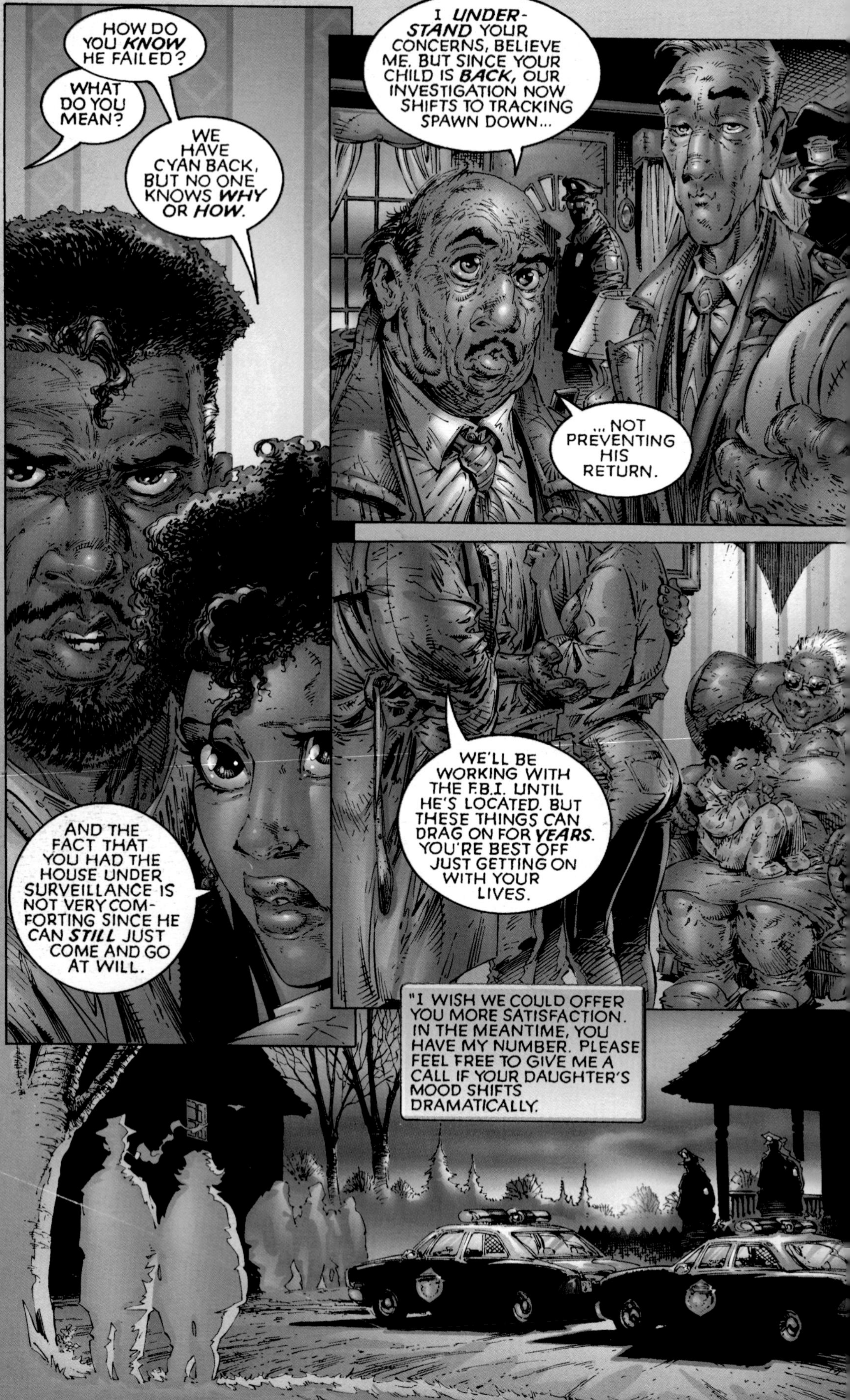
HOW DO YOU KNOW HE FAILED?
WHAT DO YOU MEAN?
WE HAVE CYAN BACK, BUT NO ONE KNOWS WHY OR HOW.
I UNDER-STAND YOUR CONCERNS, BELIEVE ME. BUT SINCE YOUR CHILD IS BACK, OUR INVESTIGATION NOW SHIFTS TO TRACKING SPAWN DOWN...
... NOT PREVENTING HIS RETURN.
AND THE FACT THAT YOU HAD THE HOUSE UNDER SURVEILLANCE IS NOT VERY COM-FORTING SINCE HE CAN STILL JUST COME AND GO AT WILL.
WE'LL BE WORKING WITH THE F.B.I. UNTIL HE'S LOCATED. BUT THESE THINGS CAN DRAG ON FOR YEARS. YOU'RE BEST OFF JUST GETTING ON WITH YOUR LIVES.
"I WISH WE COULD OFFER YOU MORE SATISFACTION. IN THE MEANTIME, YOU HAVE MY NUMBER. PLEASE FEEL FREE TO GIVE ME A CALL IF YOUR DAUGHTER'S MOOD SHIFTS DRAMATICALLY.

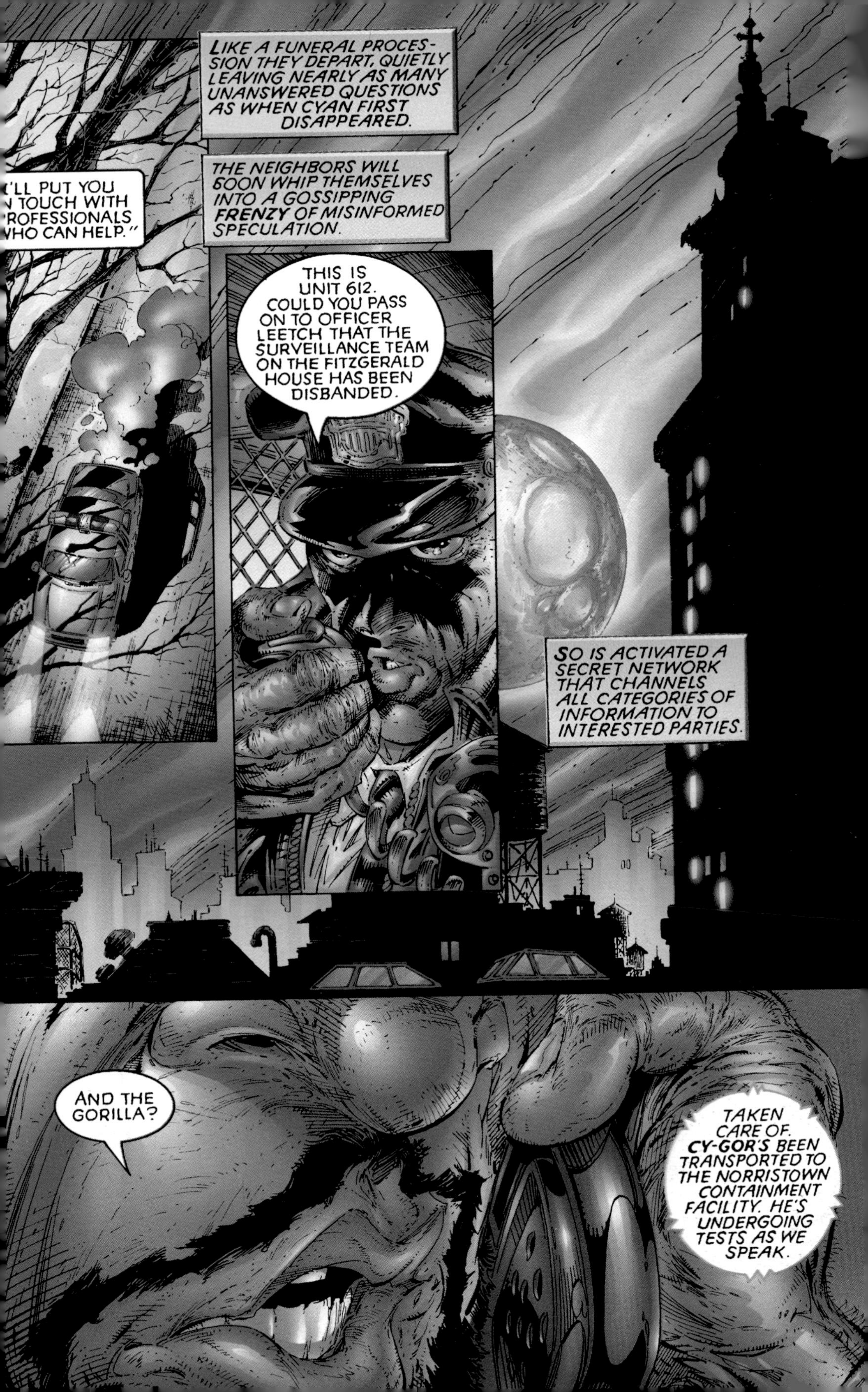
LIKE A FUNERAL PROCESSION THEY DEPART, QUIETLY LEAVING NEARLY AS MANY UNANSWERED QUESTIONS AS WHEN CYAN FIRST DISAPPEARED.
'LL PUT YOU N TOUCH WITH ROFESSIONALS WHO CAN HELP."
THE NEIGHBORS WILL SOON WHIP THEMSELVES INTO A GOSSIPPING FRENZY OF MISINFORMED SPECULATION.
THIS IS UNIT 612. COULD YOU PASS ON TO OFFICER LEETCH THAT THE SURVEILLANCE TEAM ON THE FITZGERALD HOUSE HAS BEEN DISBANDED.
SO IS ACTIVATED A SECRET NETWORK THAT CHANNELS ALL CATEGORIES OF INFORMATION TO INTERESTED PARTIES.
AND THE GORILLA?
TAKEN CARE OF. CY-GOR'S BEEN TRANSPORTED TO THE NORRISTOWN CONTAINMENT FACILITY. HE'S UNDERGOING TESTS AS WE SPEAK.

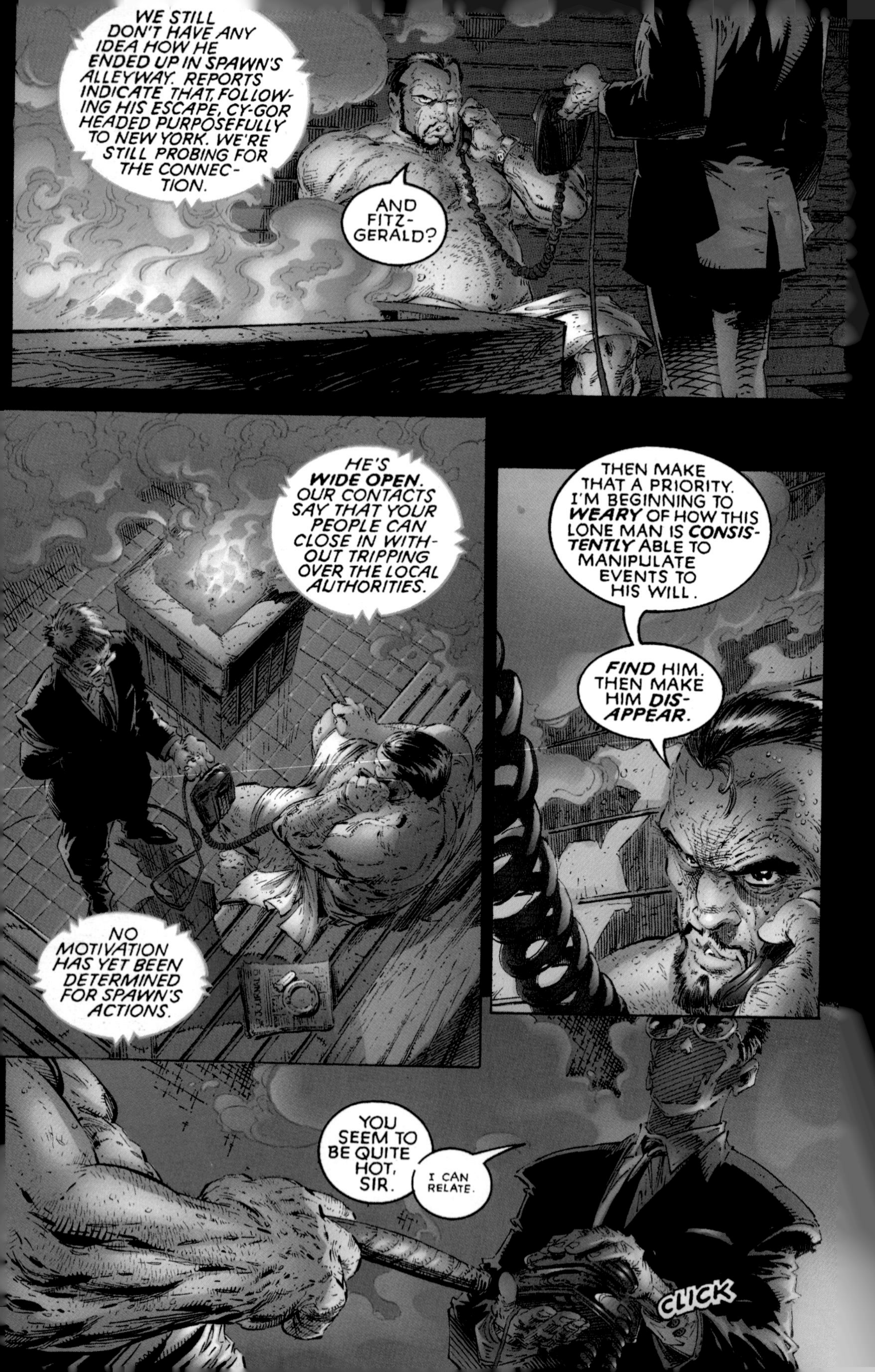
WE STILL DON'T HAVE ANY IDEA HOW HE ENDED UP IN SPAWN'S ALLEYWAY. REPORTS INDICATE THAT, FOLLOWING HIS ESCAPE, CY-GOR HEADED PURPOSEFULLY TO NEW YORK. WE'RE STILL PROBING FOR THE CONNECTION.
AND FITZGERALD?
HE'S WIDE OPEN. OUR CONTACTS SAY THAT YOUR PEOPLE CAN CLOSE IN WITHOUT TRIPPING OVER THE LOCAL AUTHORITIES.
NO MOTIVATION HAS YET BEEN DETERMINED FOR SPAWN'S ACTIONS.
THEN MAKE THAT A PRIORITY. I'M BEGINNING TO WEARY OF HOW THIS LONE MAN IS CONSISTENTLY ABLE TO MANIPULATE EVENTS TO HIS WILL.
FIND HIM. THEN MAKE HIM DISAPPEAR.
YOU SEEM TO BE QUITE HOT, SIR.
I CAN RELATE.
CLICK

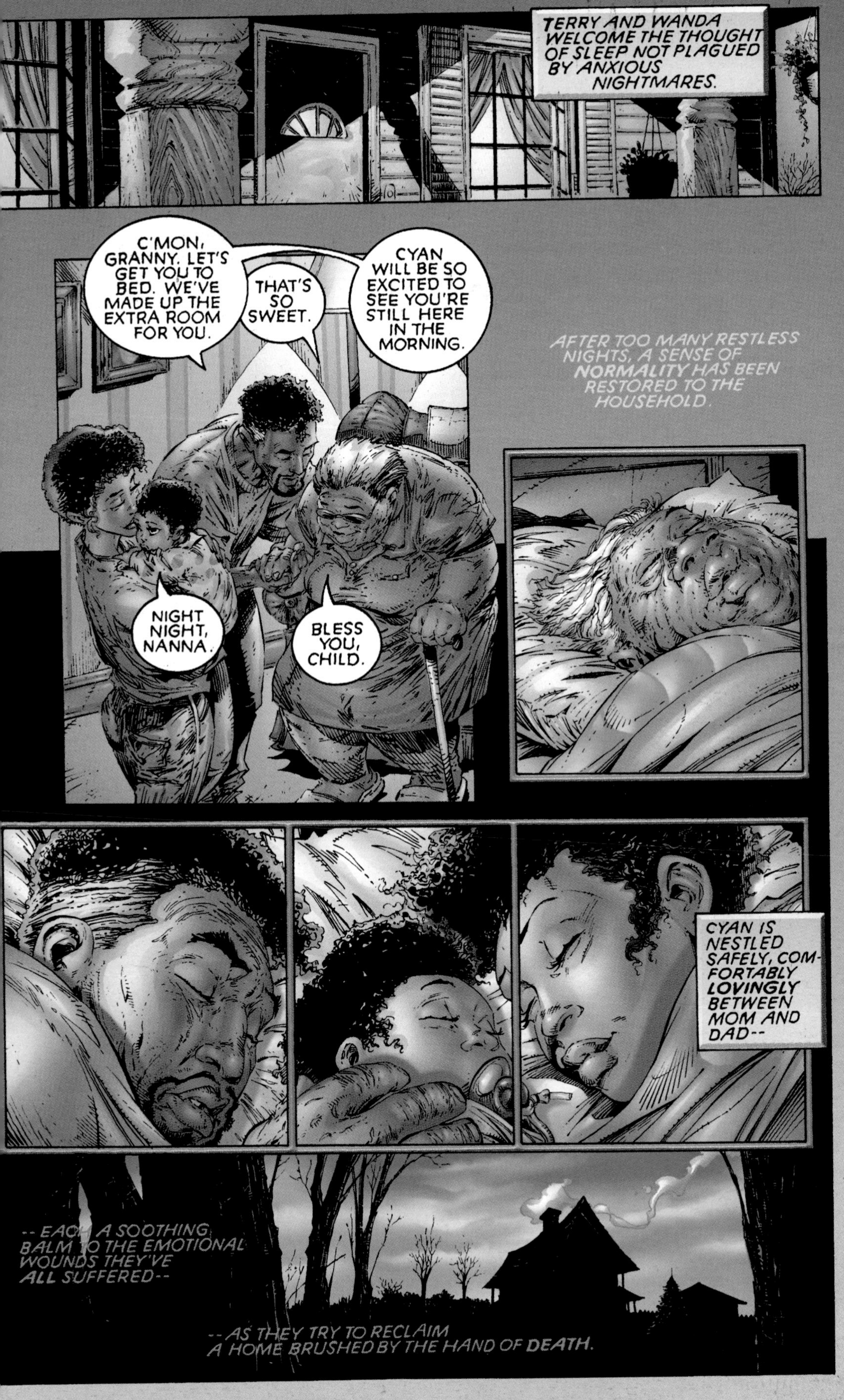
TERRY AND WANDA WELCOME THE THOUGHT OF SLEEP NOT PLAGUED BY ANXIOUS NIGHTMARES.
C'MON, GRANNY. LET'S GET YOU TO BED. WE'VE MADE UP THE EXTRA ROOM FOR YOU.
THAT'S SO SWEET.
CYAN WILL BE SO EXCITED TO SEE YOU'RE STILL HERE IN THE MORNING.
NIGHT NIGHT, NANNA.
BLESS YOU, CHILD.
AFTER TOO MANY RESTLESS NIGHTS, A SENSE OF NORMALITY HAS BEEN RESTORED TO THE HOUSEHOLD.
CYAN IS NESTLED SAFELY, COM-FORTABLY LOVINGLY BETWEEN MOM AND DAD--
-- EACH A SOOTHING BALM TO THE EMOTIONAL WOUNDS THEY'VE ALL SUFFERED--
-- AS THEY TRY TO RECLAIM A HOME BRUSHED BY THE HAND OF DEATH.

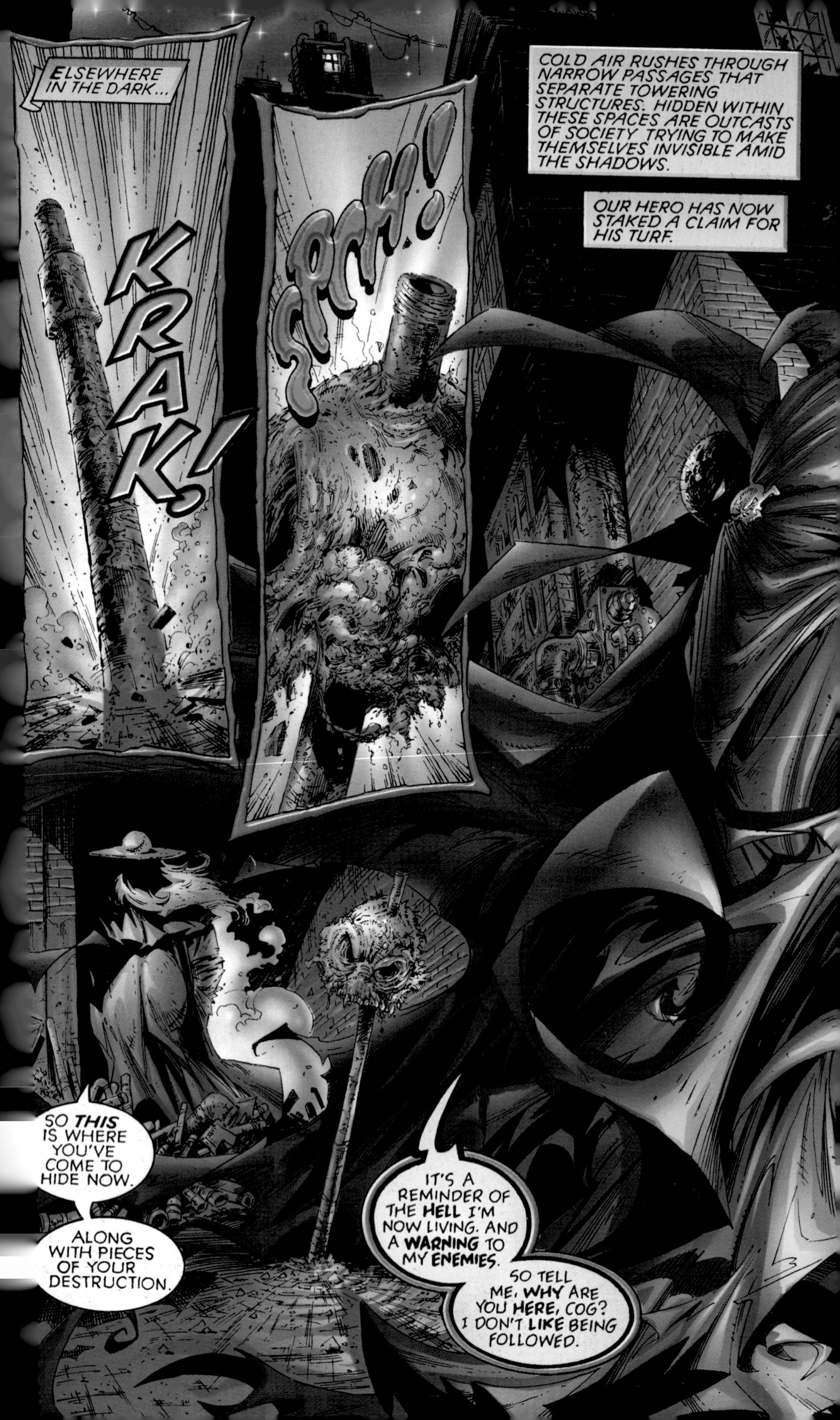
ELSEWHERE IN THE DARK...
KRAK!
SPCHH!
COLD AIR RUSHES THROUGH NARROW PASSAGES THAT SEPARATE TOWERING STRUCTURES. HIDDEN WITHIN THESE SPACES ARE OUTCASTS OF SOCIETY TRYING TO MAKE THEMSELVES INVISIBLE AMID THE SHADOWS.
OUR HERO HAS NOW STAKED A CLAIM FOR HIS TURF.
SO THIS IS WHERE YOU'VE COME TO HIDE NOW.
ALONG WITH PIECES OF YOUR DESTRUCTION.
IT'S A REMINDER OF THE HELL I'M NOW LIVING. AND A WARNING TO MY ENEMIES.
SO TELL ME, WHY ARE YOU HERE, COG? I DON'T LIKE BEING FOLLOWED.

I'M HERE TO HELP YOU.

WHY?

BECAUSE SOMEONE NEEDS TO SHOW YOU WHAT THE TRUE FACE OF YOUR ENEMY LOOKS LIKE.

I ALREADY KNOW WHO THEY ARE. IT'S JUST TAKEN ME A WHILE TO DO SOMETHING ABOUT IT.

YOU'VE ACCOMPLISHED NOTHING! FOR ALL YOUR POWER YOU STILL DON'T UNDERSTAND HOW THIS NEW LIFE WORKS.

THOUGH YOU MAY BELIEVE OTHERWISE, VIOLATOR ISN'T DEAD, NO MATTER WHAT MAY HAVE HAPPENED TO ITS HUMAN FORM. *

THERE IS ONE PROPER WAY TO KILL A DEMON... WHICH, OBVIOUSLY, YOU HAVEN'T LEARNED.

JUST AS WITH THAT ANGEL YOU BELIEVED VANQUISHED, THINGS ARE NOT WHAT THEY APPEAR TO BE.

LOOK, OLD MAN. I'M NOT INTERESTED IN YOUR MUMBO JUMBO. RIGHT NOW, THOUGH, YOU AND I ARE DUE FOR A GOOD LONG TALK.

* LAST ISSUE-- Tom.

SO, NOW WHAT?

NOW I GET MY POUND OF FLE BEFORE CLOWN POPPED UP I W ON MY WAY TO WIPE OUT WYN AND AFTER THA CHAPEL.

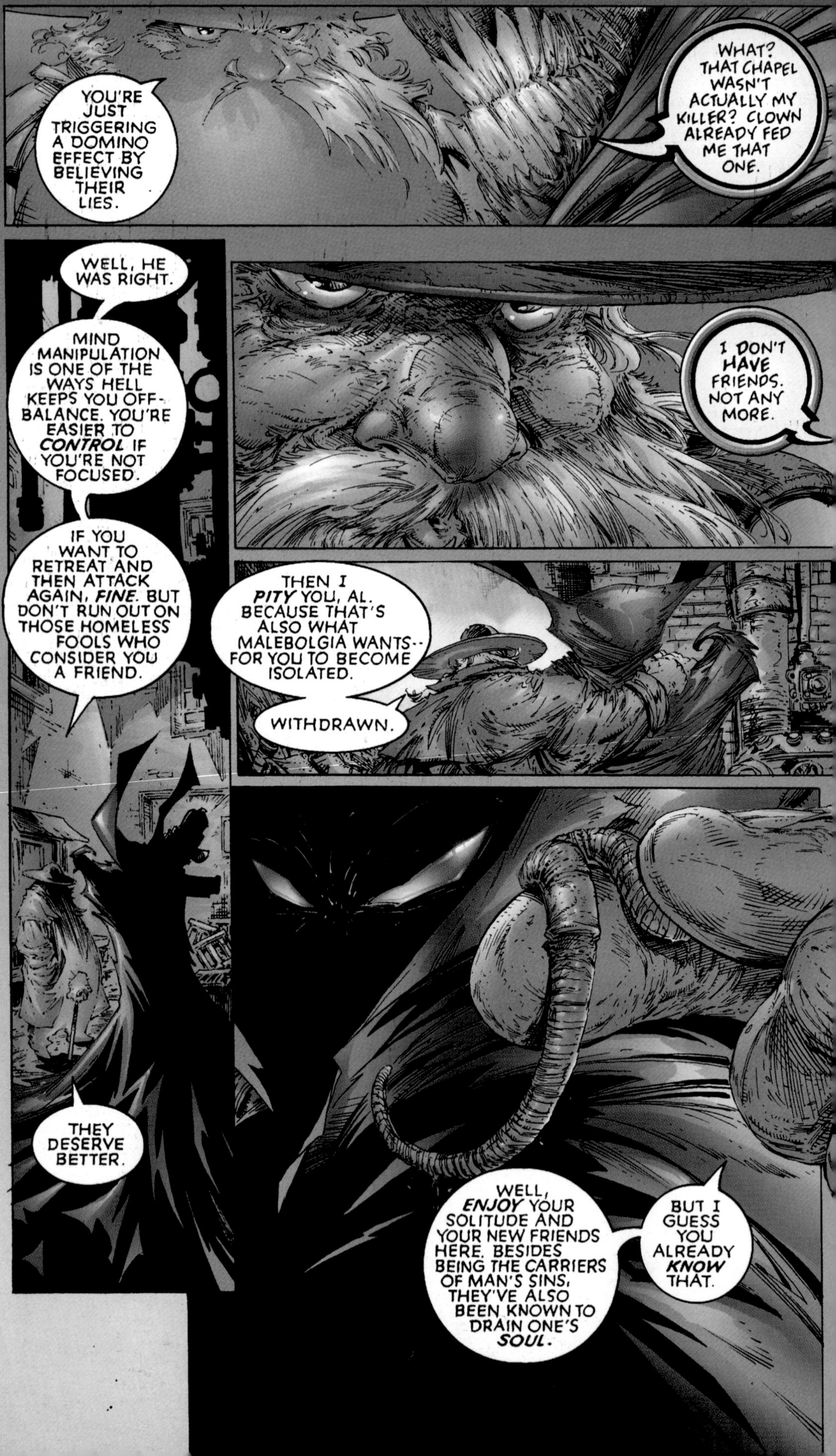
YOU'RE JUST TRIGGERING A DOMINO EFFECT BY BELIEVING THEIR LIES.
WHAT? THAT CHAPEL WASN'T ACTUALLY MY KILLER? CLOWN ALREADY FED ME THAT ONE.
WELL, HE WAS RIGHT.
MIND MANIPULATION IS ONE OF THE WAYS HELL KEEPS YOU OFF-BALANCE. YOU'RE EASIER TO CONTROL IF YOU'RE NOT FOCUSED.
IF YOU WANT TO RETREAT AND THEN ATTACK AGAIN, FINE. BUT DON'T RUN OUT ON THOSE HOMELESS FOOLS WHO CONSIDER YOU A FRIEND.
I DON'T HAVE FRIENDS. NOT ANY MORE.
THEN I PITY YOU, AL. BECAUSE THAT'S ALSO WHAT MALEBOLGIA WANTS-- FOR YOU TO BECOME ISOLATED.
WITHDRAWN.
THEY DESERVE BETTER.
BUT I GUESS YOU ALREADY KNOW THAT.
WELL, ENJOY YOUR SOLITUDE AND YOUR NEW FRIENDS HERE. BESIDES BEING THE CARRIERS OF MAN'S SINS, THEY'VE ALSO BEEN KNOWN TO DRAIN ONE'S SOUL.

ELL
NDA
ALLY
OYED
ELF
DAY,
RY.

HOPEFULLY SHE'LL FIND STRENGTH TO GET HERSELF PAST ALL THIS. ESPECIALLY FOR CYAN'S SAKE. THAT LITTLE GIRL'S GOING TO NEED ALL THE ATTENTION SHE CAN GET FROM BOTH OF YOU THE NEXT FEW DAYS.

WE KNOW, GRANNY.

YOUR BEING THERE TODAY IS APPRECIATED MORE THAN YOU'LL EVER KNOW.

WANDA'S STILL A BIT SHAKEN, AND I KNOW SHE'S GOING TO WANT TO PUT ALL HER ENERGY TOWARDS CYAN AND IGNORE HERSELF.

SHE'LL NEED SOMEONE TO DISTRACT HER, TO RELIEVE SOME OF THE PRESSURE.

I'LL DO WHAT-EVER I CAN.

I'M COUNTING ON IT.

NOW YOU'RE SURE YOU DON'T NEED ANY HELP TO YOUR HOUSE?

YOU ASK ME THAT EVERY TIME, TERRY.

I MAY BE OLD AND BLIND BUT I CAN STILL WALK A FEW STEPS WITHOUT FALLING DOWN DEAD. Hee hee!

LORD BLESS YOU FOR ALWAYS CARING.

KISS CYAN AGAIN FOR ME.

BEFORE THE DOOR IS FULLY OPENED, THE ELDERLY WOMAN SENSES SOMETHING.

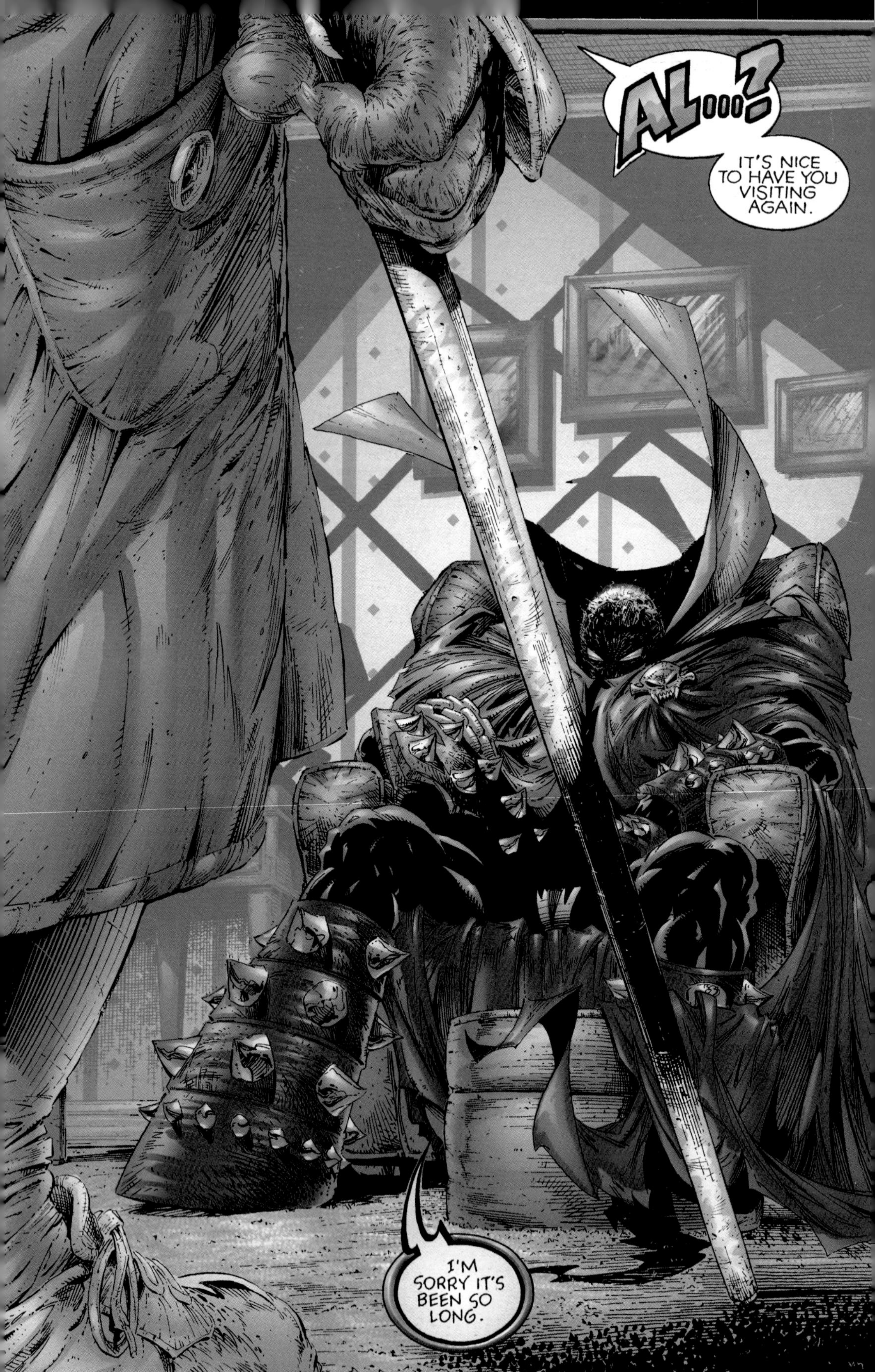
ALooo?
IT'S NICE TO HAVE YOU VISITING AGAIN.
I'M SORRY IT'S BEEN SO LONG.

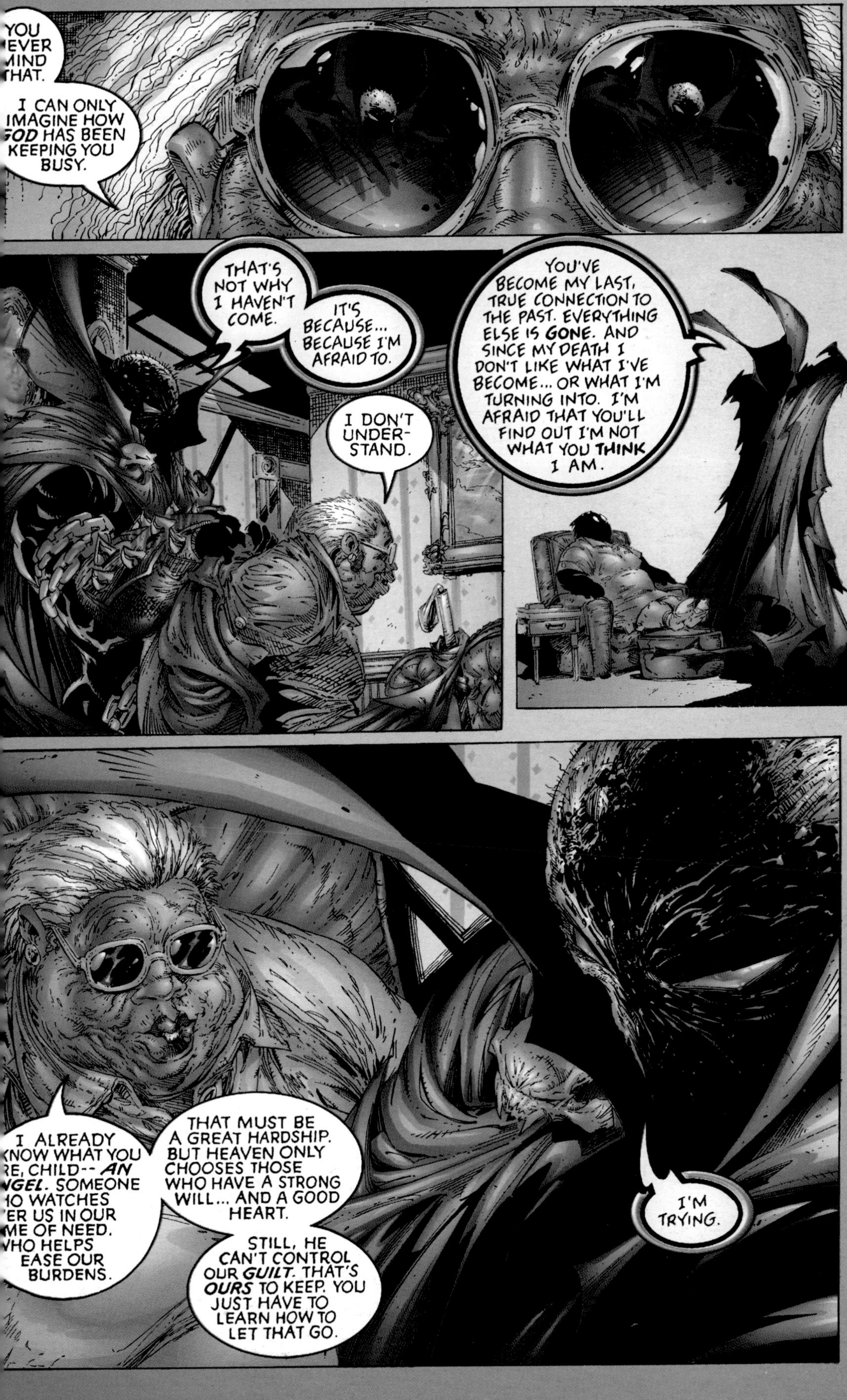

YOU EVER MIND THAT.
I CAN ONLY IMAGINE HOW GOD HAS BEEN KEEPING YOU BUSY.
THAT'S NOT WHY I HAVEN'T COME.
IT'S BECAUSE... BECAUSE I'M AFRAID TO.
I DON'T UNDER-STAND.
YOU'VE BECOME MY LAST, TRUE CONNECTION TO THE PAST. EVERYTHING ELSE IS GONE. AND SINCE MY DEATH I DON'T LIKE WHAT I'VE BECOME... OR WHAT I'M TURNING INTO. I'M AFRAID THAT YOU'LL FIND OUT I'M NOT WHAT YOU THINK I AM.
I ALREADY KNOW WHAT YOU ARE, CHILD-- AN ANGEL. SOMEONE WHO WATCHES OVER US IN OUR TIME OF NEED. WHO HELPS EASE OUR BURDENS.
THAT MUST BE A GREAT HARDSHIP. BUT HEAVEN ONLY CHOOSES THOSE WHO HAVE A STRONG WILL... AND A GOOD HEART.
STILL, HE CAN'T CONTROL OUR GUILT. THAT'S OURS TO KEEP. YOU JUST HAVE TO LEARN HOW TO LET THAT GO.
I'M TRYING.

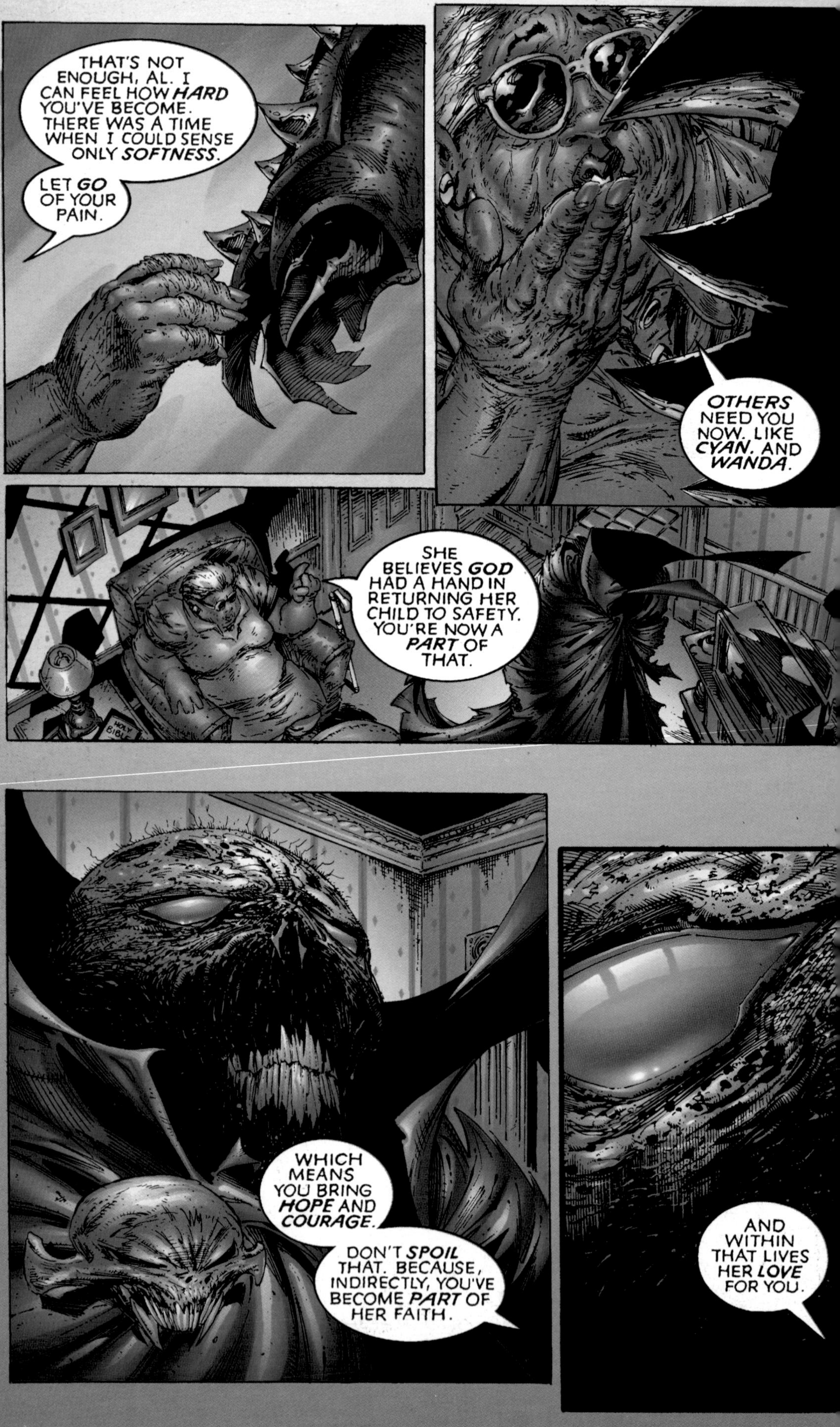
THAT'S NOT ENOUGH, AL. I CAN FEEL HOW HARD YOU'VE BECOME. THERE WAS A TIME WHEN I COULD SENSE ONLY SOFTNESS.
LET GO OF YOUR PAIN.
OTHERS NEED YOU NOW. LIKE CYAN. AND WANDA.
SHE BELIEVES GOD HAD A HAND IN RETURNING HER CHILD TO SAFETY. YOU'RE NOW A PART OF THAT.
HOLY BIBLE
WHICH MEANS YOU BRING HOPE AND COURAGE.
DON'T SPOIL THAT. BECAUSE, INDIRECTLY, YOU'VE BECOME PART OF HER FAITH.
AND WITHIN THAT LIVES HER LOVE FOR YOU.

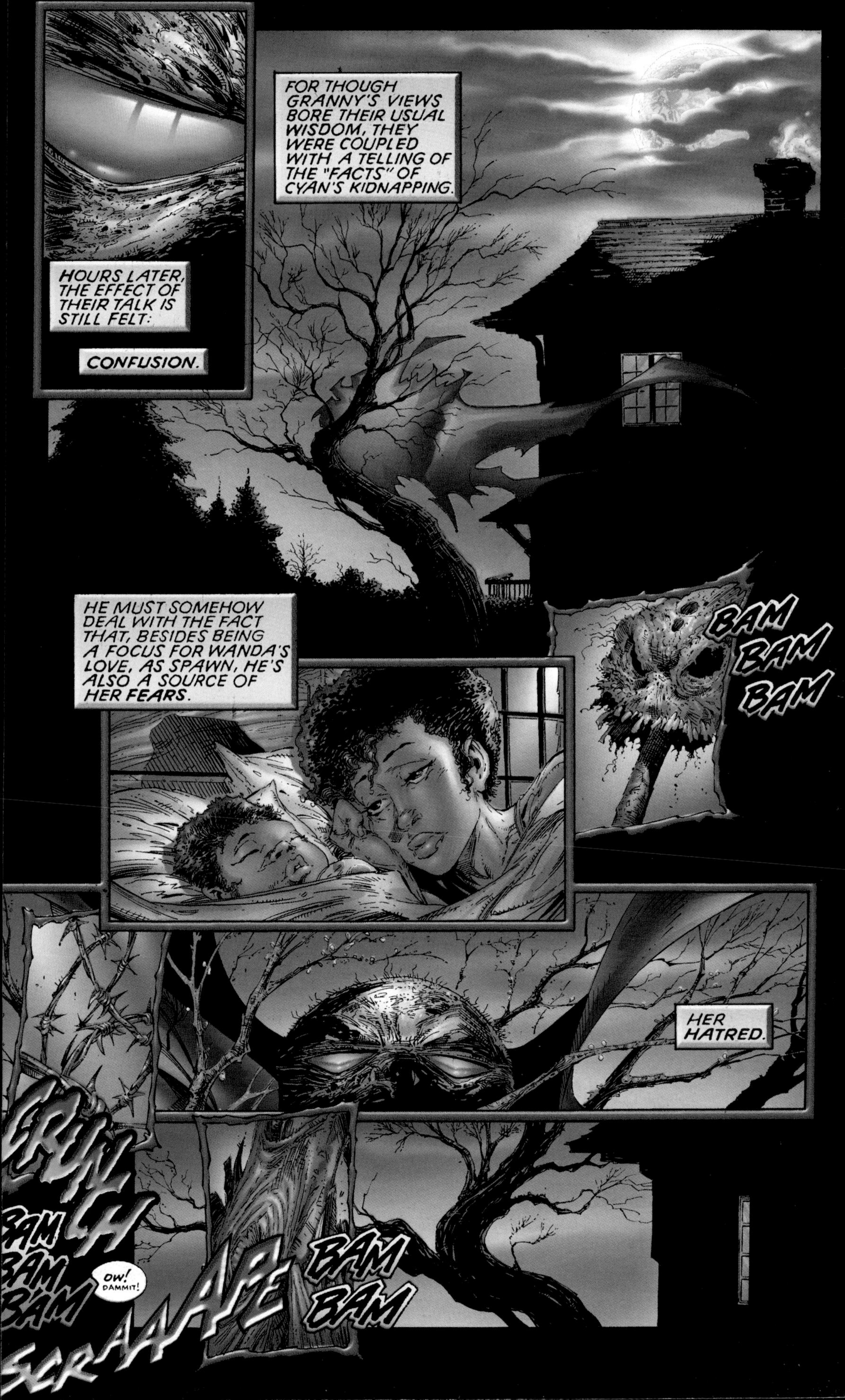
FOR THOUGH GRANNY'S VIEWS BORE THEIR USUAL WISDOM, THEY WERE COUPLED WITH A TELLING OF THE "FACTS" OF CYAN'S KIDNAPPING.
HOURS LATER, THE EFFECT OF THEIR TALK IS STILL FELT:
CONFUSION.
HE MUST SOMEHOW DEAL WITH THE FACT THAT, BESIDES BEING A FOCUS FOR WANDA'S LOVE, AS SPAWN, HE'S ALSO A SOURCE OF HER FEARS.
BAM BAM BAM
HER HATRED.
CRUNCH
BAM BAM BAM
OW! DAMMIT!
SCRAAAPE
BAM BAM

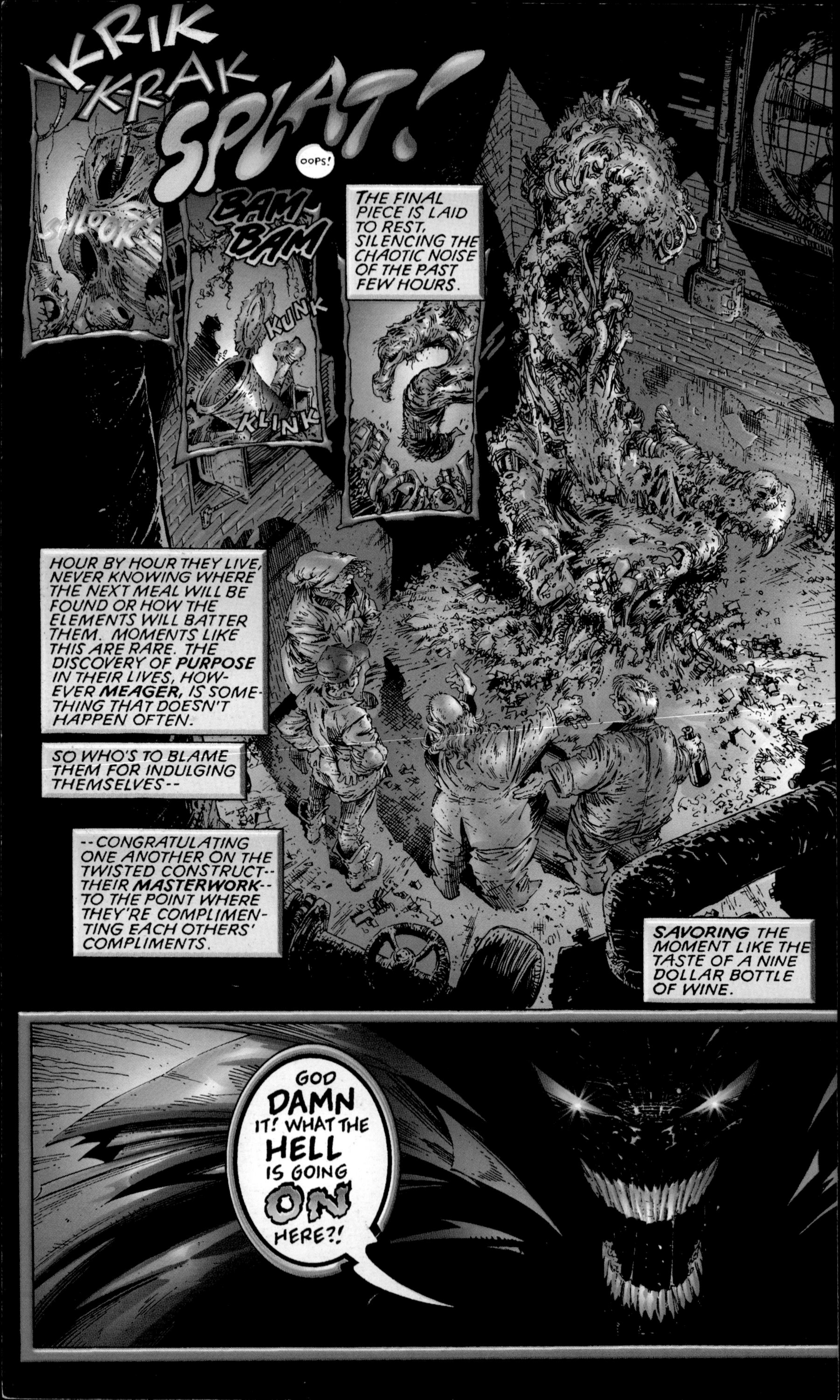

KRIK KRAK SPLAT!
OOPS!
SHLOOOK!
BAM-BAM
KUNK
KLINK
THE FINAL PIECE IS LAID TO REST, SILENCING THE CHAOTIC NOISE OF THE PAST FEW HOURS.
HOUR BY HOUR THEY LIVE, NEVER KNOWING WHERE THE NEXT MEAL WILL BE FOUND OR HOW THE ELEMENTS WILL BATTER THEM. MOMENTS LIKE THIS ARE RARE. THE DISCOVERY OF PURPOSE IN THEIR LIVES, HOWEVER MEAGER, IS SOMETHING THAT DOESN'T HAPPEN OFTEN.
SO WHO'S TO BLAME THEM FOR INDULGING THEMSELVES--
--CONGRATULATING ONE ANOTHER ON THE TWISTED CONSTRUCT--THEIR MASTERWORK--TO THE POINT WHERE THEY'RE COMPLIMENTING EACH OTHERS' COMPLIMENTS.
SAVORING THE MOMENT LIKE THE TASTE OF A NINE DOLLAR BOTTLE OF WINE.
GOD DAMN IT! WHAT THE HELL IS GOING ON HERE?!

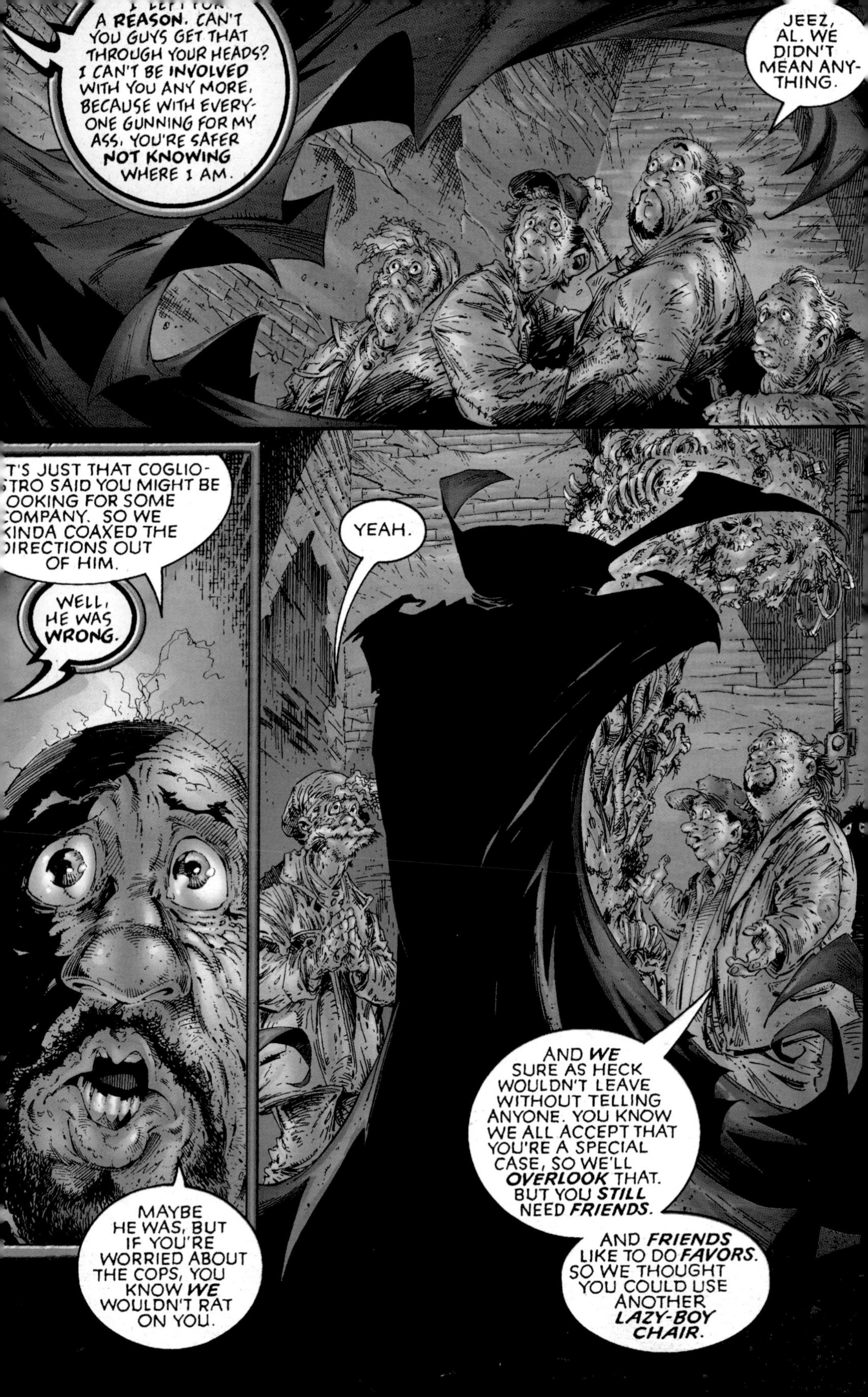
A REASON. CAN'T YOU GUYS GET THAT THROUGH YOUR HEADS? I CAN'T BE INVOLVED WITH YOU ANY MORE, BECAUSE WITH EVERY-ONE GUNNING FOR MY ASS, YOU'RE SAFER NOT KNOWING WHERE I AM.
JEEZ, AL. WE DIDN'T MEAN ANY-THING.
T'S JUST THAT COGLIO-STRO SAID YOU MIGHT BE OOKING FOR SOME COMPANY. SO WE KINDA COAXED THE DIRECTIONS OUT OF HIM.
WELL, HE WAS WRONG.
YEAH.
MAYBE HE WAS, BUT IF YOU'RE WORRIED ABOUT THE COPS, YOU KNOW WE WOULDN'T RAT ON YOU.
AND WE SURE AS HECK WOULDN'T LEAVE WITHOUT TELLING ANYONE. YOU KNOW WE ALL ACCEPT THAT YOU'RE A SPECIAL CASE, SO WE'LL OVERLOOK THAT. BUT YOU STILL NEED FRIENDS.
AND FRIENDS LIKE TO DO FAVORS. SO WE THOUGHT YOU COULD USE ANOTHER LAZY-BOY CHAIR.

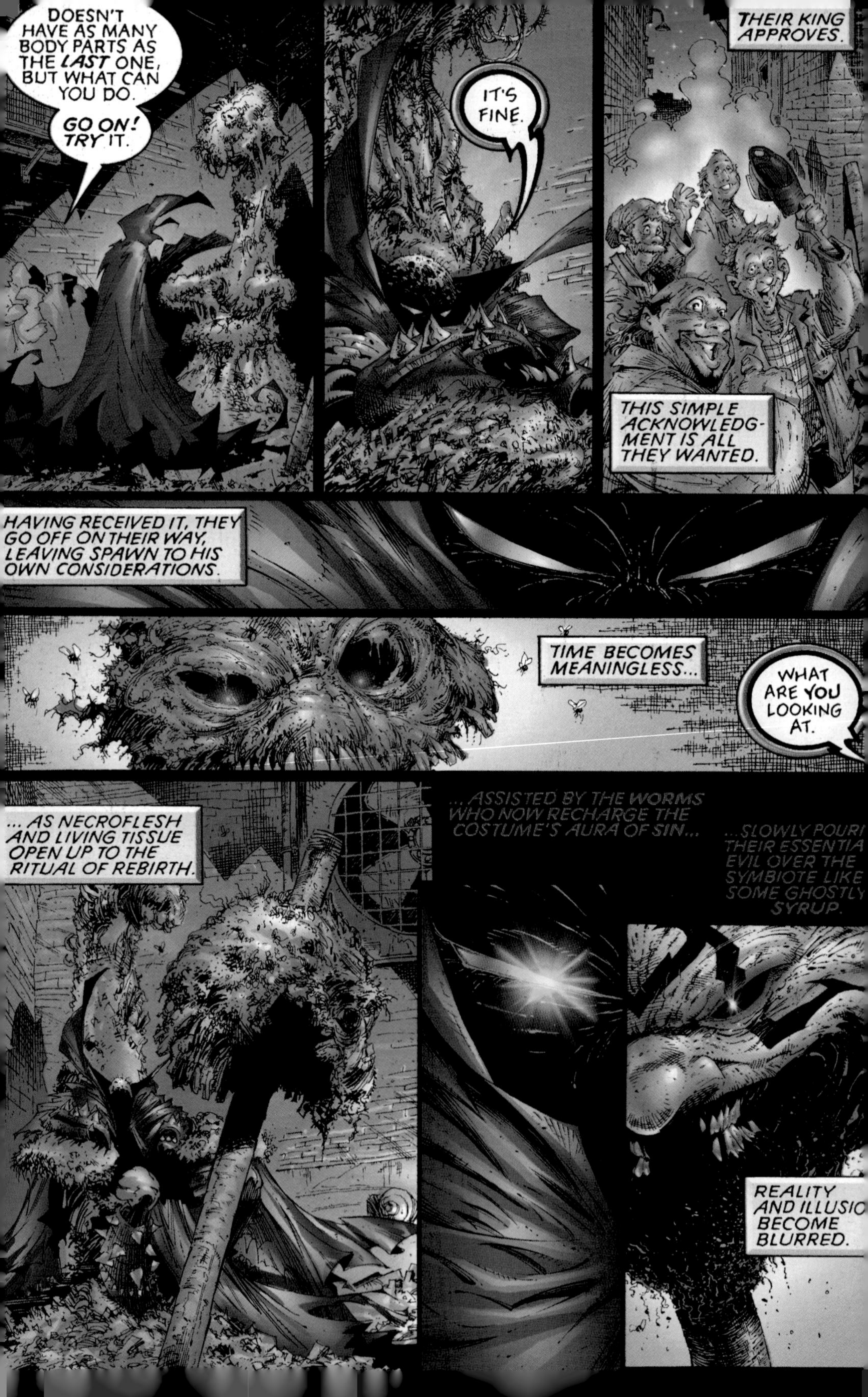
DOESN'T HAVE AS MANY BODY PARTS AS THE LAST ONE, BUT WHAT CAN YOU DO.
GO ON! TRY IT.
IT'S FINE.
THEIR KING APPROVES.
THIS SIMPLE ACKNOWLEDGMENT IS ALL THEY WANTED.
HAVING RECEIVED IT, THEY GO OFF ON THEIR WAY, LEAVING SPAWN TO HIS OWN CONSIDERATIONS.
TIME BECOMES MEANINGLESS...
WHAT ARE YOU LOOKING AT.
...AS NECROFLESH AND LIVING TISSUE OPEN UP TO THE RITUAL OF REBIRTH.
...ASSISTED BY THE WORMS WHO NOW RECHARGE THE COSTUME'S AURA OF SIN...
...SLOWLY POURI THEIR ESSENTIA EVIL OVER THE SYMBIOTE LIKE SOME GHOSTLY SYRUP.
REALITY AND ILLUSIO BECOME BLURRED.

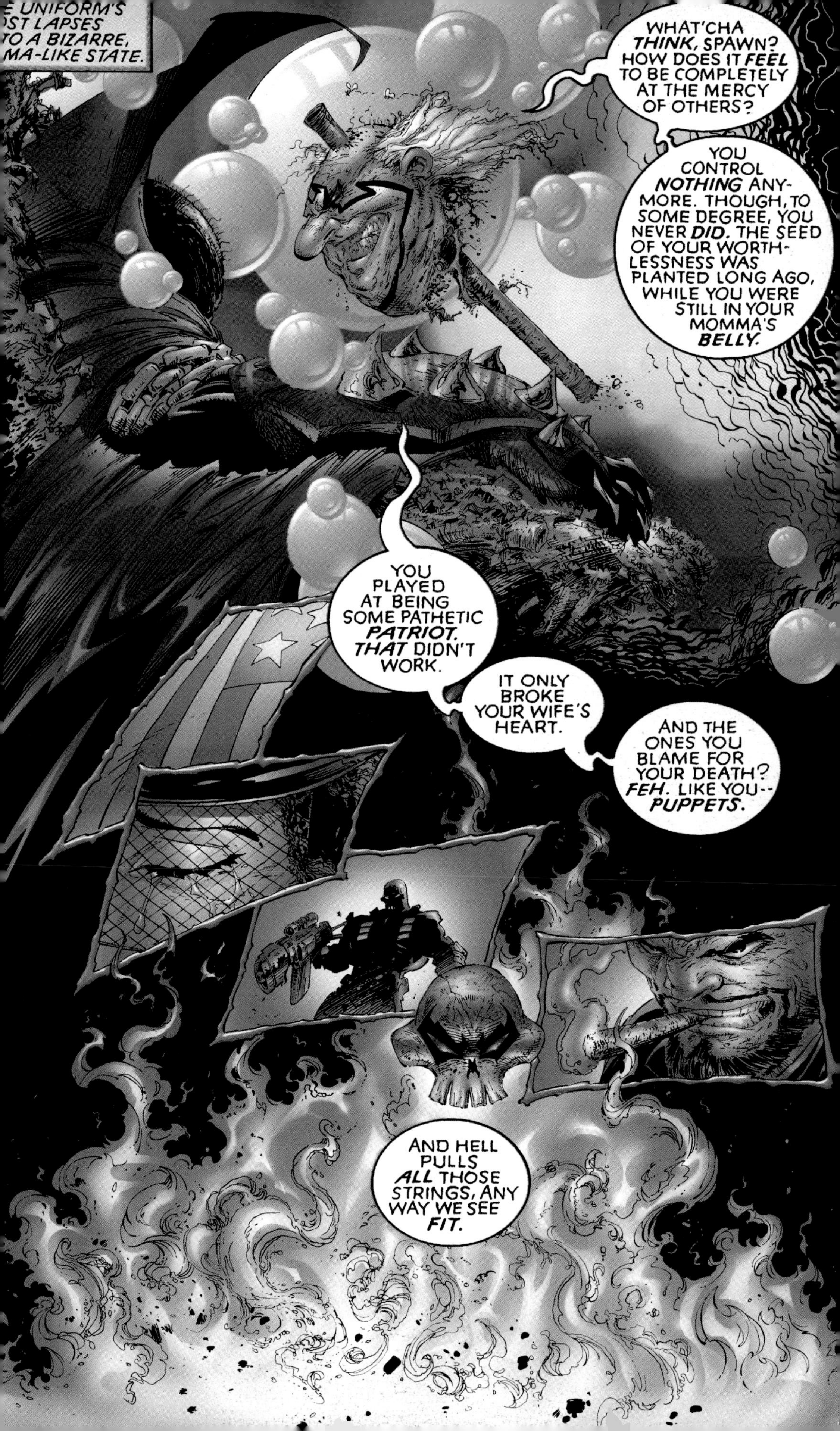
E UNIFORM'S
OST LAPSES
TO A BIZARRE,
MA-LIKE STATE.
WHAT'CHA THINK, SPAWN? HOW DOES IT FEEL TO BE COMPLETELY AT THE MERCY OF OTHERS?
YOU CONTROL NOTHING ANYMORE. THOUGH, TO SOME DEGREE, YOU NEVER DID. THE SEED OF YOUR WORTHLESSNESS WAS PLANTED LONG AGO, WHILE YOU WERE STILL IN YOUR MOMMA'S BELLY.
YOU PLAYED AT BEING SOME PATHETIC PATRIOT. THAT DIDN'T WORK.
IT ONLY BROKE YOUR WIFE'S HEART.
AND THE ONES YOU BLAME FOR YOUR DEATH? FEH. LIKE YOU-- PUPPETS.
AND HELL PULLS ALL THOSE STRINGS, ANY WAY WE SEE FIT.

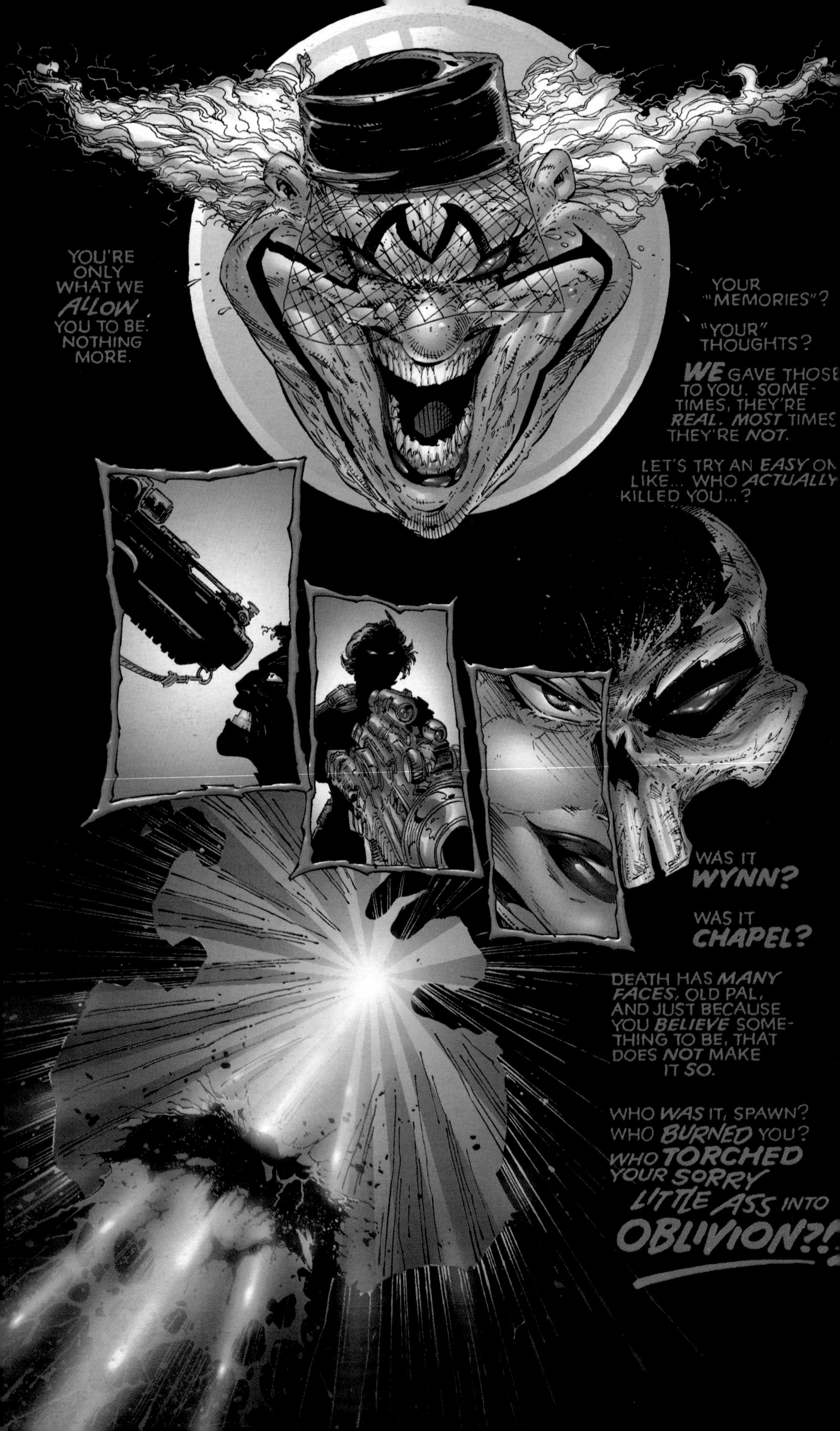

YOU'RE ONLY WHAT WE ALLOW YOU TO BE. NOTHING MORE.
YOUR "MEMORIES"?
"YOUR" THOUGHTS?
WE GAVE THOSE TO YOU. SOMETIMES, THEY'RE REAL. MOST TIMES THEY'RE NOT.
LET'S TRY AN EASY ONE LIKE... WHO ACTUALLY KILLED YOU...?
WAS IT WYNN?
WAS IT CHAPEL?
DEATH HAS MANY FACES, OLD PAL, AND JUST BECAUSE YOU BELIEVE SOMETHING TO BE, THAT DOES NOT MAKE IT SO.
WHO WAS IT, SPAWN? WHO BURNED YOU? WHO TORCHED YOUR SORRY LITTLE ASS INTO OBLIVION?!

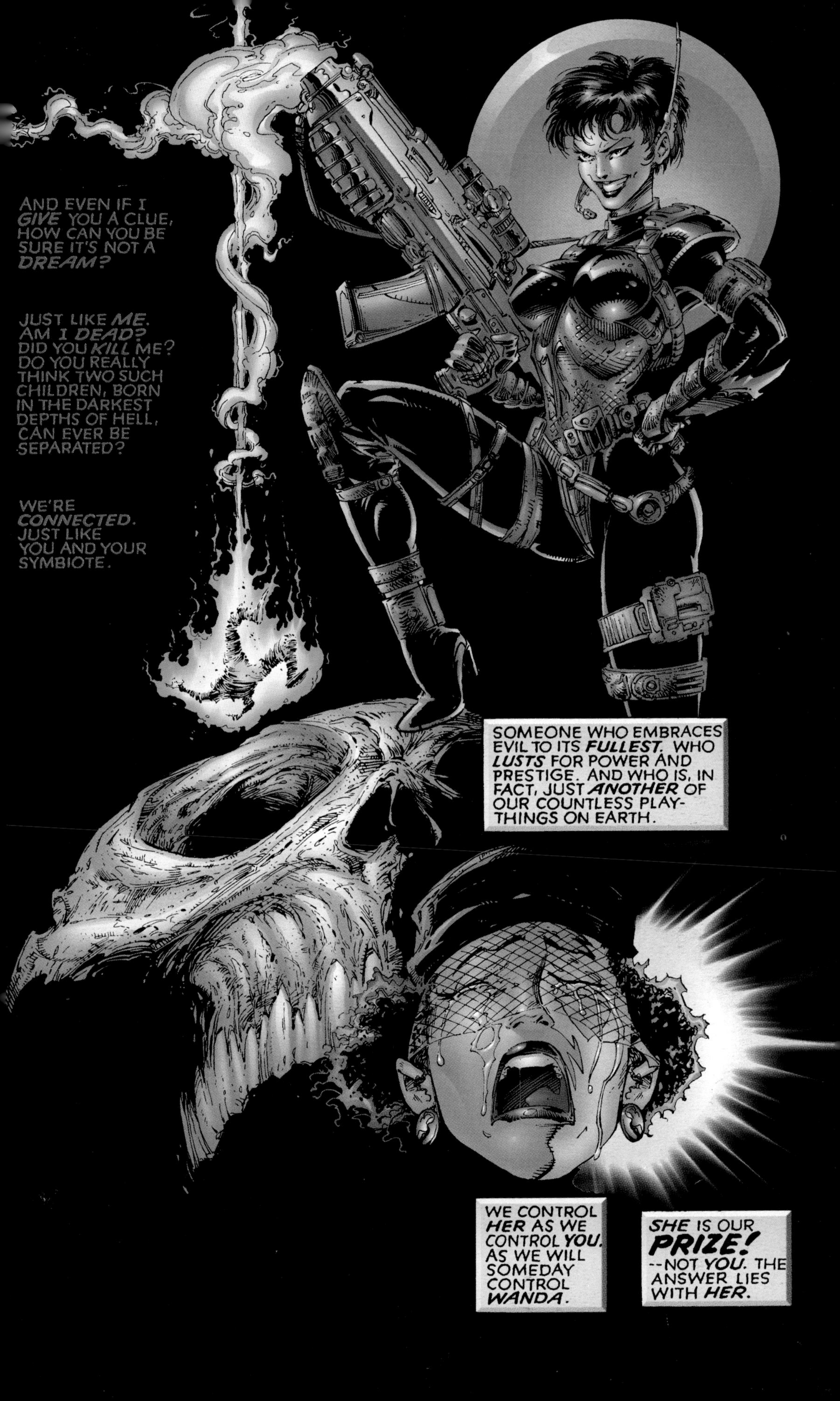
AND EVEN IF I GIVE YOU A CLUE, HOW CAN YOU BE SURE IT'S NOT A DREAM?
JUST LIKE ME. AM I DEAD? DID YOU KILL ME? DO YOU REALLY THINK TWO SUCH CHILDREN, BORN IN THE DARKEST DEPTHS OF HELL, CAN EVER BE SEPARATED?
WE'RE CONNECTED. JUST LIKE YOU AND YOUR SYMBIOTE.
SOMEONE WHO EMBRACES EVIL TO ITS FULLEST. WHO LUSTS FOR POWER AND PRESTIGE. AND WHO IS, IN FACT, JUST ANOTHER OF OUR COUNTLESS PLAY-THINGS ON EARTH.
WE CONTROL HER AS WE CONTROL YOU. AS WE WILL SOMEDAY CONTROL WANDA.
SHE IS OUR PRIZE! --NOT YOU. THE ANSWER LIES WITH HER.

"**SHE'S** WHAT HELL'S AFTER AND YOU ARE **LEADING** US TO HER. HA HA HA HA HAA"

SO ANOTHER PIECE OF SPAWN'S UNHOLY TAPESTRY IS WOVEN--

--AND HIDDEN WITHIN ITS DESIGN, A FEW MORE ANSWERS--

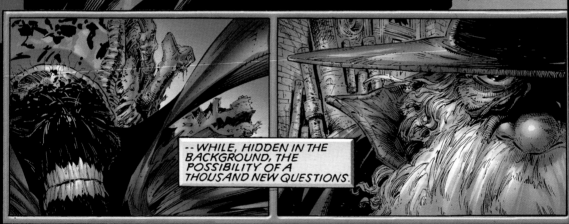

--WHILE, HIDDEN IN THE BACKGROUND, THE POSSIBILITY OF A THOUSAND NEW QUESTIONS.

OUR HERO FEELS FORCED INTO AN ABYSS OF PAIN AND TURMOIL. ANY THOUGHT OF REDEMPTION SEEMS A DELUDED FANTASY. YET, HE HOPES FOR RELEASE.

THE OTHERS ARE LEFT **HELPLESS** BUT TO WATCH FOR THE OUTCOME.

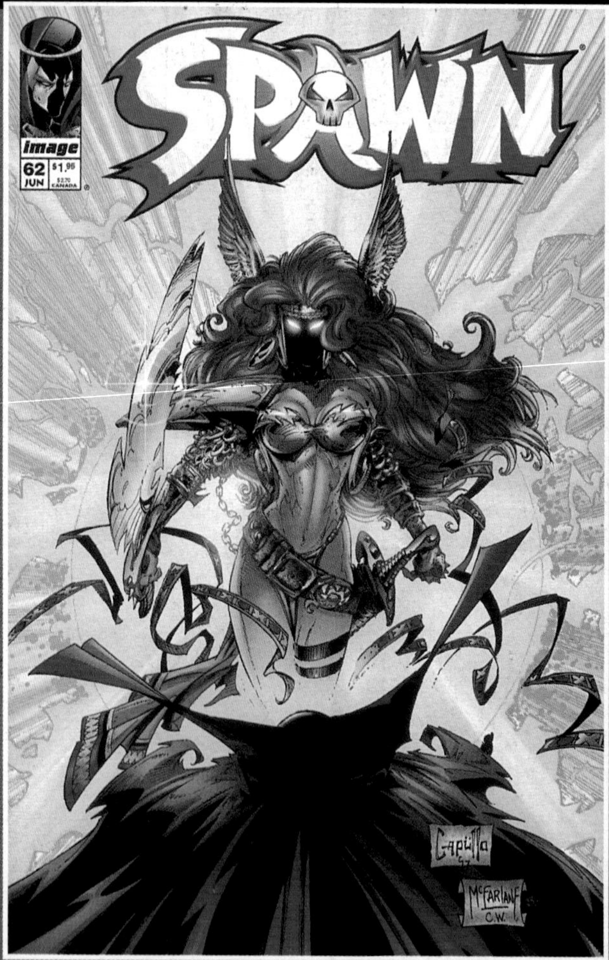
image
62
JUN
$1.95
$2.70 KANADA
SPAWN
Capullo
McFarlane
C.W.

R E T U R N

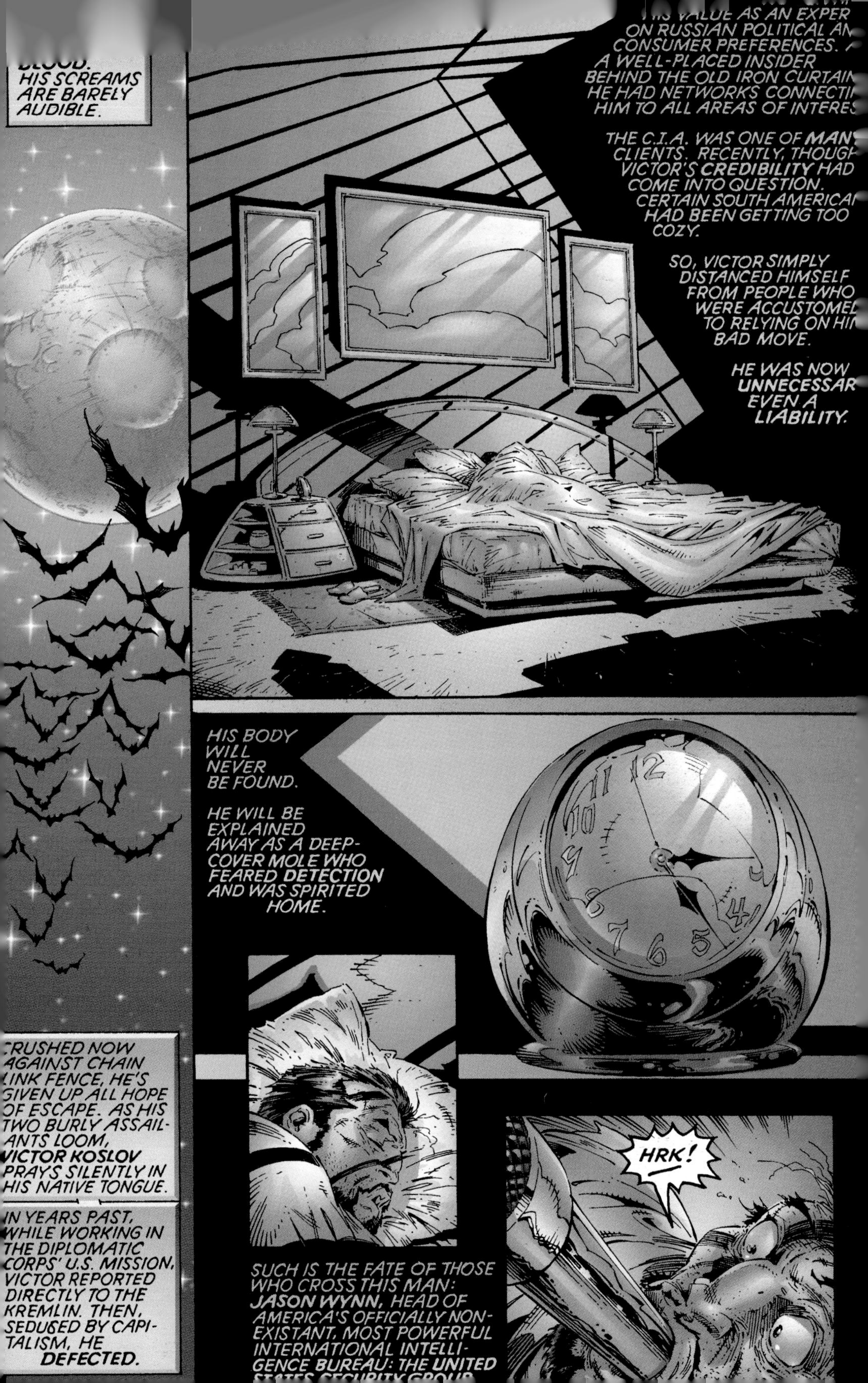
BLOOD. HIS SCREAMS ARE BARELY AUDIBLE.
...HIS VALUE AS AN EXPER ON RUSSIAN POLITICAL AN CONSUMER PREFERENCES. A WELL-PLACED INSIDER BEHIND THE OLD IRON CURTAIN HE HAD NETWORKS CONNECTI HIM TO ALL AREAS OF INTERES
THE C.I.A. WAS ONE OF MANY CLIENTS. RECENTLY, THOUGH VICTOR'S CREDIBILITY HAD COME INTO QUESTION. CERTAIN SOUTH AMERICA HAD BEEN GETTING TOO COZY.
SO, VICTOR SIMPLY DISTANCED HIMSELF FROM PEOPLE WHO WERE ACCUSTOMED TO RELYING ON HIM BAD MOVE.
HE WAS NOW UNNECESSAR EVEN A LIABILITY.
CRUSHED NOW AGAINST CHAIN LINK FENCE, HE'S GIVEN UP ALL HOPE OF ESCAPE. AS HIS TWO BURLY ASSAIL-ANTS LOOM, VICTOR KOSLOV PRAYS SILENTLY IN HIS NATIVE TONGUE.
IN YEARS PAST, WHILE WORKING IN THE DIPLOMATIC CORPS' U.S. MISSION, VICTOR REPORTED DIRECTLY TO THE KREMLIN. THEN, SEDUCED BY CAPI-TALISM, HE DEFECTED.
HIS BODY WILL NEVER BE FOUND.
HE WILL BE EXPLAINED AWAY AS A DEEP-COVER MOLE WHO FEARED DETECTION AND WAS SPIRITED HOME.
SUCH IS THE FATE OF THOSE WHO CROSS THIS MAN: JASON WYNN, HEAD OF AMERICA'S OFFICIALLY NON-EXISTANT, MOST POWERFUL INTERNATIONAL INTELLI-GENCE BUREAU: THE UNITED
HRK!

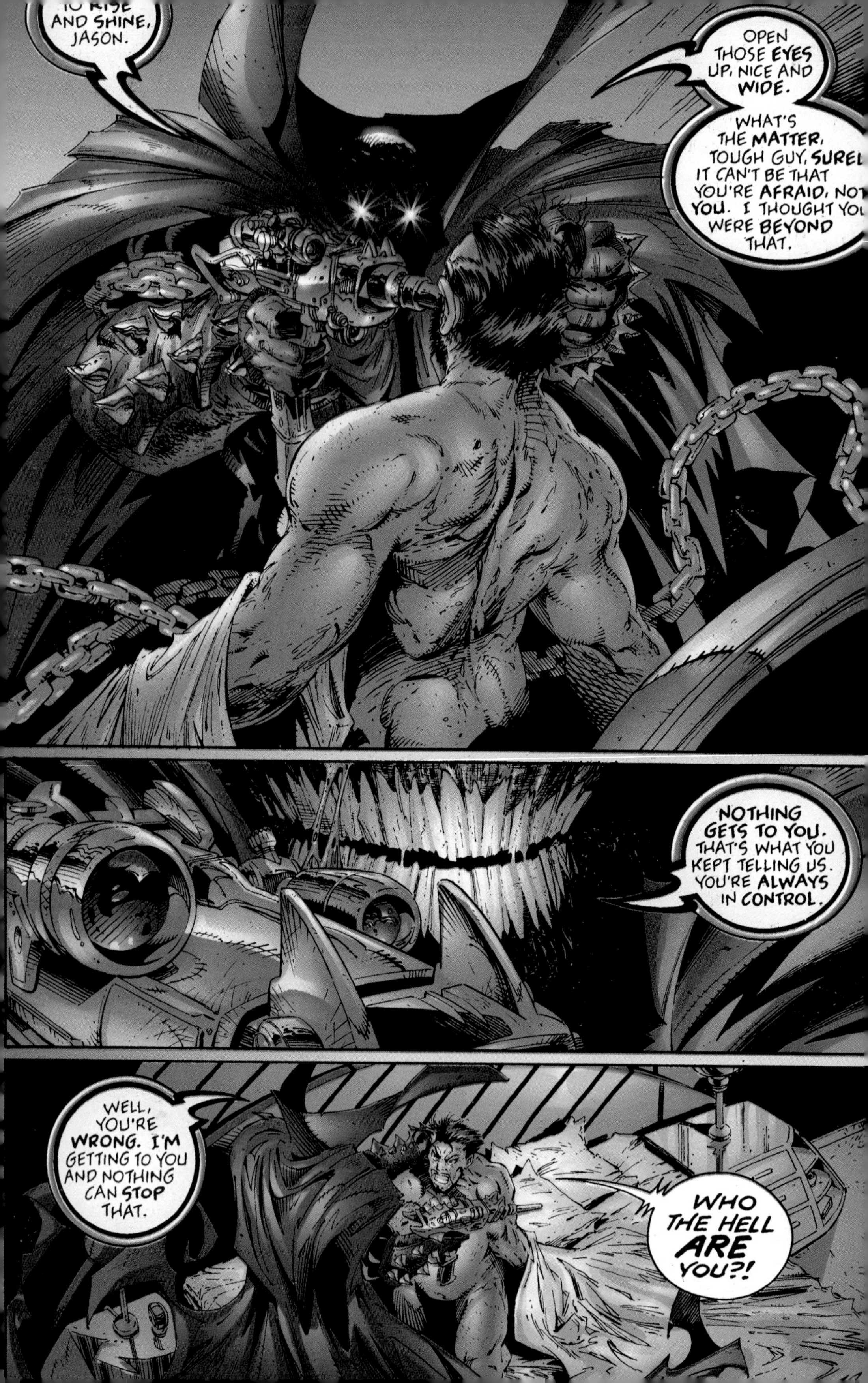
RISE AND SHINE, JASON.
OPEN THOSE EYES UP, NICE AND WIDE.
WHAT'S THE MATTER, TOUGH GUY, SUREL IT CAN'T BE THAT YOU'RE AFRAID, NOT YOU. I THOUGHT YOU WERE BEYOND THAT.
NOTHING GETS TO YOU. THAT'S WHAT YOU KEPT TELLING US. YOU'RE ALWAYS IN CONTROL.
WELL, YOU'RE WRONG. I'M GETTING TO YOU AND NOTHING CAN STOP THAT.
WHO THE HELL ARE YOU?!

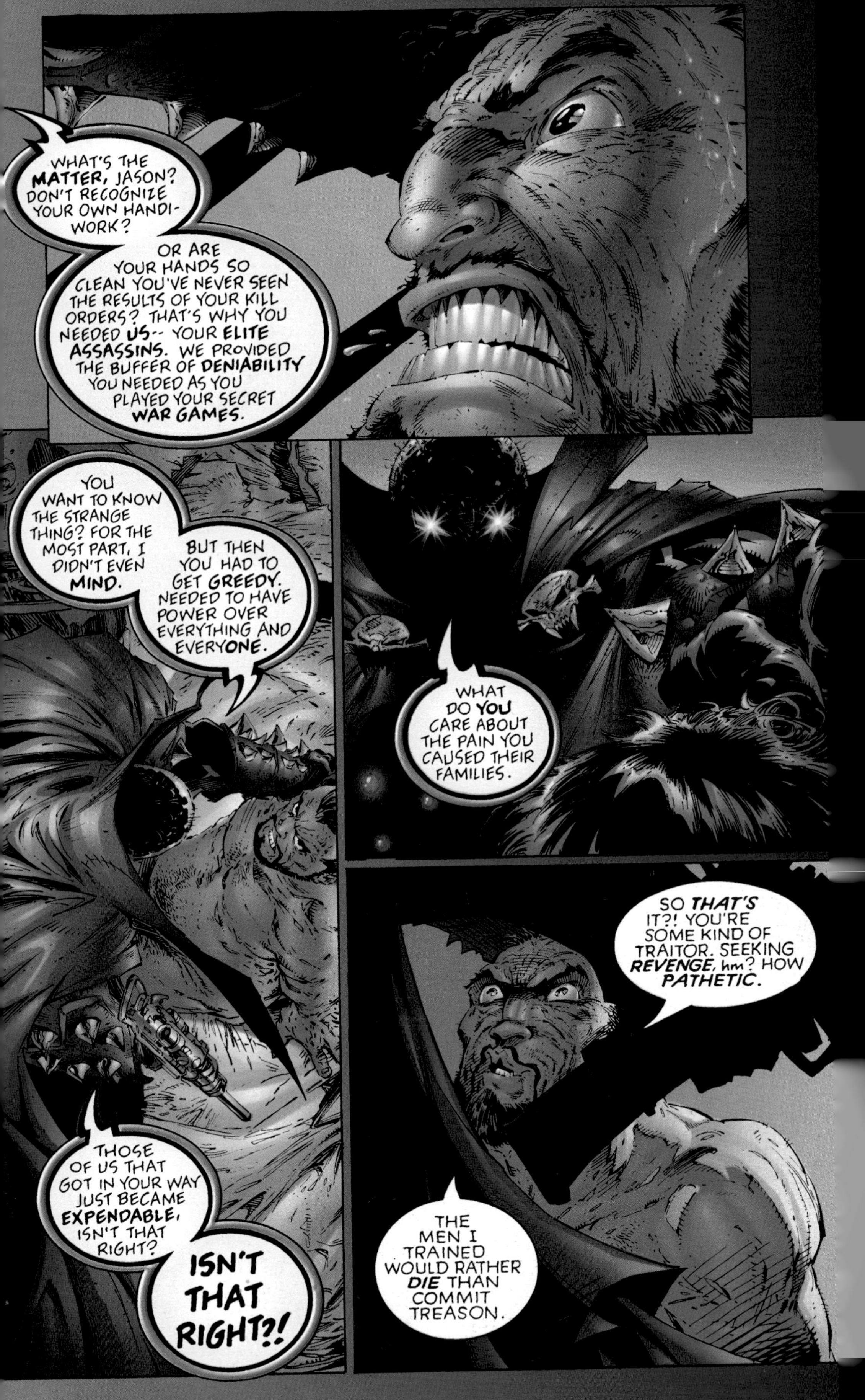

WHAT'S THE MATTER, JASON? DON'T RECOGNIZE YOUR OWN HANDI-WORK?
OR ARE YOUR HANDS SO CLEAN YOU'VE NEVER SEEN THE RESULTS OF YOUR KILL ORDERS? THAT'S WHY YOU NEEDED US-- YOUR ELITE ASSASSINS. WE PROVIDED THE BUFFER OF DENIABILITY YOU NEEDED AS YOU PLAYED YOUR SECRET WAR GAMES.
YOU WANT TO KNOW THE STRANGE THING? FOR THE MOST PART, I DIDN'T EVEN MIND.
BUT THEN YOU HAD TO GET GREEDY. NEEDED TO HAVE POWER OVER EVERYTHING AND EVERYONE.
THOSE OF US THAT GOT IN YOUR WAY JUST BECAME EXPENDABLE, ISN'T THAT RIGHT?
ISN'T THAT RIGHT?!
WHAT DO YOU CARE ABOUT THE PAIN YOU CAUSED THEIR FAMILIES.
SO THAT'S IT?! YOU'RE SOME KIND OF TRAITOR. SEEKING REVENGE, hm? HOW PATHETIC.
THE MEN I TRAINED WOULD RATHER DIE THAN COMMIT TREASON.

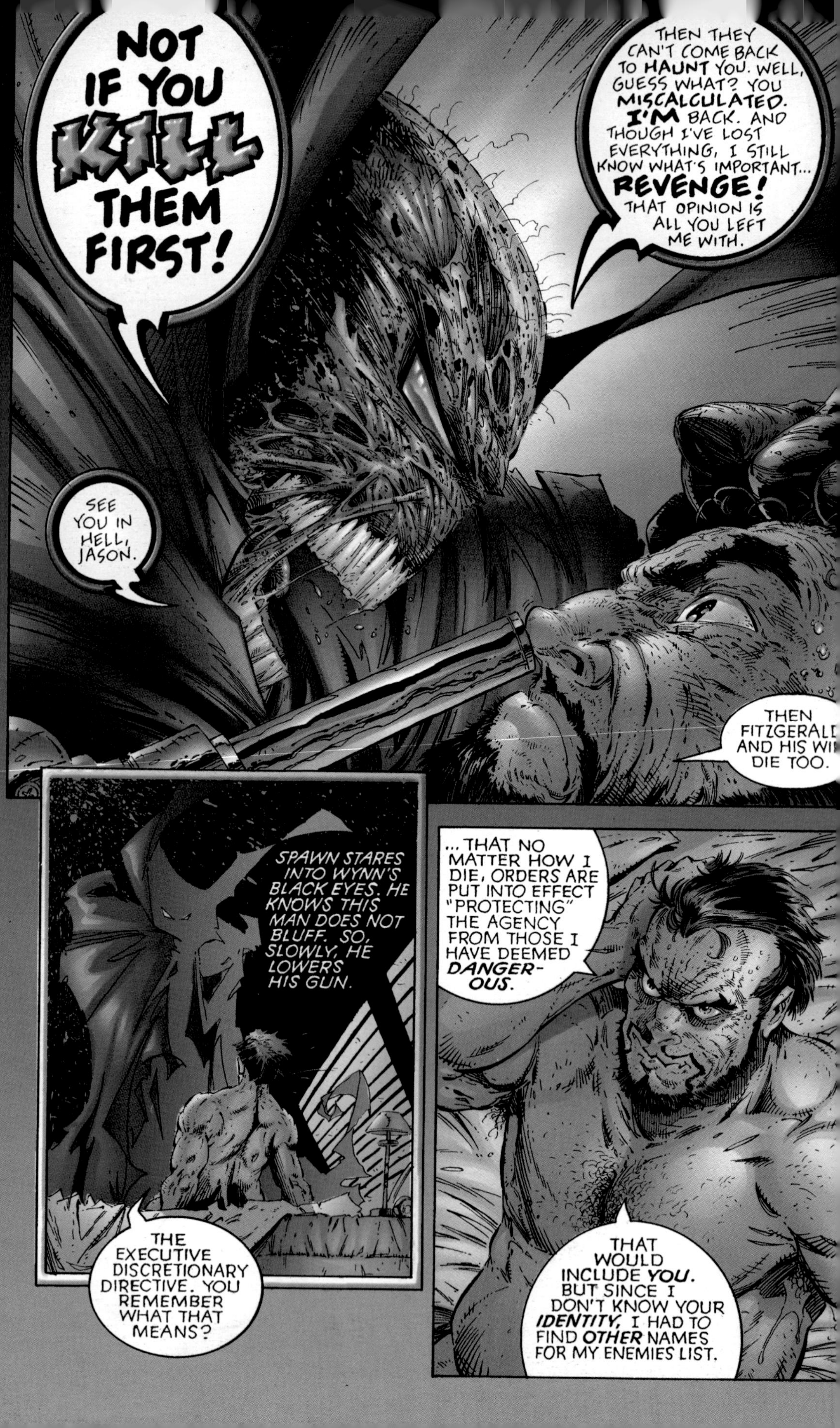
NOT IF YOU KILL THEM FIRST!
THEN THEY CAN'T COME BACK TO HAUNT YOU. WELL, GUESS WHAT? YOU MISCALCULATED. I'M BACK. AND THOUGH I'VE LOST EVERYTHING, I STILL KNOW WHAT'S IMPORTANT... REVENGE! THAT OPINION IS ALL YOU LEFT ME WITH.
SEE YOU IN HELL, JASON.
THEN FITZGERALD AND HIS WI DIE TOO.
SPAWN STARES INTO WYNN'S BLACK EYES. HE KNOWS THIS MAN DOES NOT BLUFF. SO, SLOWLY, HE LOWERS HIS GUN.
THE EXECUTIVE DISCRETIONARY DIRECTIVE. YOU REMEMBER WHAT THAT MEANS?
...THAT NO MATTER HOW I DIE, ORDERS ARE PUT INTO EFFECT "PROTECTING" THE AGENCY FROM THOSE I HAVE DEEMED DANGER-OUS.
THAT WOULD INCLUDE YOU. BUT SINCE I DON'T KNOW YOUR IDENTITY, I HAD TO FIND OTHER NAMES FOR MY ENEMIES LIST.

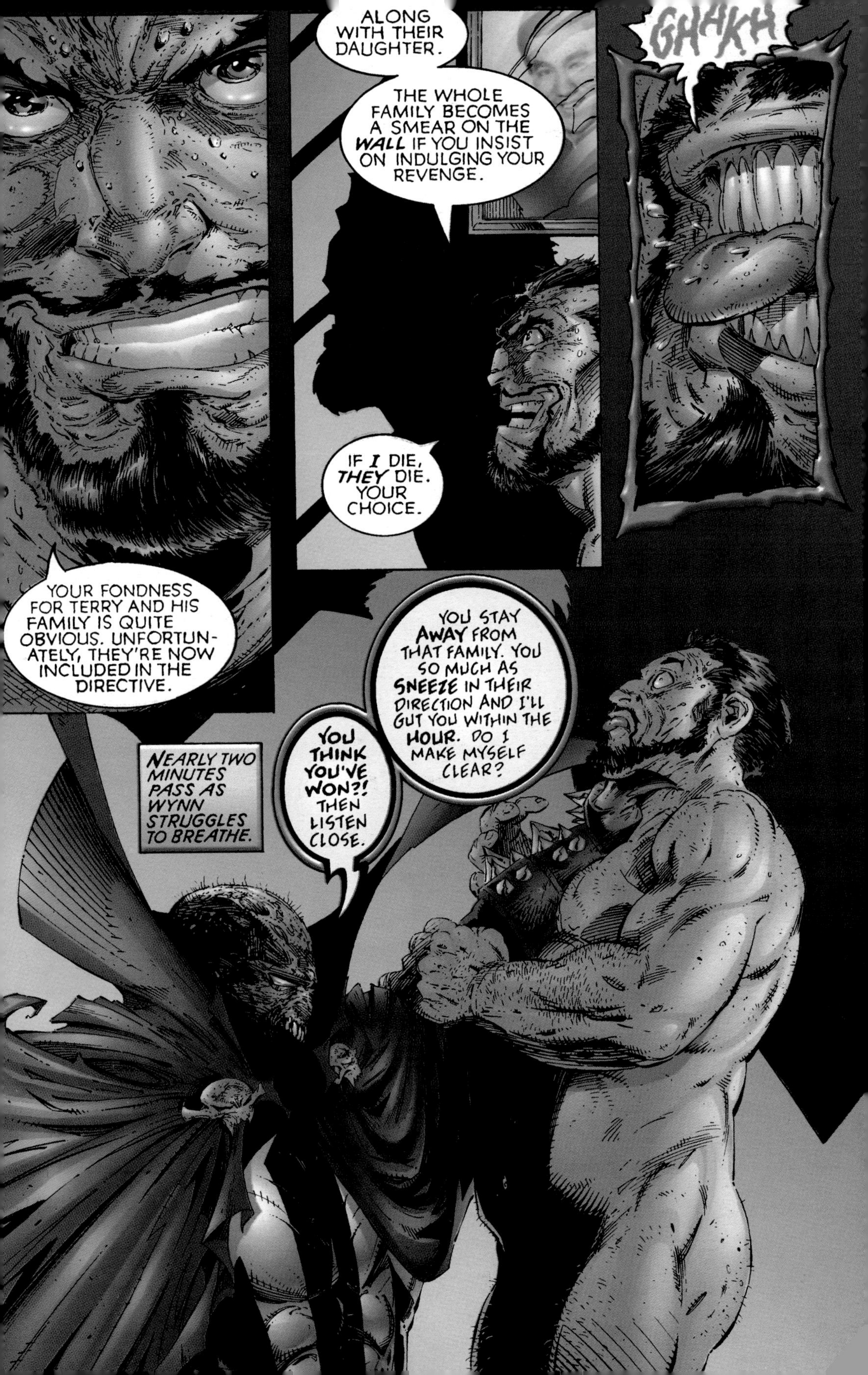
ALONG WITH THEIR DAUGHTER.
THE WHOLE FAMILY BECOMES A SMEAR ON THE WALL IF YOU INSIST ON INDULGING YOUR REVENGE.
IF I DIE, THEY DIE. YOUR CHOICE.
GHHKH
YOUR FONDNESS FOR TERRY AND HIS FAMILY IS QUITE OBVIOUS. UNFORTUN-ATELY, THEY'RE NOW INCLUDED IN THE DIRECTIVE.
YOU STAY AWAY FROM THAT FAMILY. YOU SO MUCH AS SNEEZE IN THEIR DIRECTION AND I'LL GUT YOU WITHIN THE HOUR. DO I MAKE MYSELF CLEAR?
NEARLY TWO MINUTES PASS AS WYNN STRUGGLES TO BREATHE.
YOU THINK YOU'VE WON?! THEN LISTEN CLOSE.

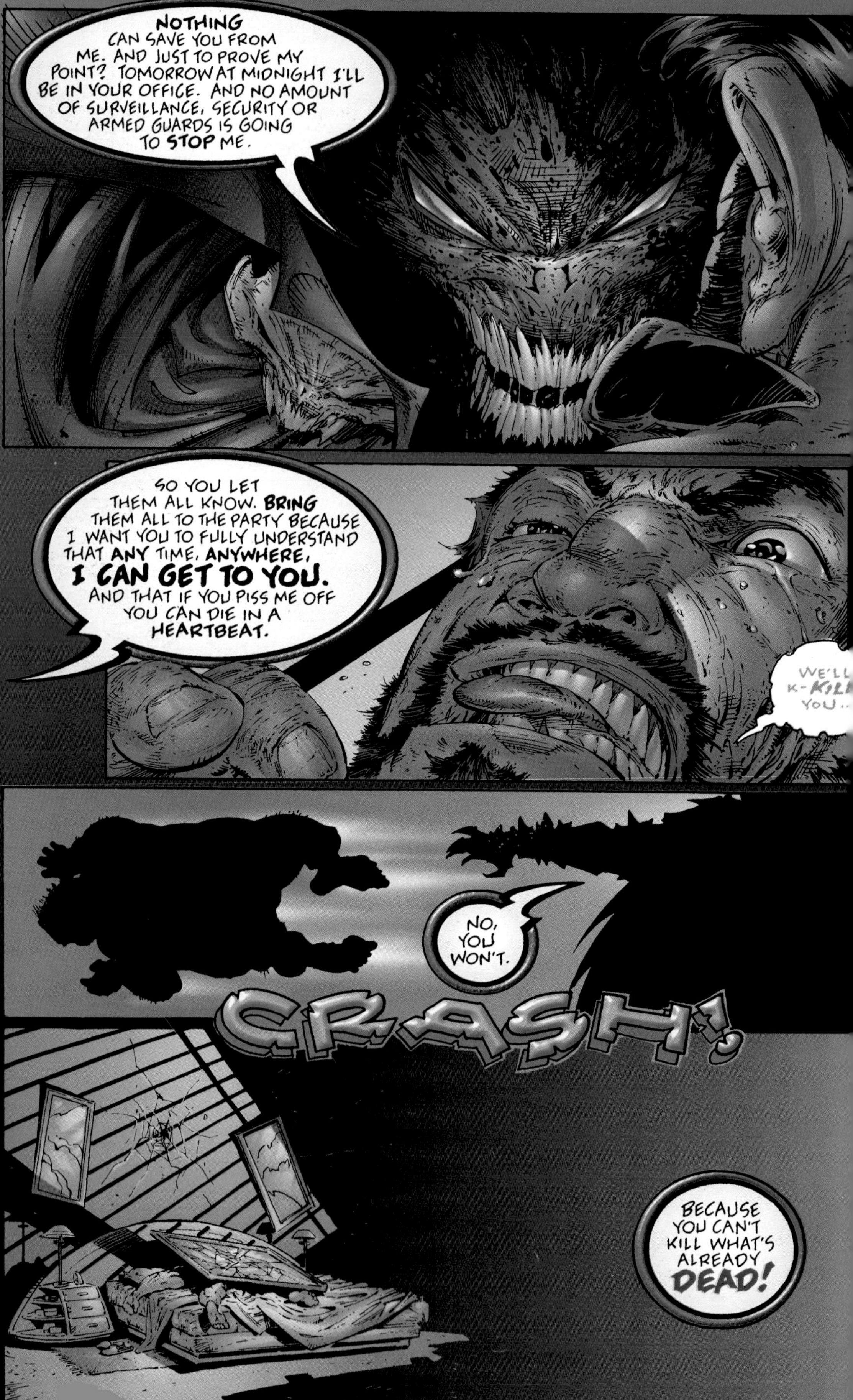
NOTHING CAN SAVE YOU FROM ME. AND JUST TO PROVE MY POINT? TOMORROW AT MIDNIGHT I'LL BE IN YOUR OFFICE. AND NO AMOUNT OF SURVEILLANCE, SECURITY OR ARMED GUARDS IS GOING TO STOP ME.
SO YOU LET THEM ALL KNOW. BRING THEM ALL TO THE PARTY BECAUSE I WANT YOU TO FULLY UNDERSTAND THAT ANY TIME, ANYWHERE, I CAN GET TO YOU. AND THAT IF YOU PISS ME OFF YOU CAN DIE IN A HEARTBEAT.
WE'LL K-KILL YOU...
NO, YOU WON'T.
CRASH!
BECAUSE YOU CAN'T KILL WHAT'S ALREADY DEAD!

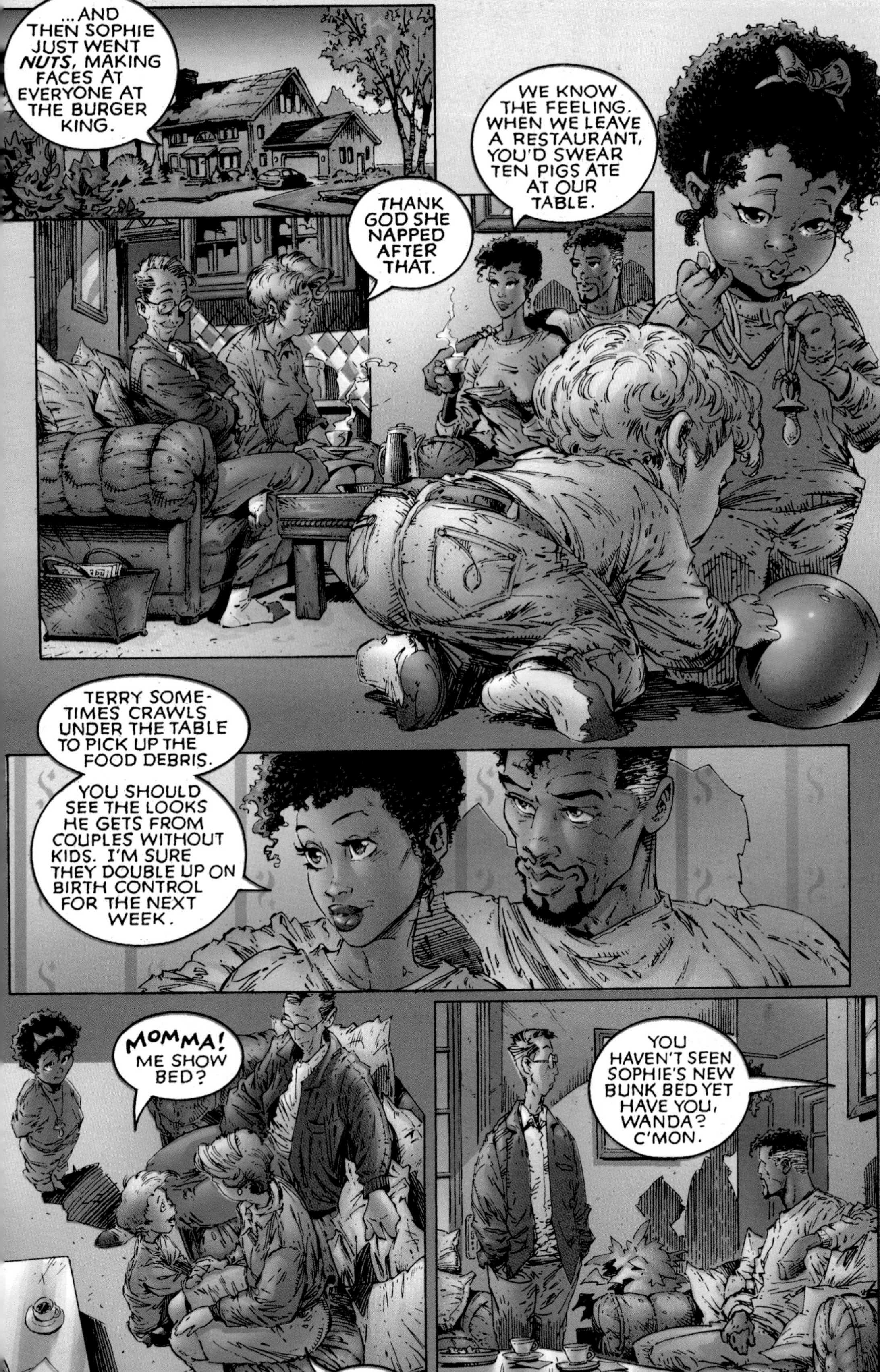
...AND THEN SOPHIE JUST WENT *NUTS*, MAKING FACES AT EVERYONE AT THE BURGER KING.
THANK GOD SHE NAPPED AFTER THAT.
WE KNOW THE FEELING. WHEN WE LEAVE A RESTAURANT, YOU'D SWEAR TEN PIGS ATE AT OUR TABLE.
TERRY SOMETIMES CRAWLS UNDER THE TABLE TO PICK UP THE FOOD DEBRIS.
YOU SHOULD SEE THE LOOKS HE GETS FROM COUPLES WITHOUT KIDS. I'M SURE THEY DOUBLE UP ON BIRTH CONTROL FOR THE NEXT WEEK.
MOMMA! ME SHOW BED?
SURE, HONEY.
YOU HAVEN'T SEEN SOPHIE'S NEW BUNK BED YET HAVE YOU, WANDA? C'MON.

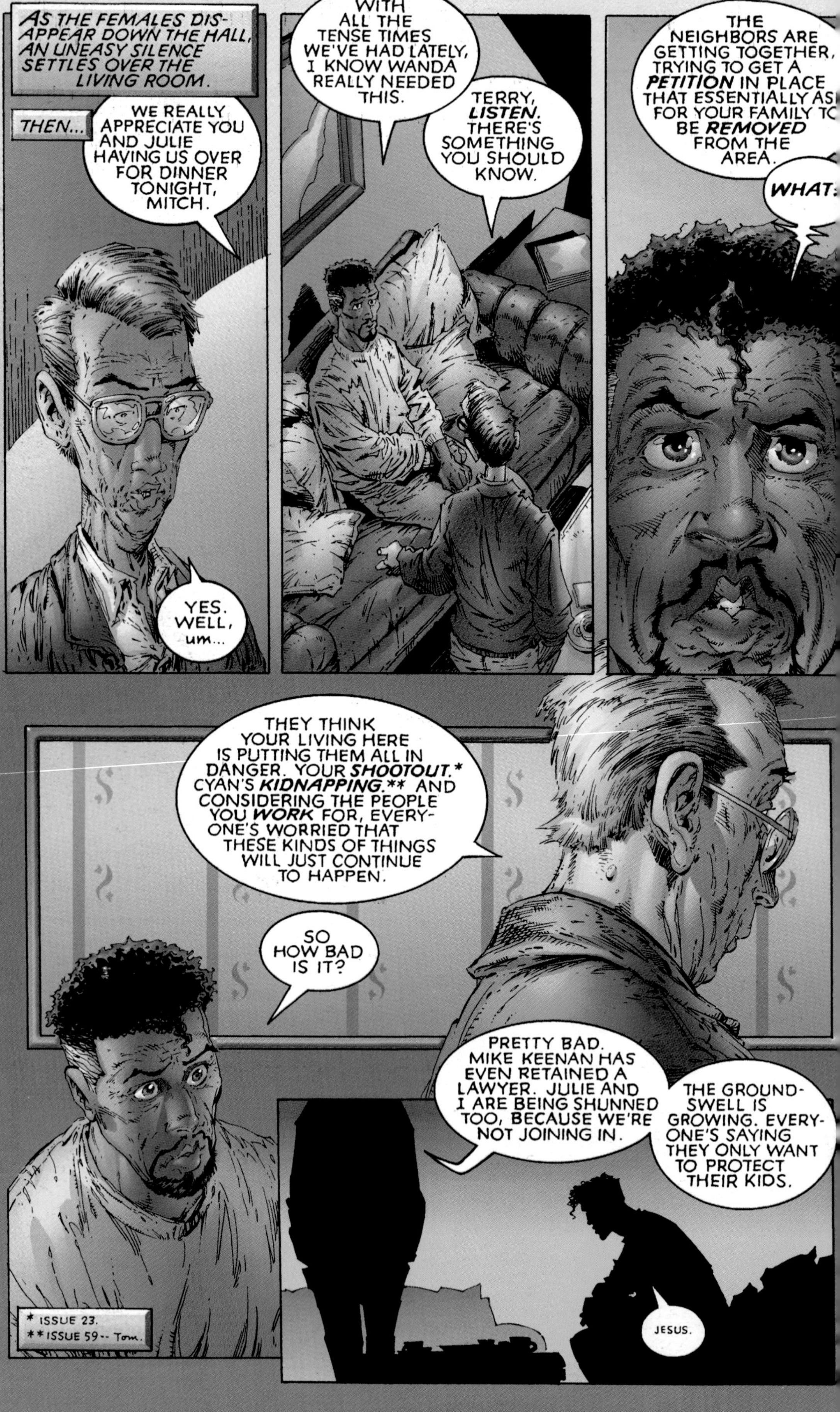
AS THE FEMALES DIS-APPEAR DOWN THE HALL, AN UNEASY SILENCE SETTLES OVER THE LIVING ROOM.
THEN...
WE REALLY APPRECIATE YOU AND JULIE HAVING US OVER FOR DINNER TONIGHT, MITCH.
YES. WELL, um...
WITH ALL THE TENSE TIMES WE'VE HAD LATELY, I KNOW WANDA REALLY NEEDED THIS.
TERRY, LISTEN. THERE'S SOMETHING YOU SHOULD KNOW.
THE NEIGHBORS ARE GETTING TOGETHER, TRYING TO GET A PETITION IN PLACE THAT ESSENTIALLY AS FOR YOUR FAMILY TO BE REMOVED FROM THE AREA.
WHAT
THEY THINK YOUR LIVING HERE IS PUTTING THEM ALL IN DANGER. YOUR SHOOTOUT.* CYAN'S KIDNAPPING.** AND CONSIDERING THE PEOPLE YOU WORK FOR, EVERY-ONE'S WORRIED THAT THESE KINDS OF THINGS WILL JUST CONTINUE TO HAPPEN.
SO HOW BAD IS IT?
PRETTY BAD. MIKE KEENAN HAS EVEN RETAINED A LAWYER. JULIE AND I ARE BEING SHUNNED TOO, BECAUSE WE'RE NOT JOINING IN.
THE GROUND-SWELL IS GROWING. EVERY-ONE'S SAYING THEY ONLY WANT TO PROTECT THEIR KIDS.
* ISSUE 23.
** ISSUE 59 -- Tom.
JESUS.

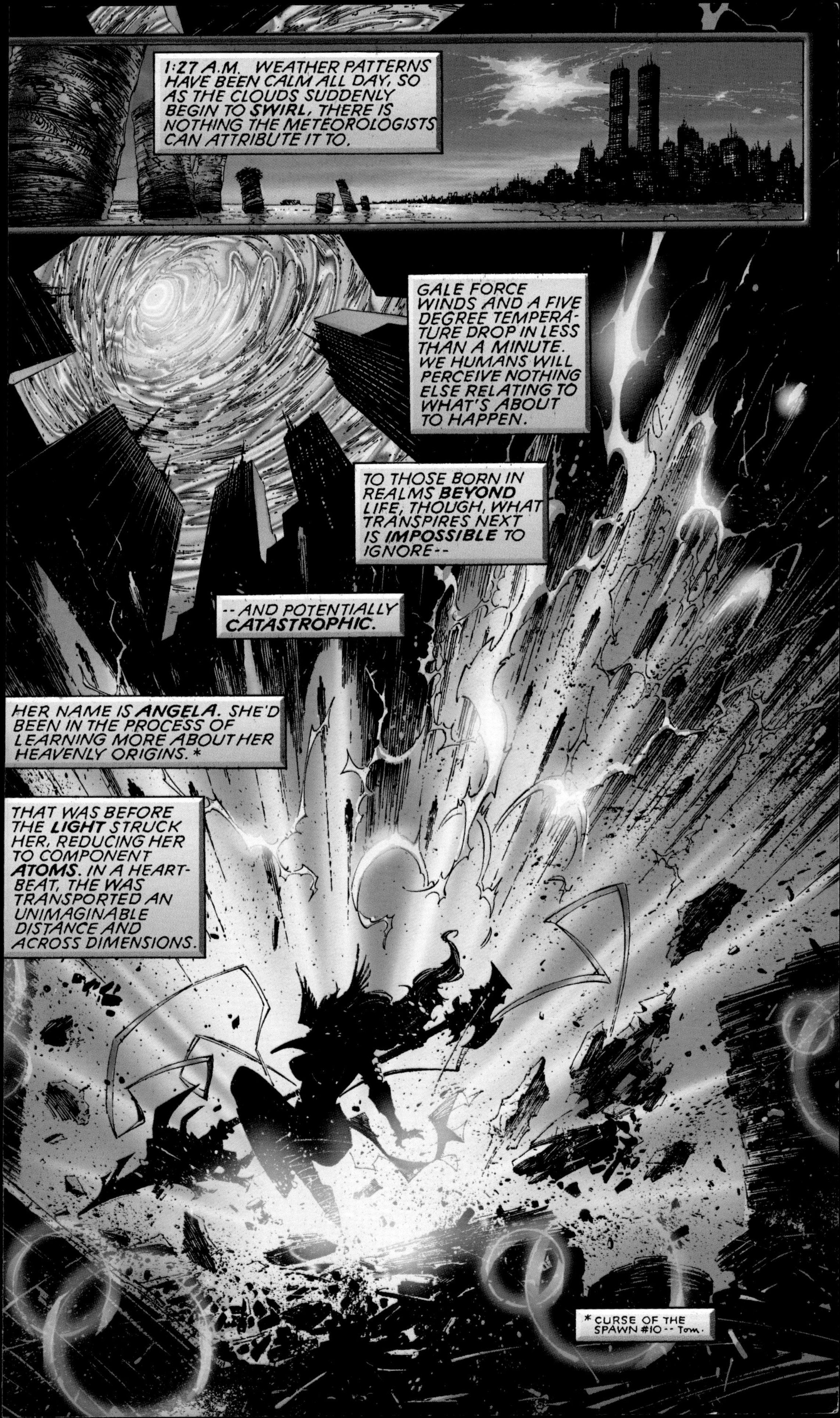
1:27 A.M. WEATHER PATTERNS HAVE BEEN CALM ALL DAY, SO AS THE CLOUDS SUDDENLY BEGIN TO SWIRL, THERE IS NOTHING THE METEOROLOGISTS CAN ATTRIBUTE IT TO.
GALE FORCE WINDS AND A FIVE DEGREE TEMPERATURE DROP IN LESS THAN A MINUTE. WE HUMANS WILL PERCEIVE NOTHING ELSE RELATING TO WHAT'S ABOUT TO HAPPEN.
TO THOSE BORN IN REALMS BEYOND LIFE, THOUGH, WHAT TRANSPIRES NEXT IS IMPOSSIBLE TO IGNORE--
--AND POTENTIALLY CATASTROPHIC.
HER NAME IS ANGELA. SHE'D BEEN IN THE PROCESS OF LEARNING MORE ABOUT HER HEAVENLY ORIGINS.*
THAT WAS BEFORE THE LIGHT STRUCK HER, REDUCING HER TO COMPONENT ATOMS. IN A HEART-BEAT, THE WAS TRANSPORTED AN UNIMAGINABLE DISTANCE AND ACROSS DIMENSIONS.
*CURSE OF THE SPAWN #10 -- Tom.

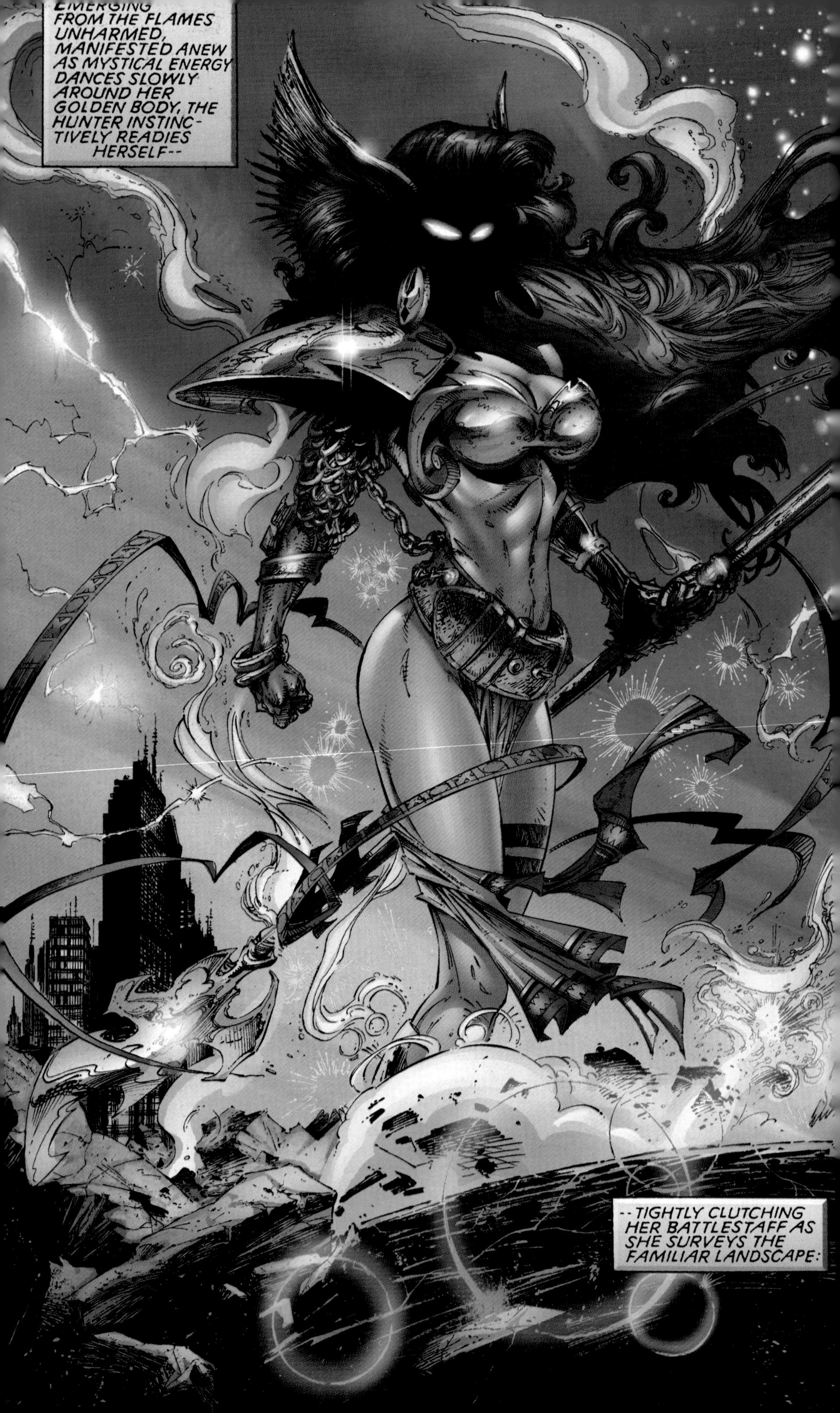
EMERGING FROM THE FLAMES UNHARMED, MANIFESTED ANEW AS MYSTICAL ENERGY DANCES SLOWLY AROUND HER GOLDEN BODY, THE HUNTER INSTINCTIVELY READIES HERSELF--
--TIGHTLY CLUTCHING HER BATTLESTAFF AS SHE SURVEYS THE FAMILIAR LANDSCAPE:

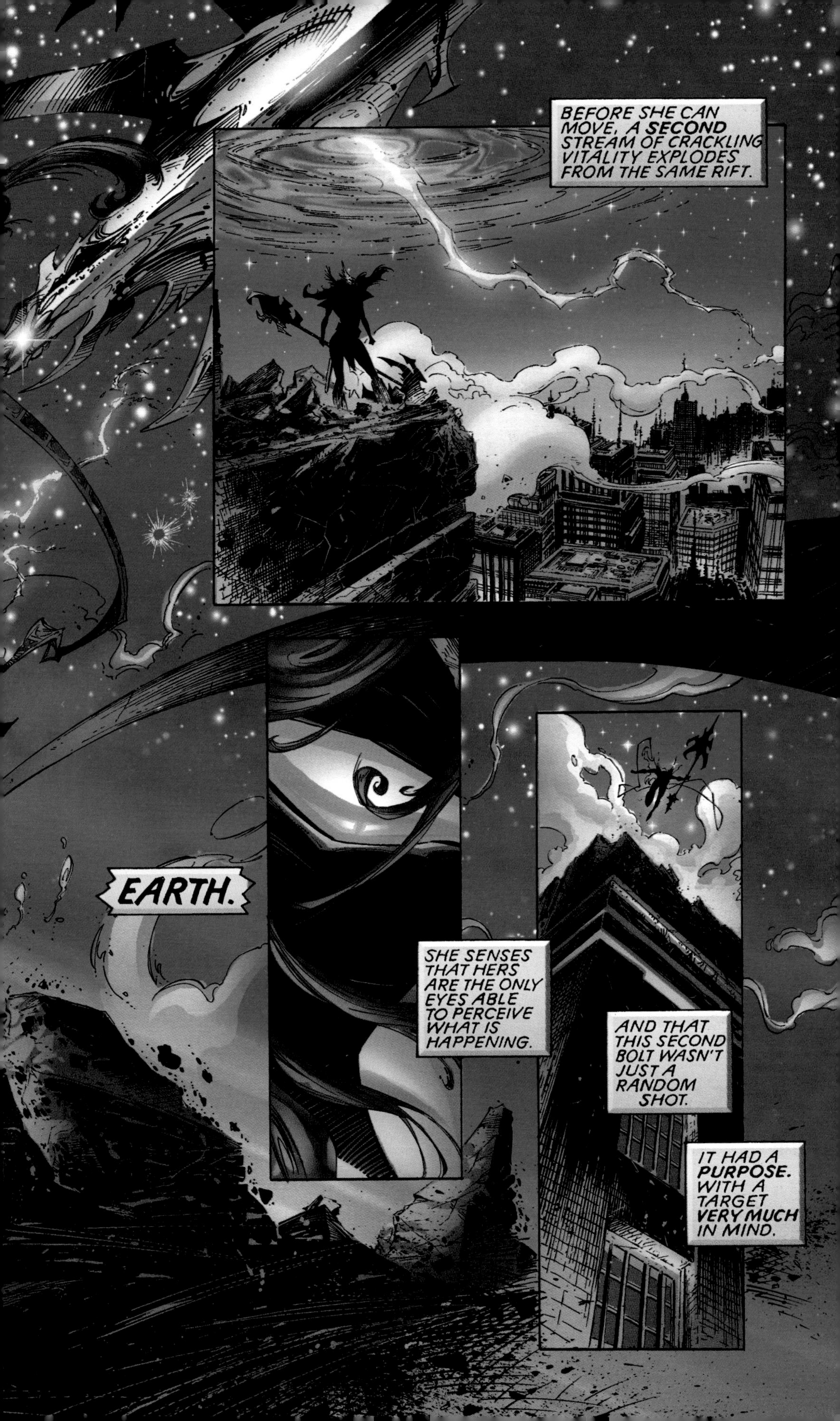
BEFORE SHE CAN MOVE, A SECOND STREAM OF CRACKLING VITALITY EXPLODES FROM THE SAME RIFT.
EARTH.
SHE SENSES THAT HERS ARE THE ONLY EYES ABLE TO PERCEIVE WHAT IS HAPPENING.
AND THAT THIS SECOND BOLT WASN'T JUST A RANDOM SHOT.
IT HAD A PURPOSE. WITH A TARGET VERY MUCH IN MIND.

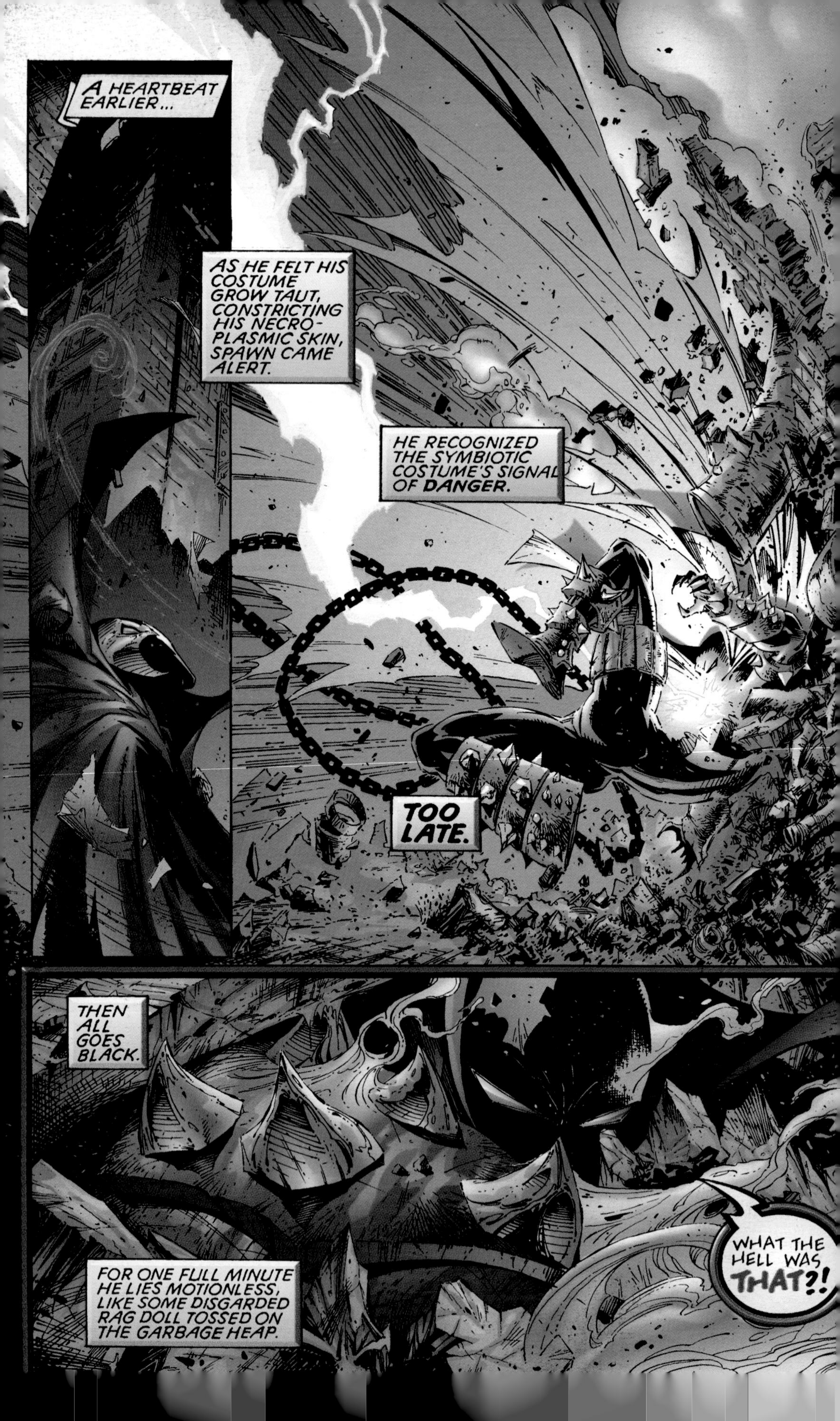
A HEARTBEAT EARLIER...
AS HE FELT HIS COSTUME GROW TAUT, CONSTRICTING HIS NECRO-PLASMIC SKIN, SPAWN CAME ALERT.
HE RECOGNIZED THE SYMBIOTIC COSTUME'S SIGNAL OF DANGER.
TOO LATE.
THEN ALL GOES BLACK.
FOR ONE FULL MINUTE HE LIES MOTIONLESS, LIKE SOME DISGARDED RAG DOLL TOSSED ON THE GARBAGE HEAP.
WHAT THE HELL WAS THAT?!

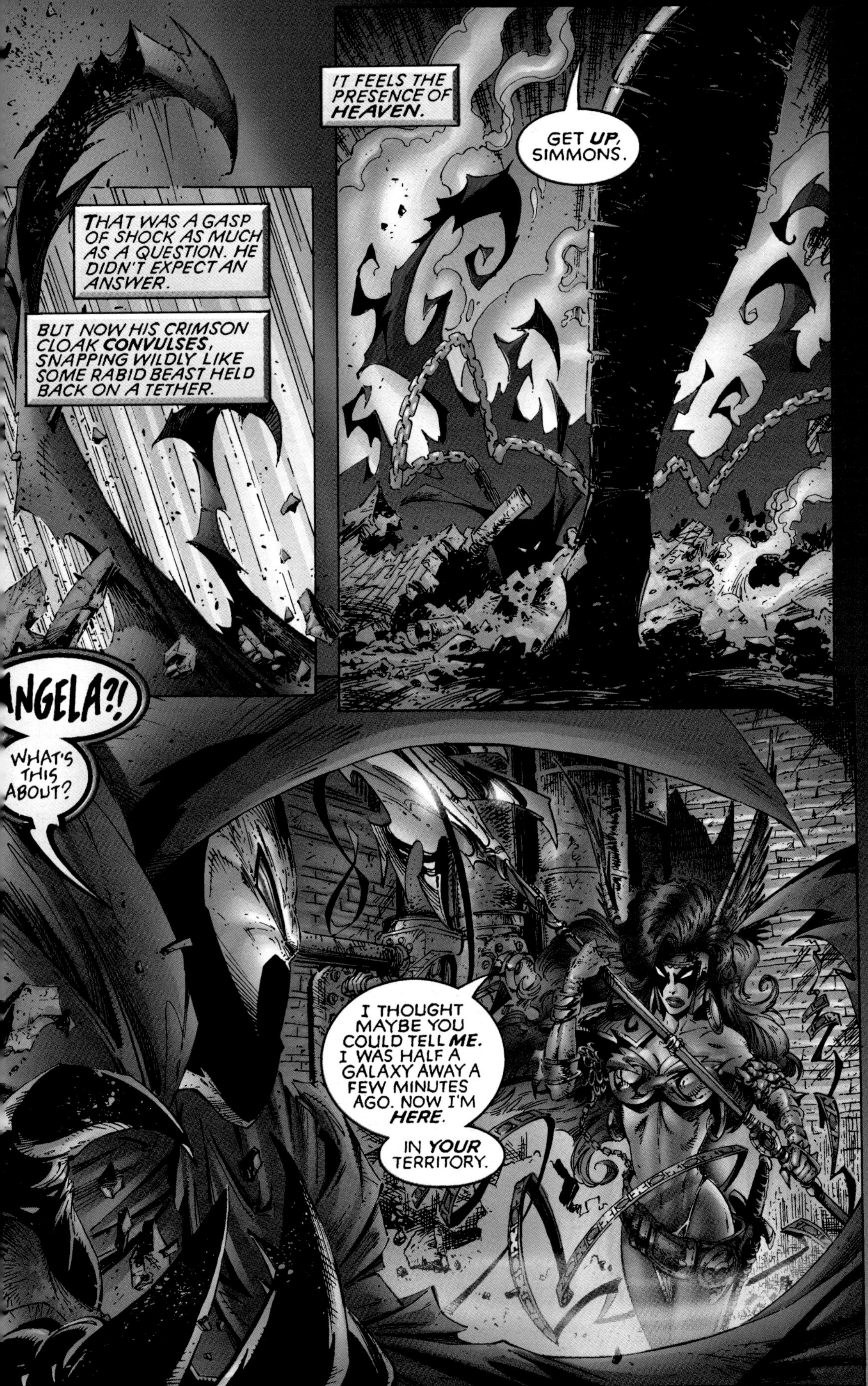
THAT WAS A GASP OF SHOCK AS MUCH AS A QUESTION. HE DIDN'T EXPECT AN ANSWER.
BUT NOW HIS CRIMSON CLOAK **CONVULSES**, SNAPPING WILDLY LIKE SOME RABID BEAST HELD BACK ON A TETHER.
IT FEELS THE PRESENCE OF **HEAVEN**.
GET **UP**, SIMMONS.
NGELA?!
WHAT'S THIS ABOUT?
I THOUGHT MAYBE YOU COULD TELL **ME**. I WAS HALF A GALAXY AWAY A FEW MINUTES AGO. NOW I'M **HERE**.
IN **YOUR** TERRITORY.

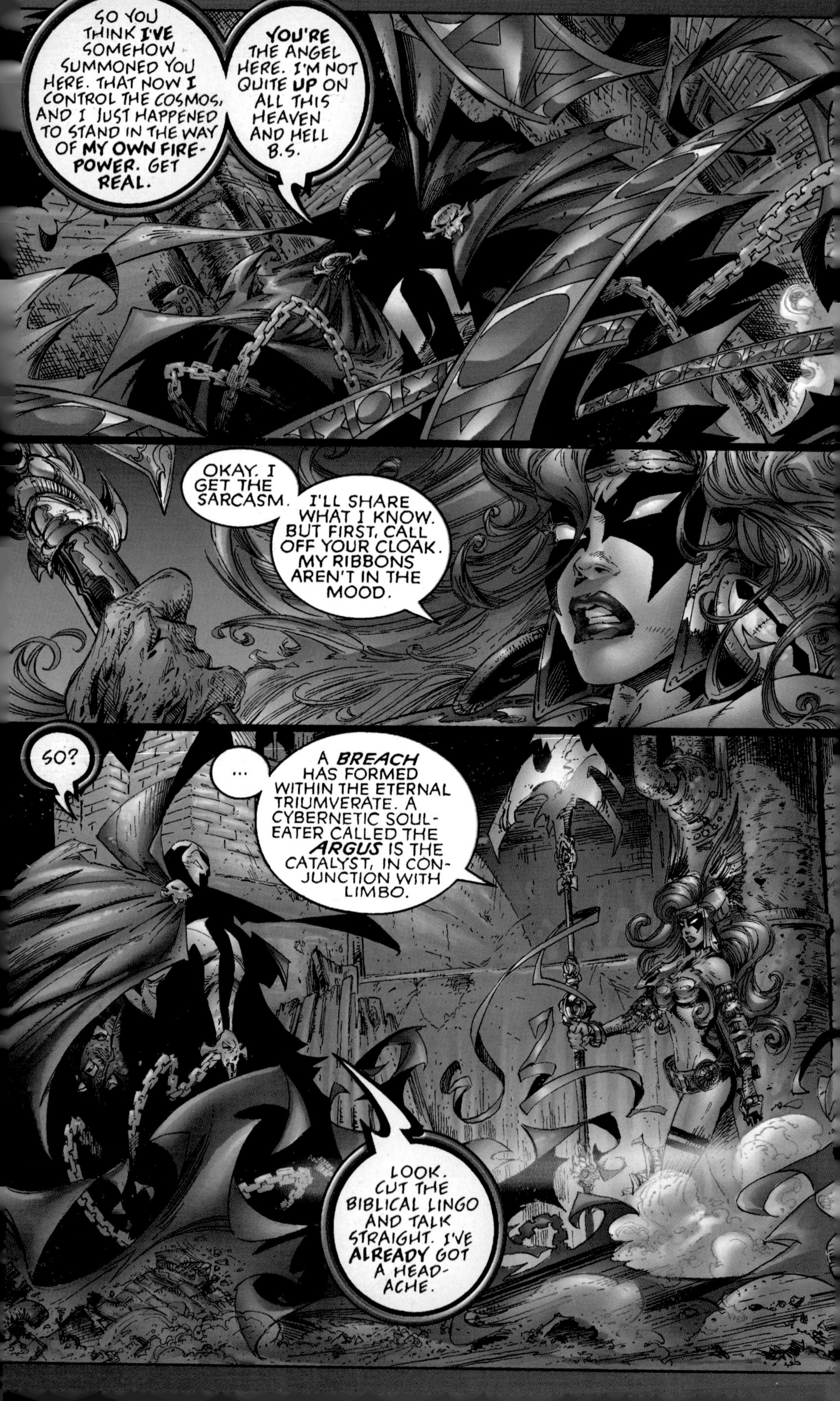
SO YOU THINK I'VE SOMEHOW SUMMONED YOU HERE. THAT NOW I CONTROL THE COSMOS, AND I JUST HAPPENED TO STAND IN THE WAY OF MY OWN FIRE-POWER. GET REAL.
YOU'RE THE ANGEL HERE. I'M NOT QUITE UP ON ALL THIS HEAVEN AND HELL B.S.
OKAY. I GET THE SARCASM.
I'LL SHARE WHAT I KNOW. BUT FIRST, CALL OFF YOUR CLOAK. MY RIBBONS AREN'T IN THE MOOD.
SO?
...
A BREACH HAS FORMED WITHIN THE ETERNAL TRIUMVERATE. A CYBERNETIC SOUL-EATER CALLED THE ARGUS IS THE CATALYST, IN CONJUNCTION WITH LIMBO.
LOOK. CUT THE BIBLICAL LINGO AND TALK STRAIGHT. I'VE ALREADY GOT A HEADACHE.

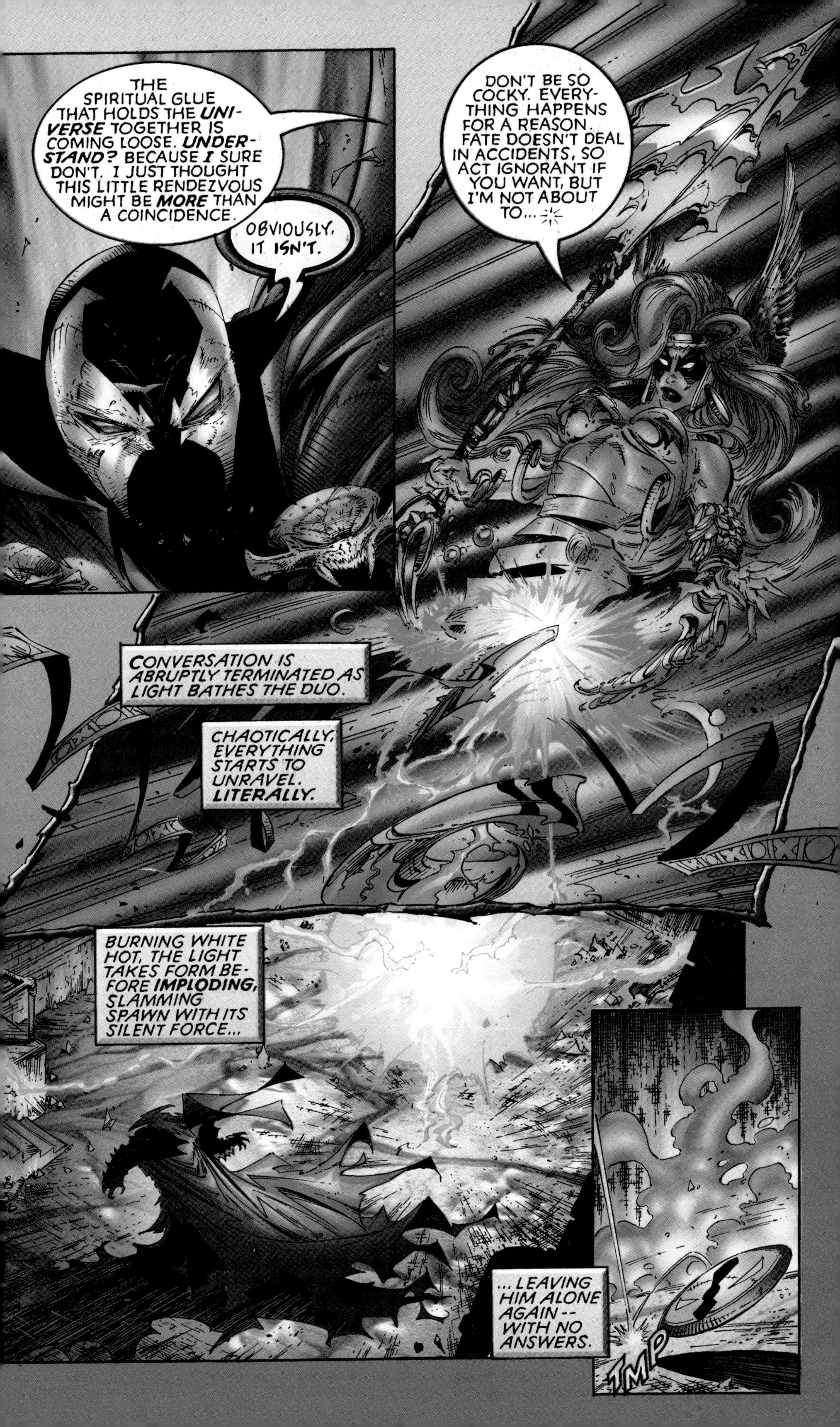
THE SPIRITUAL GLUE THAT HOLDS THE UNIVERSE TOGETHER IS COMING LOOSE. UNDERSTAND? BECAUSE I SURE DON'T. I JUST THOUGHT THIS LITTLE RENDEZVOUS MIGHT BE MORE THAN A COINCIDENCE.
OBVIOUSLY, IT ISN'T.
DON'T BE SO COCKY. EVERYTHING HAPPENS FOR A REASON. FATE DOESN'T DEAL IN ACCIDENTS, SO ACT IGNORANT IF YOU WANT, BUT I'M NOT ABOUT TO...
CONVERSATION IS ABRUPTLY TERMINATED AS LIGHT BATHES THE DUO.
CHAOTICALLY, EVERYTHING STARTS TO UNRAVEL. LITERALLY.
BURNING WHITE HOT, THE LIGHT TAKES FORM BEFORE IMPLODING, SLAMMING SPAWN WITH ITS SILENT FORCE...
...LEAVING HIM ALONE AGAIN--WITH NO ANSWERS.
TMP

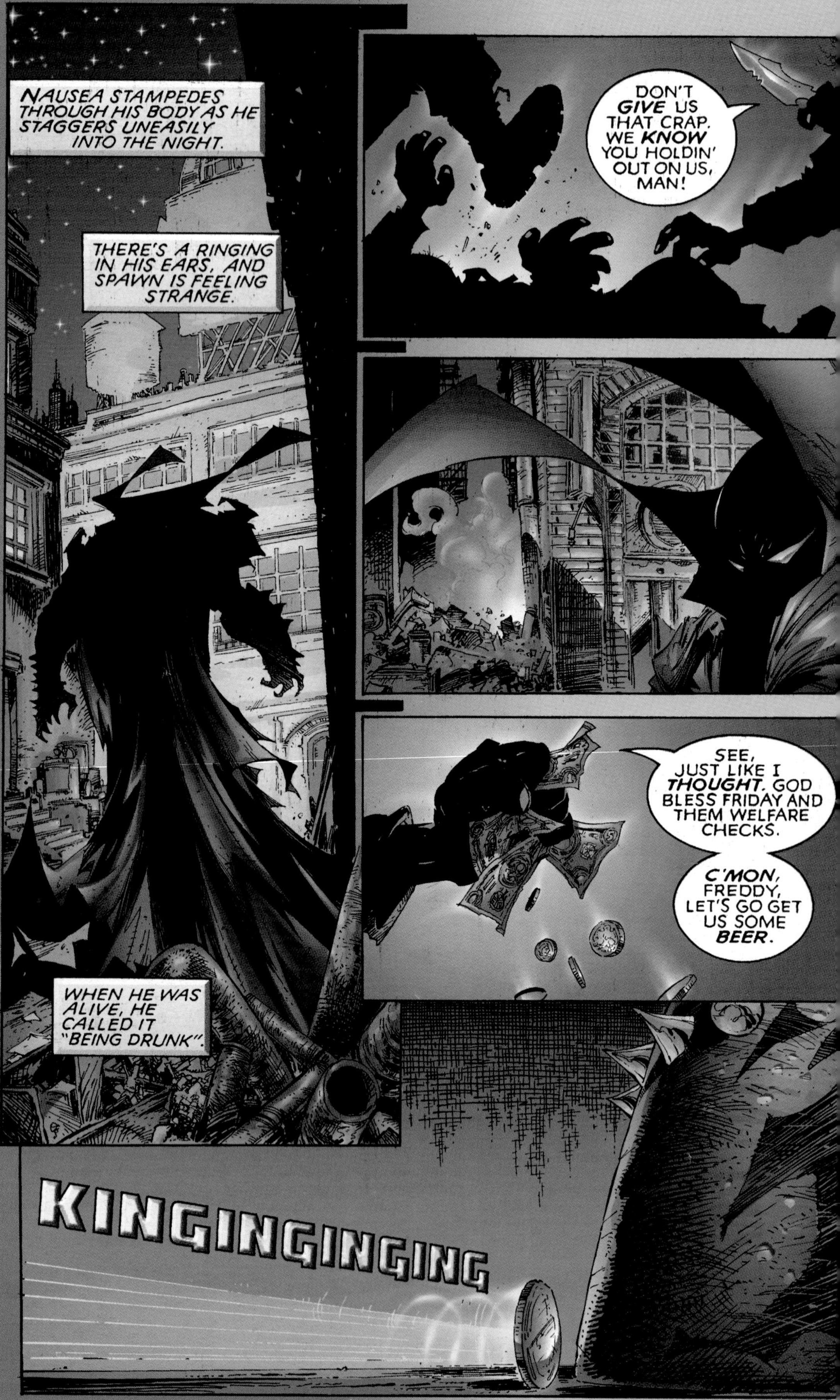
NAUSEA STAMPEDES THROUGH HIS BODY AS HE STAGGERS UNEASILY INTO THE NIGHT.
THERE'S A RINGING IN HIS EARS, AND SPAWN IS FEELING STRANGE.
WHEN HE WAS ALIVE, HE CALLED IT "BEING DRUNK".
DON'T GIVE US THAT CRAP. WE KNOW YOU HOLDIN' OUT ON US, MAN!
SEE, JUST LIKE I THOUGHT. GOD BLESS FRIDAY AND THEM WELFARE CHECKS.
C'MON, FREDDY, LET'S GO GET US SOME BEER.
KINGINGINGING

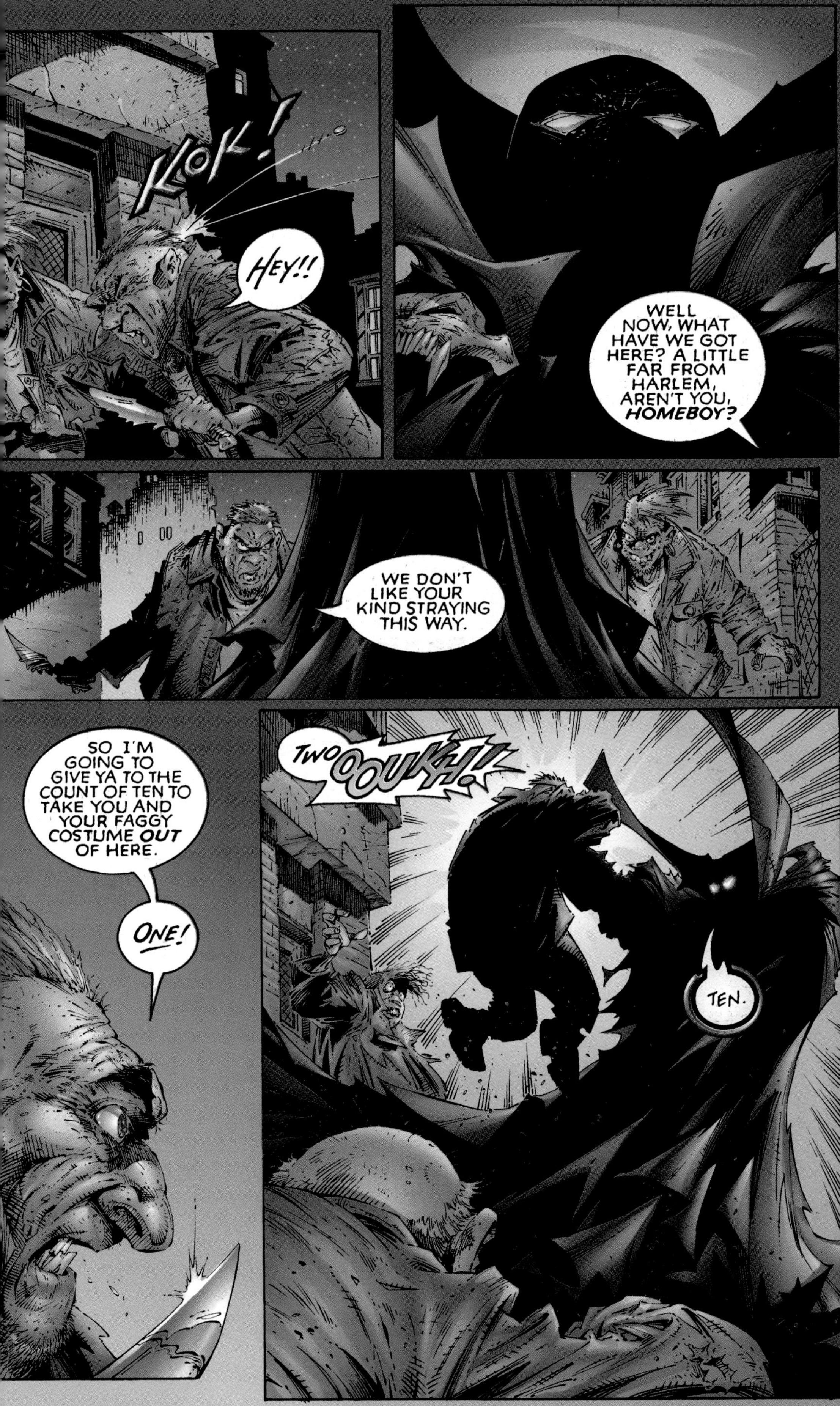
KLOK!
HEY!!
WELL NOW, WHAT HAVE WE GOT HERE? A LITTLE FAR FROM HARLEM, AREN'T YOU, HOMEBOY?
WE DON'T LIKE YOUR KIND STRAYING THIS WAY.
SO I'M GOING TO GIVE YA TO THE COUNT OF TEN TO TAKE YOU AND YOUR FAGGY COSTUME OUT OF HERE.
ONE!
TWO OOOUKH!
TEN.

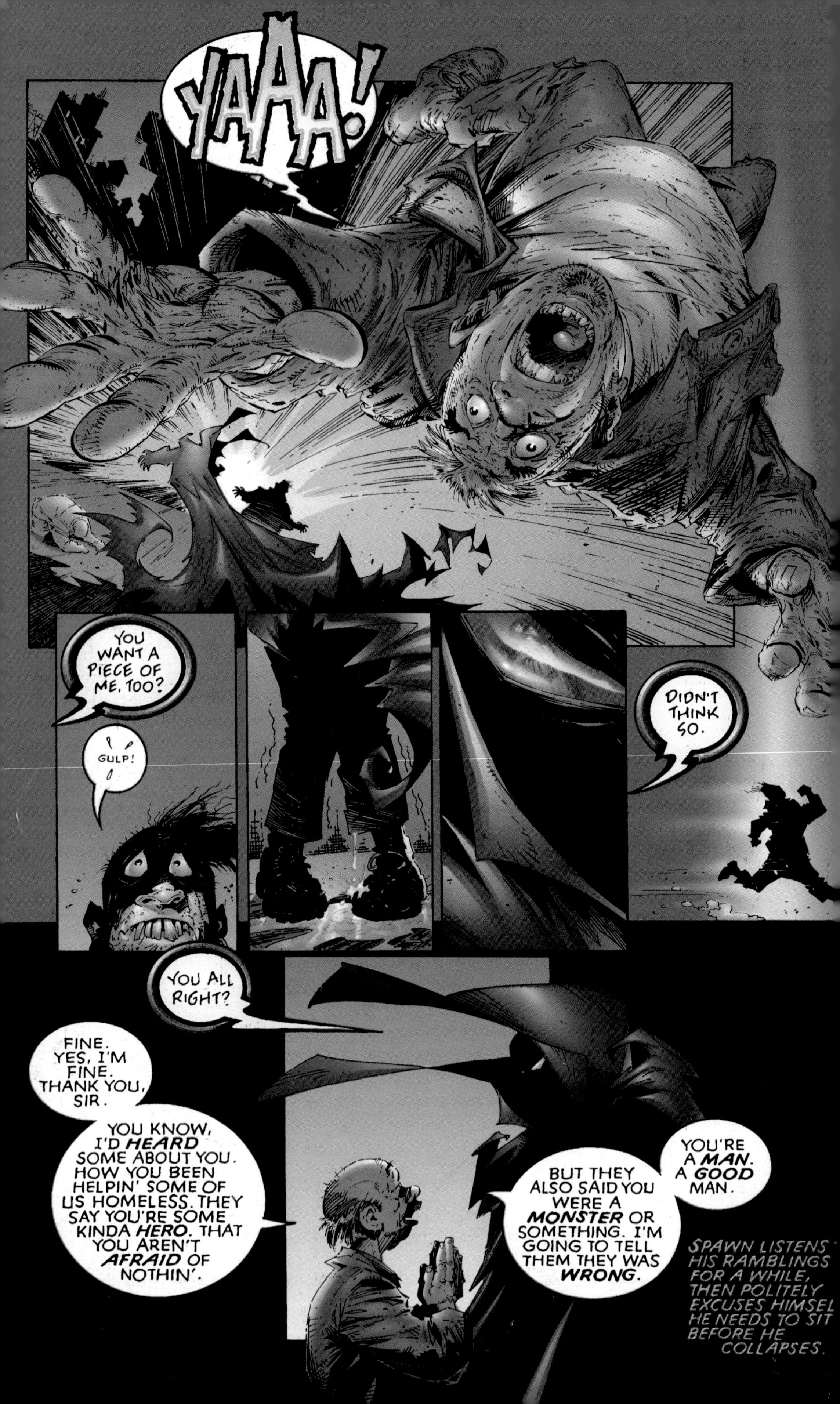
YAAA!
YOU WANT A PIECE OF ME, TOO?
GULP!
DIDN'T THINK SO.
YOU ALL RIGHT?
FINE. YES, I'M FINE. THANK YOU, SIR.
YOU KNOW, I'D HEARD SOME ABOUT YOU. HOW YOU BEEN HELPIN' SOME OF US HOMELESS. THEY SAY YOU'RE SOME KINDA HERO. THAT YOU AREN'T AFRAID OF NOTHIN'.
BUT THEY ALSO SAID YOU WERE A MONSTER OR SOMETHING. I'M GOING TO TELL THEM THEY WAS WRONG.
YOU'RE A MAN. A GOOD MAN.
SPAWN LISTENS HIS RAMBLINGS FOR A WHILE, THEN POLITELY EXCUSES HIMSEL HE NEEDS TO SIT BEFORE HE COLLAPSES.

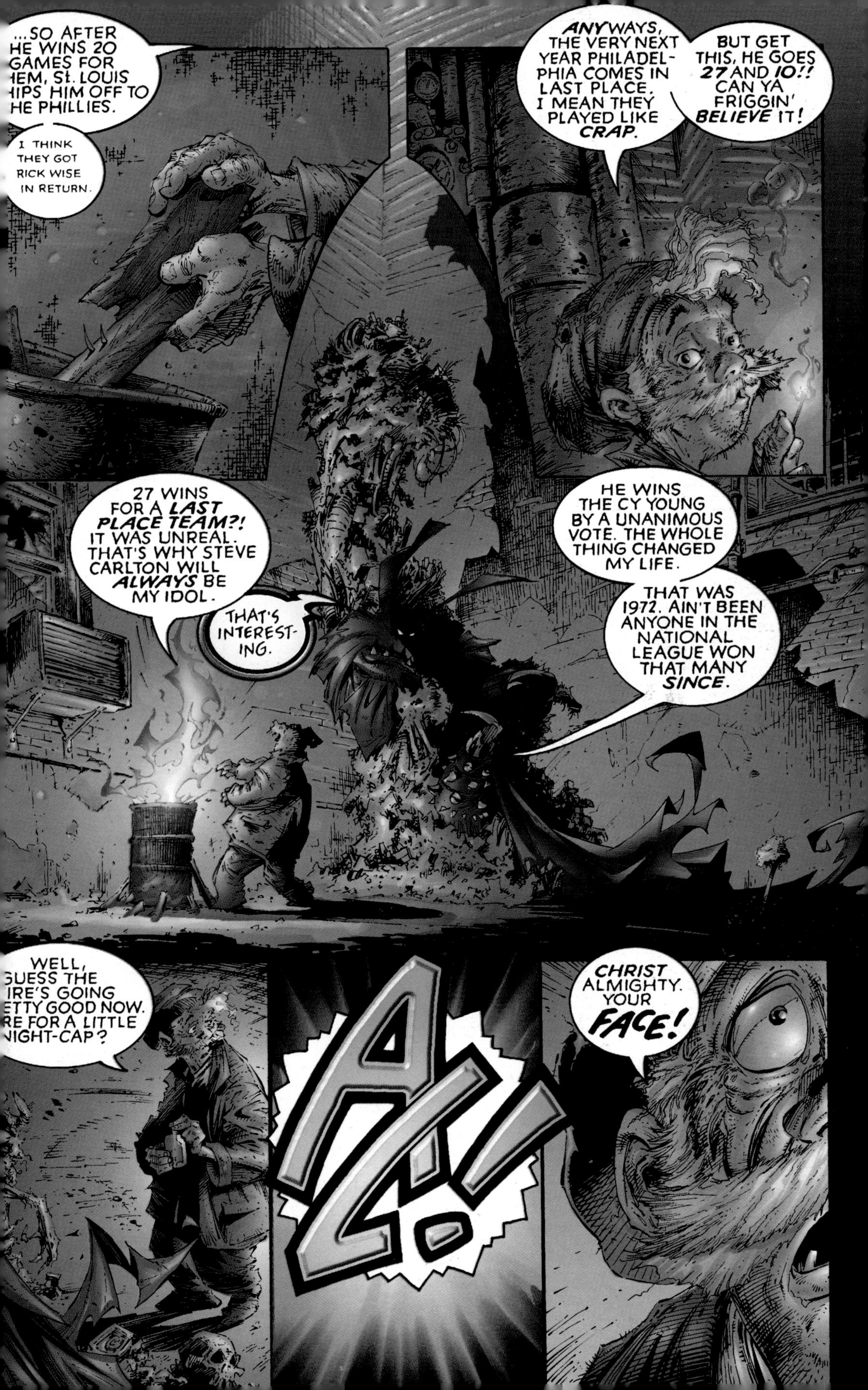
...SO AFTER HE WINS 20 GAMES FOR HEM, St. LOUIS HIPS HIM OFF TO HE PHILLIES.
I THINK THEY GOT RICK WISE IN RETURN.
ANYWAYS, THE VERY NEXT YEAR PHILADELPHIA COMES IN LAST PLACE. I MEAN THEY PLAYED LIKE CRAP.
BUT GET THIS, HE GOES 27 AND 10!! CAN YA FRIGGIN' BELIEVE IT!
27 WINS FOR A LAST PLACE TEAM?! IT WAS UNREAL. THAT'S WHY STEVE CARLTON WILL ALWAYS BE MY IDOL.
THAT'S INTERESTING.
HE WINS THE CY YOUNG BY A UNANIMOUS VOTE. THE WHOLE THING CHANGED MY LIFE.
THAT WAS 1972. AIN'T BEEN ANYONE IN THE NATIONAL LEAGUE WON THAT MANY SINCE.
WELL, GUESS THE IRE'S GOING ETTY GOOD NOW. RE FOR A LITTLE NIGHT-CAP?
AH!
CHRIST ALMIGHTY. YOUR FACE!

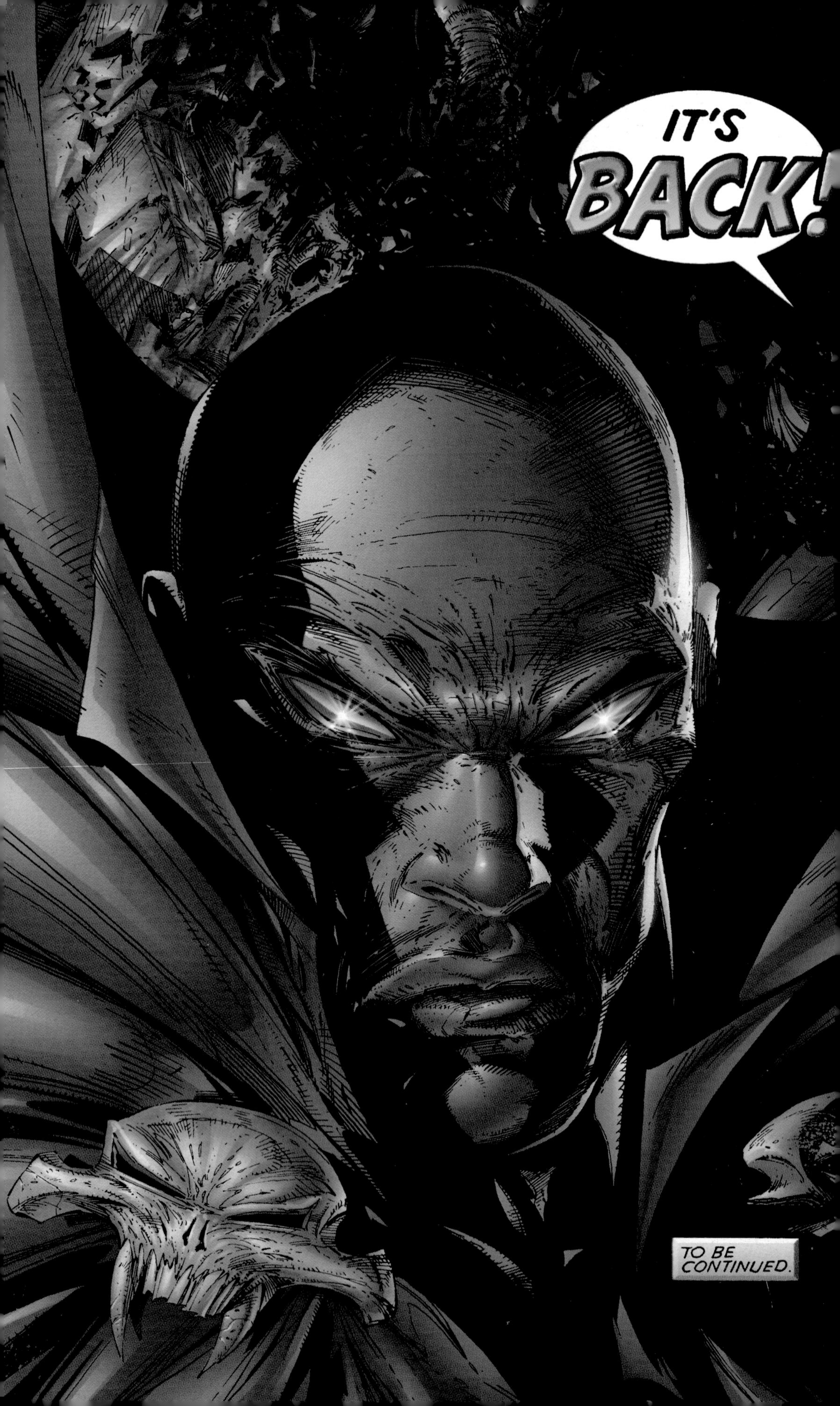
IT'S BACK!
TO BE CONTINUED.

# 5

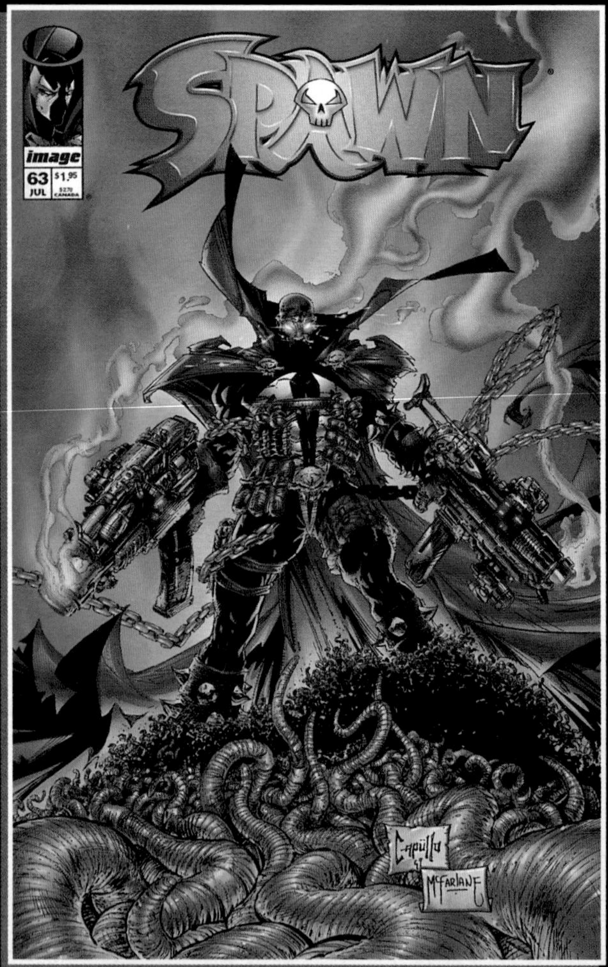
SPAWN
image
63
JUL
$1.95
$2.70 CANADA

# I D E N T I T Y

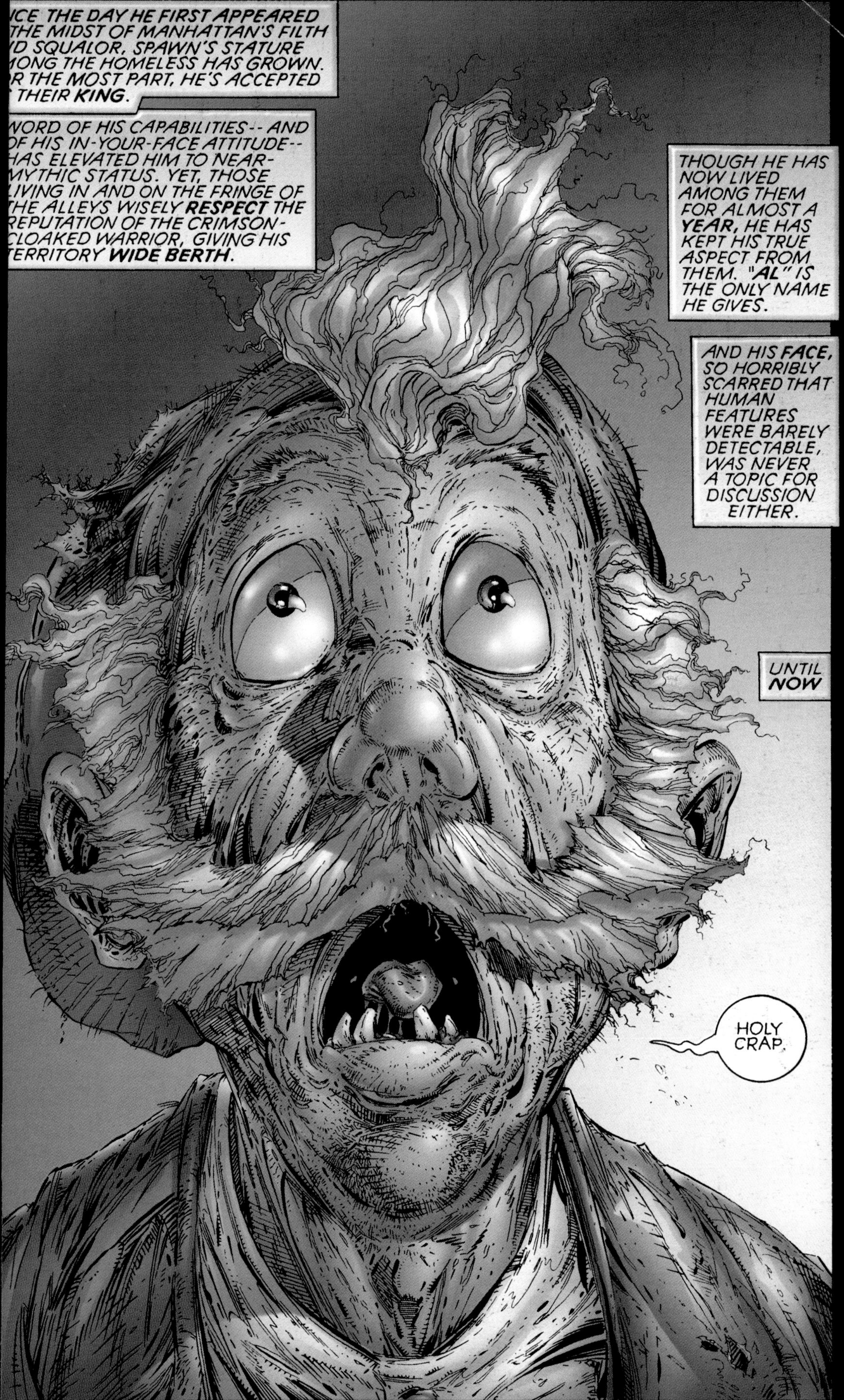
NCE THE DAY HE FIRST APPEARED THE MIDST OF MANHATTAN'S FILTH ND SQUALOR, SPAWN'S STATURE MONG THE HOMELESS HAS GROWN. R THE MOST PART, HE'S ACCEPTED THEIR KING.
WORD OF HIS CAPABILITIES-- AND OF HIS IN-YOUR-FACE ATTITUDE-- HAS ELEVATED HIM TO NEAR-MYTHIC STATUS. YET, THOSE LIVING IN AND ON THE FRINGE OF THE ALLEYS WISELY RESPECT THE REPUTATION OF THE CRIMSON-CLOAKED WARRIOR, GIVING HIS TERRITORY WIDE BERTH.
THOUGH HE HAS NOW LIVED AMONG THEM FOR ALMOST A YEAR, HE HAS KEPT HIS TRUE ASPECT FROM THEM. "AL" IS THE ONLY NAME HE GIVES.
AND HIS FACE, SO HORRIBLY SCARRED THAT HUMAN FEATURES WERE BARELY DETECTABLE, WAS NEVER A TOPIC FOR DISCUSSION EITHER.
UNTIL NOW
HOLY CRAP.

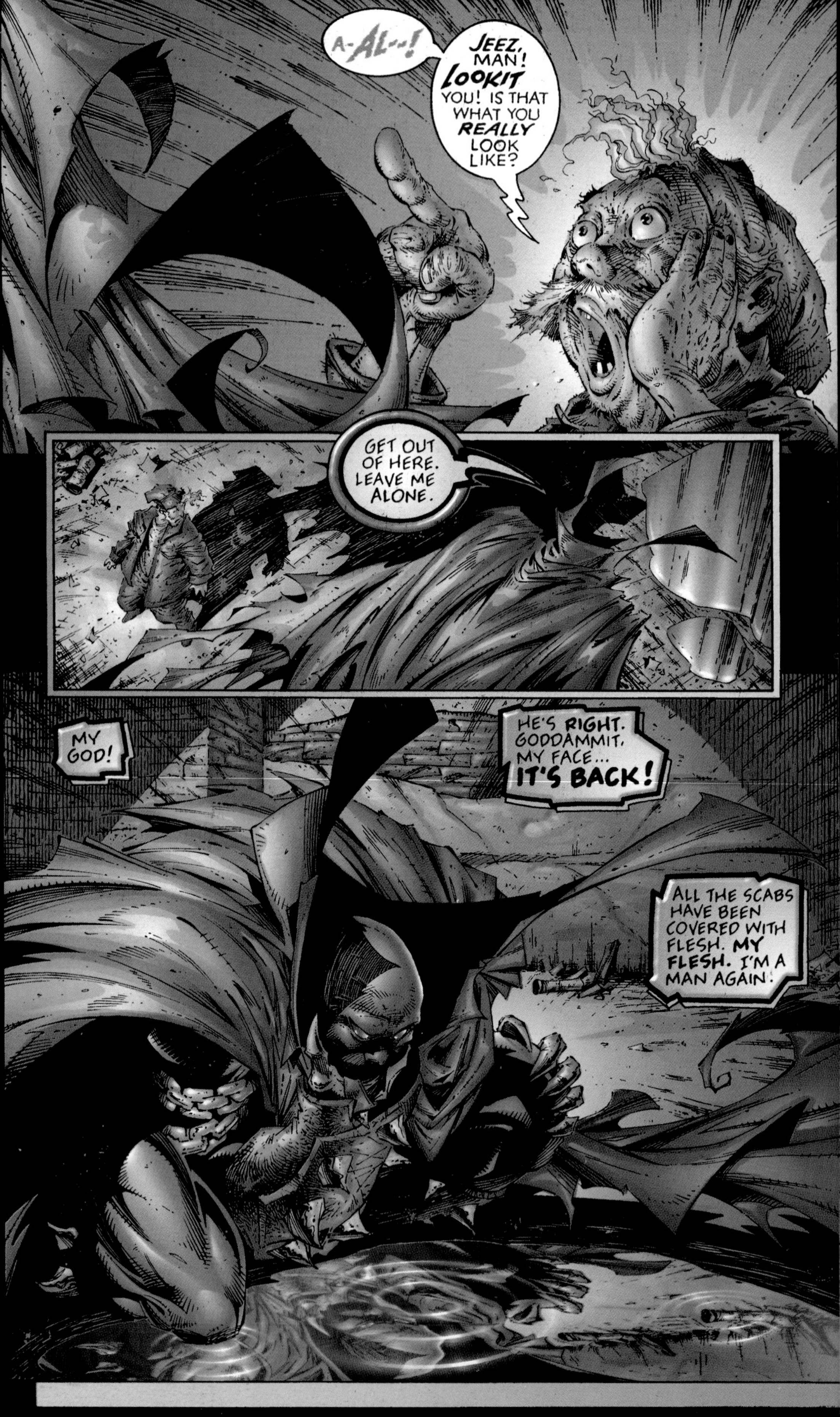
A-AL--!
JEEZ, MAN! LOOKIT YOU! IS THAT WHAT YOU REALLY LOOK LIKE?
GET OUT OF HERE. LEAVE ME ALONE.
MY GOD!
HE'S RIGHT. GODDAMMIT. MY FACE... IT'S BACK!
ALL THE SCABS HAVE BEEN COVERED WITH FLESH. MY FLESH. I'M A MAN AGAIN.

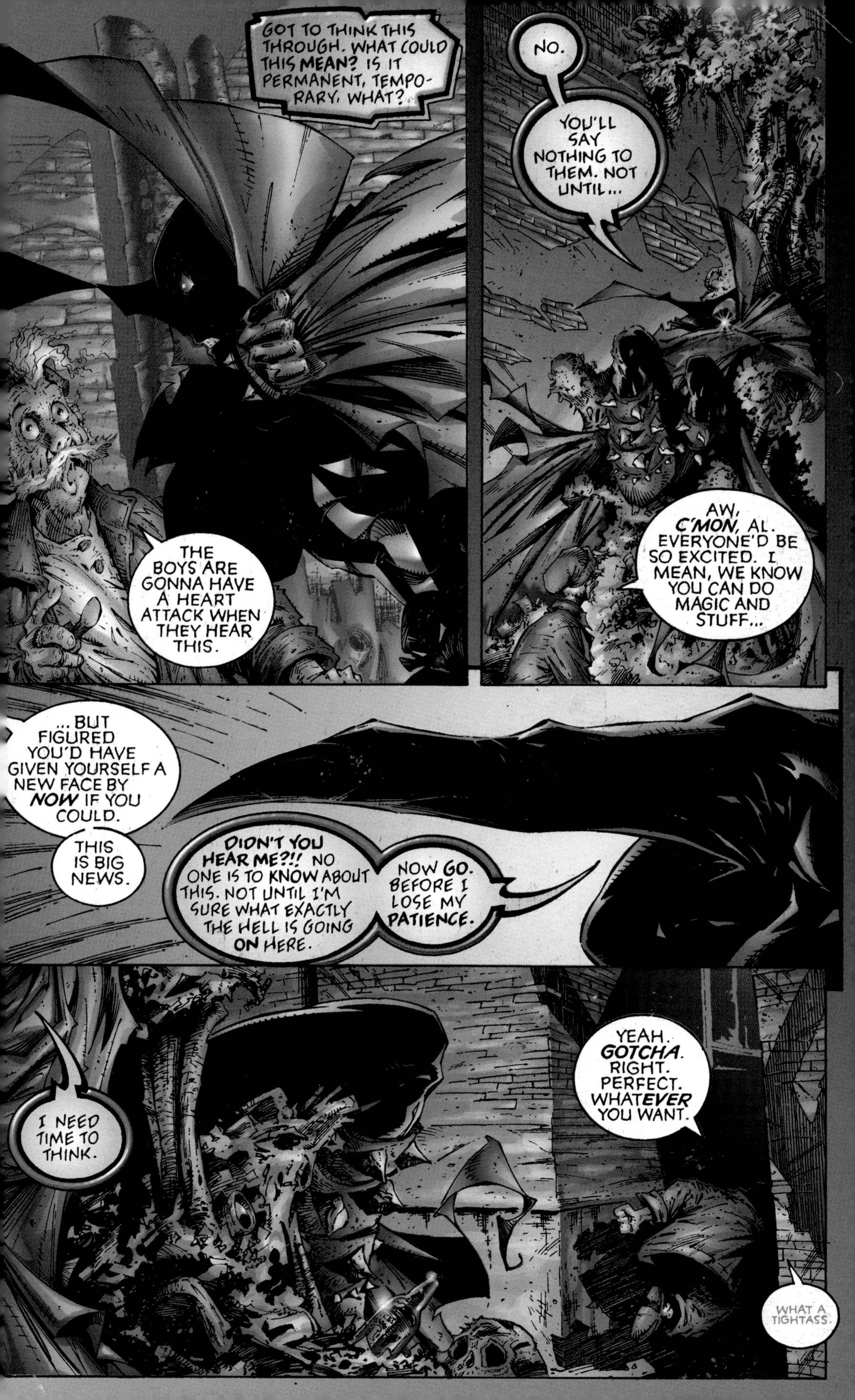
GOT TO THINK THIS THROUGH. WHAT COULD THIS MEAN? IS IT PERMANENT, TEMPORARY, WHAT?
THE BOYS ARE GONNA HAVE A HEART ATTACK WHEN THEY HEAR THIS.
NO.
YOU'LL SAY NOTHING TO THEM. NOT UNTIL...
AW, C'MON, AL. EVERYONE'D BE SO EXCITED. I MEAN, WE KNOW YOU CAN DO MAGIC AND STUFF...
...BUT FIGURED YOU'D HAVE GIVEN YOURSELF A NEW FACE BY NOW IF YOU COULD.
THIS IS BIG NEWS.
DIDN'T YOU HEAR ME?!! NO ONE IS TO KNOW ABOUT THIS. NOT UNTIL I'M SURE WHAT EXACTLY THE HELL IS GOING ON HERE.
NOW GO. BEFORE I LOSE MY PATIENCE.
I NEED TIME TO THINK.
YEAH. GOTCHA. RIGHT. PERFECT. WHATEVER YOU WANT.
WHAT A TIGHTASS.

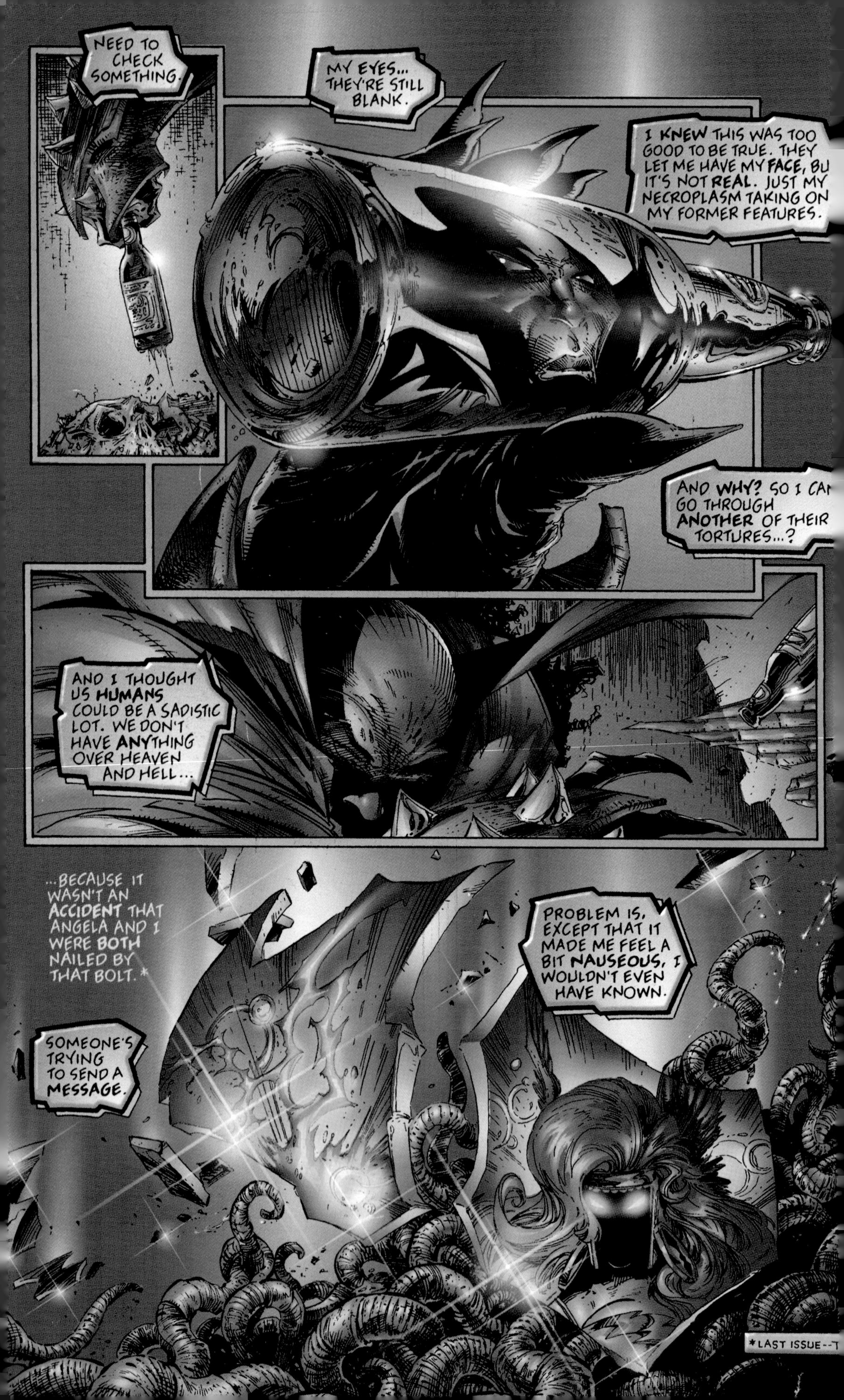
NEED TO CHECK SOMETHING.
MY EYES... THEY'RE STILL BLANK.
I KNEW THIS WAS TOO GOOD TO BE TRUE. THEY LET ME HAVE MY FACE, BU IT'S NOT REAL. JUST MY NECROPLASM TAKING ON MY FORMER FEATURES.
AND WHY? SO I CAN GO THROUGH ANOTHER OF THEIR TORTURES...?
AND I THOUGHT US HUMANS COULD BE A SADISTIC LOT. WE DON'T HAVE ANYTHING OVER HEAVEN AND HELL...
...BECAUSE IT WASN'T AN ACCIDENT THAT ANGELA AND I WERE BOTH NAILED BY THAT BOLT. *
PROBLEM IS, EXCEPT THAT IT MADE ME FEEL A BIT NAUSEOUS, I WOULDN'T EVEN HAVE KNOWN.
SOMEONE'S TRYING TO SEND A MESSAGE.
*LAST ISSUE--T

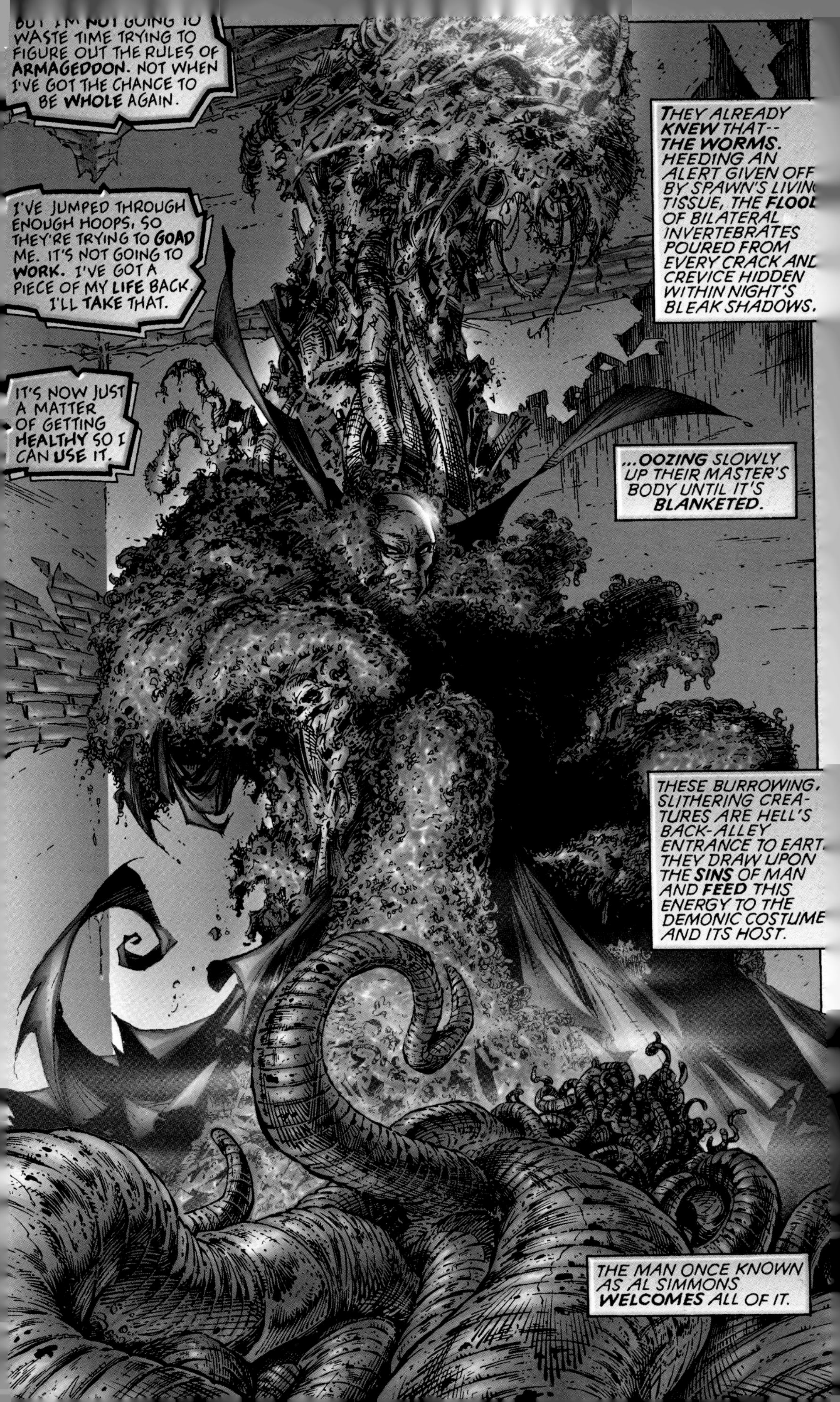

BUT I'M NOT GOING TO WASTE TIME TRYING TO FIGURE OUT THE RULES OF ARMAGEDDON. NOT WHEN I'VE GOT THE CHANCE TO BE WHOLE AGAIN.
THEY ALREADY KNEW THAT-- THE WORMS. HEEDING AN ALERT GIVEN OFF BY SPAWN'S LIVING TISSUE, THE FLOOD OF BILATERAL INVERTEBRATES POURED FROM EVERY CRACK AND CREVICE HIDDEN WITHIN NIGHT'S BLEAK SHADOWS.
I'VE JUMPED THROUGH ENOUGH HOOPS, SO THEY'RE TRYING TO GOAD ME. IT'S NOT GOING TO WORK. I'VE GOT A PIECE OF MY LIFE BACK. I'LL TAKE THAT.
IT'S NOW JUST A MATTER OF GETTING HEALTHY SO I CAN USE IT.
...OOZING SLOWLY UP THEIR MASTER'S BODY UNTIL IT'S BLANKETED.
THESE BURROWING, SLITHERING CREATURES ARE HELL'S BACK-ALLEY ENTRANCE TO EARTH. THEY DRAW UPON THE SINS OF MAN AND FEED THIS ENERGY TO THE DEMONIC COSTUME AND ITS HOST.
THE MAN ONCE KNOWN AS AL SIMMONS WELCOMES ALL OF IT.

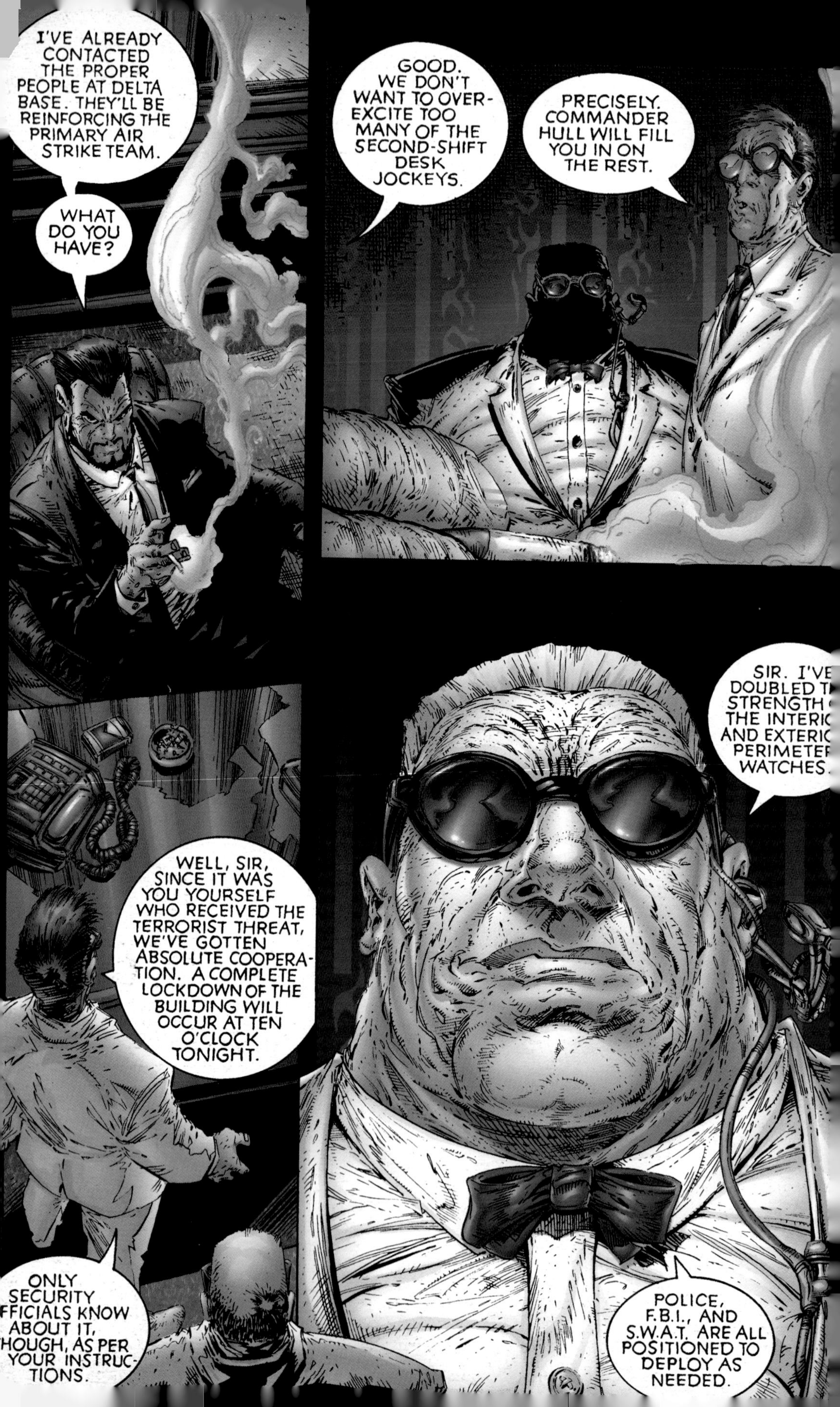
I'VE ALREADY CONTACTED THE PROPER PEOPLE AT DELTA BASE. THEY'LL BE REINFORCING THE PRIMARY AIR STRIKE TEAM.
WHAT DO YOU HAVE?
GOOD. WE DON'T WANT TO OVER-EXCITE TOO MANY OF THE SECOND-SHIFT DESK JOCKEYS.
PRECISELY. COMMANDER HULL WILL FILL YOU IN ON THE REST.
WELL, SIR, SINCE IT WAS YOU YOURSELF WHO RECEIVED THE TERRORIST THREAT, WE'VE GOTTEN ABSOLUTE COOPERATION. A COMPLETE LOCKDOWN OF THE BUILDING WILL OCCUR AT TEN O'CLOCK TONIGHT.
ONLY SECURITY FFICIALS KNOW ABOUT IT, HOUGH, AS PER YOUR INSTRUCTIONS.
SIR. I'VE DOUBLED T STRENGTH THE INTERI AND EXTERI PERIMETE WATCHES.
POLICE, F.B.I., AND S.W.A.T. ARE ALL POSITIONED TO DEPLOY AS NEEDED.

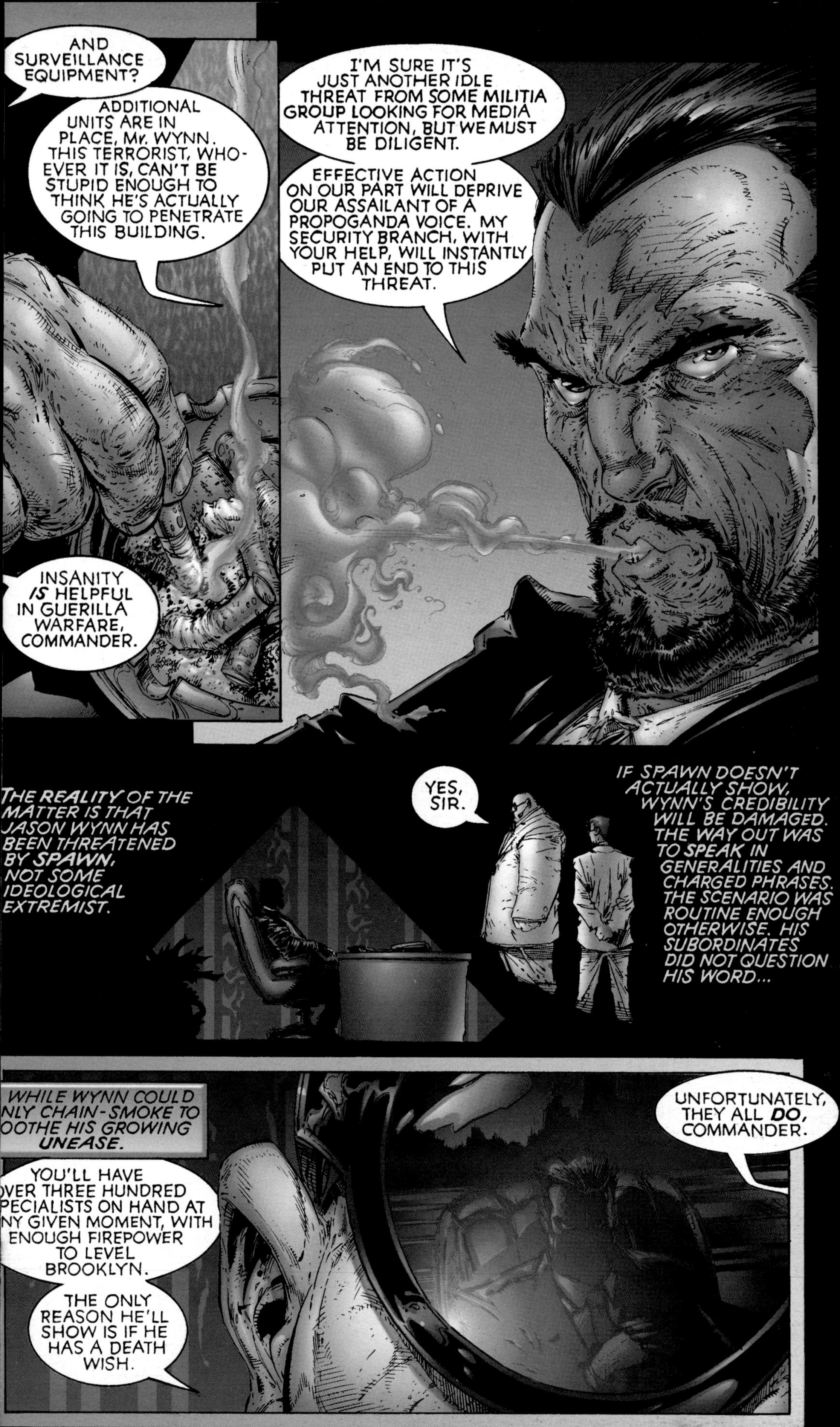
AND SURVEILLANCE EQUIPMENT?
ADDITIONAL UNITS ARE IN PLACE, Mr. WYNN. THIS TERRORIST, WHO-EVER IT IS, CAN'T BE STUPID ENOUGH TO THINK HE'S ACTUALLY GOING TO PENETRATE THIS BUILDING.
I'M SURE IT'S JUST ANOTHER IDLE THREAT FROM SOME MILITIA GROUP LOOKING FOR MEDIA ATTENTION, BUT WE MUST BE DILIGENT.
EFFECTIVE ACTION ON OUR PART WILL DEPRIVE OUR ASSAILANT OF A PROPOGANDA VOICE. MY SECURITY BRANCH, WITH YOUR HELP, WILL INSTANTLY PUT AN END TO THIS THREAT.
INSANITY IS HELPFUL IN GUERILLA WARFARE, COMMANDER.
THE REALITY OF THE MATTER IS THAT JASON WYNN HAS BEEN THREATENED BY SPAWN, NOT SOME IDEOLOGICAL EXTREMIST.
YES, SIR.
IF SPAWN DOESN'T ACTUALLY SHOW, WYNN'S CREDIBILITY WILL BE DAMAGED. THE WAY OUT WAS TO SPEAK IN GENERALITIES AND CHARGED PHRASES. THE SCENARIO WAS ROUTINE ENOUGH OTHERWISE. HIS SUBORDINATES DID NOT QUESTION HIS WORD...
WHILE WYNN COULD NLY CHAIN-SMOKE TO OOTHE HIS GROWING UNEASE.
YOU'LL HAVE VER THREE HUNDRED PECIALISTS ON HAND AT NY GIVEN MOMENT, WITH ENOUGH FIREPOWER TO LEVEL BROOKLYN.
THE ONLY REASON HE'LL SHOW IS IF HE HAS A DEATH WISH.
UNFORTUNATELY, THEY ALL DO, COMMANDER.

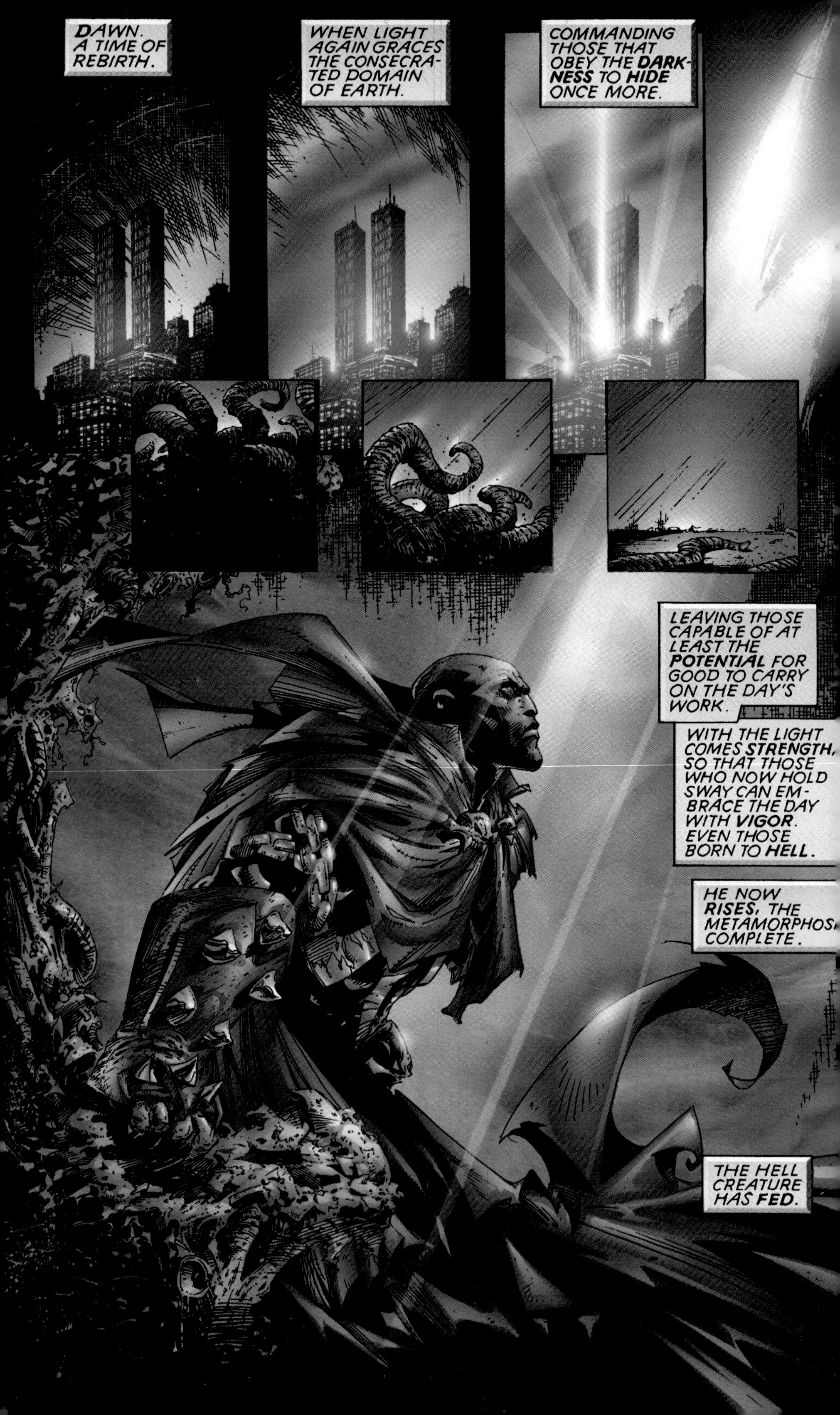
DAWN. A TIME OF REBIRTH.
WHEN LIGHT AGAIN GRACES THE CONSECRA-TED DOMAIN OF EARTH.
COMMANDING THOSE THAT OBEY THE DARK-NESS TO HIDE ONCE MORE.
LEAVING THOSE CAPABLE OF AT LEAST THE POTENTIAL FOR GOOD TO CARRY ON THE DAY'S WORK.
WITH THE LIGHT COMES STRENGTH, SO THAT THOSE WHO NOW HOLD SWAY CAN EM-BRACE THE DAY WITH VIGOR. EVEN THOSE BORN TO HELL.
HE NOW RISES, THE METAMORPHOS COMPLETE.
THE HELL CREATURE HAS FED.

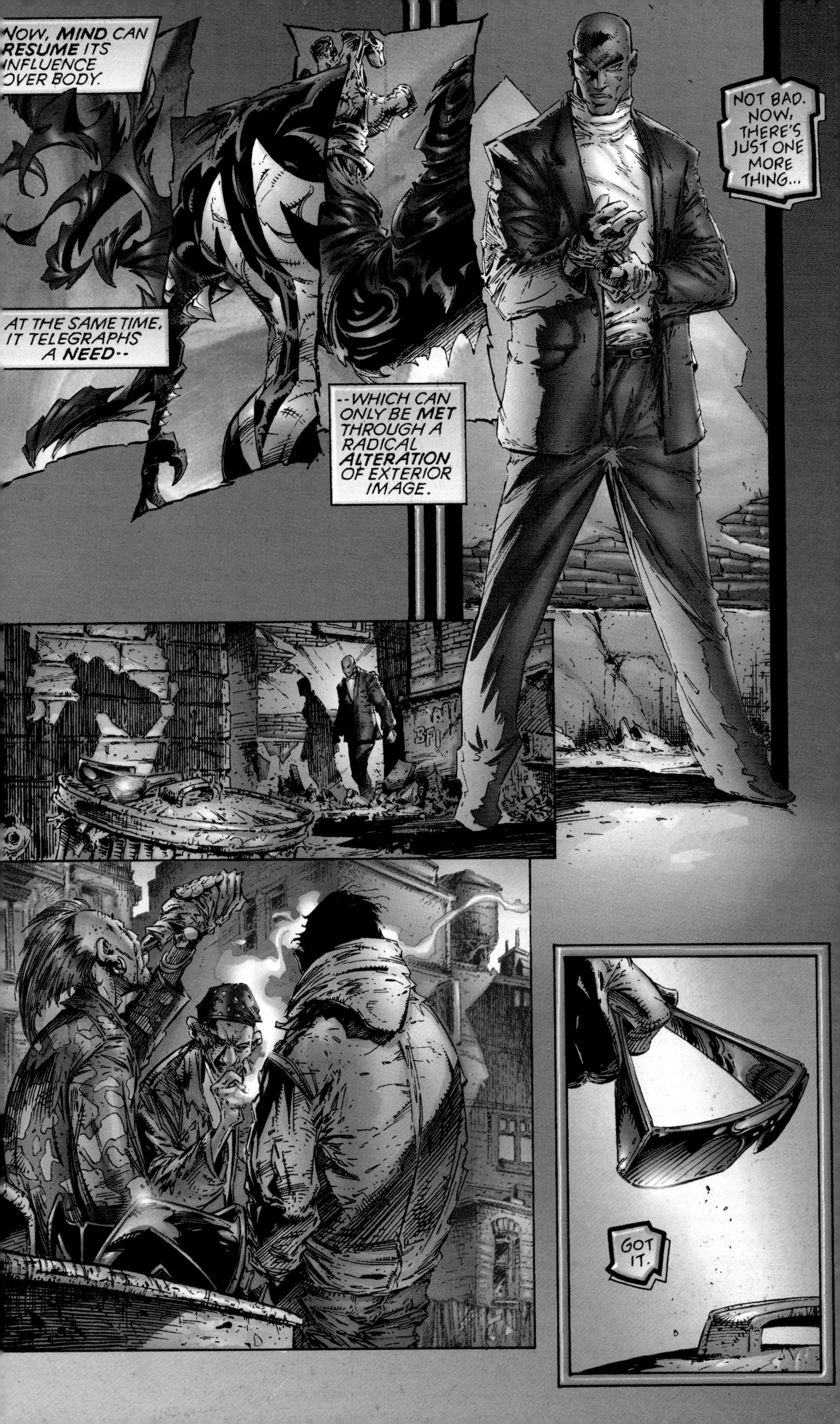

NOW, MIND CAN RESUME ITS INFLUENCE OVER BODY.
AT THE SAME TIME, IT TELEGRAPHS A NEED--
--WHICH CAN ONLY BE MET THROUGH A RADICAL ALTERATION OF EXTERIOR IMAGE.
NOT BAD. NOW, THERE'S JUST ONE MORE THING...
GOT IT.

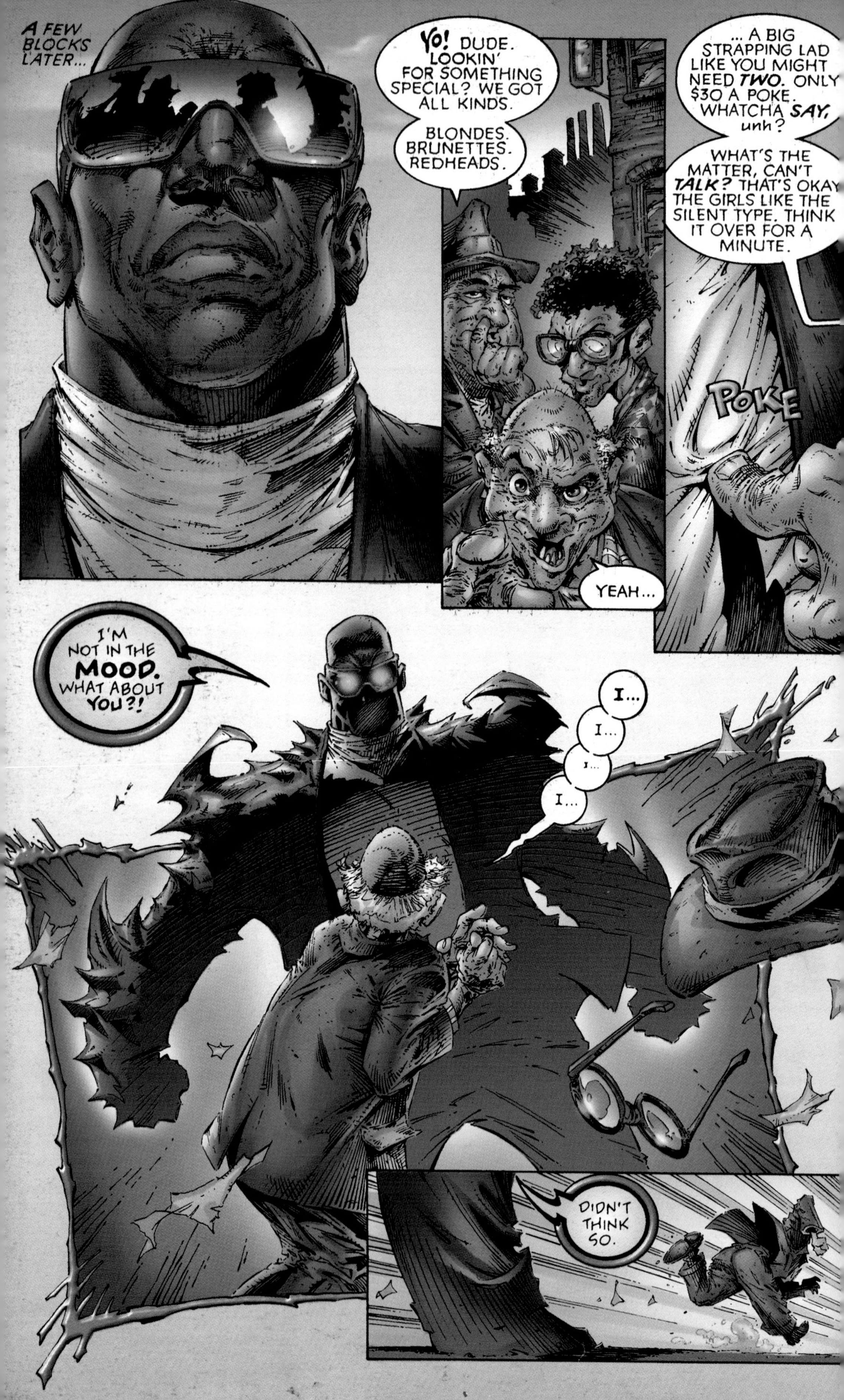
A FEW BLOCKS LATER...
YO! DUDE. LOOKIN' FOR SOMETHING SPECIAL? WE GOT ALL KINDS.
BLONDES. BRUNETTES. REDHEADS.
YEAH...
... A BIG STRAPPING LAD LIKE YOU MIGHT NEED TWO. ONLY $30 A POKE. WHATCHA SAY, unh?
WHAT'S THE MATTER, CAN'T TALK? THAT'S OKAY THE GIRLS LIKE THE SILENT TYPE. THINK IT OVER FOR A MINUTE.
POKE
I'M NOT IN THE MOOD. WHAT ABOUT YOU?!
I...
I...
I...
I...
DIDN'T THINK SO.

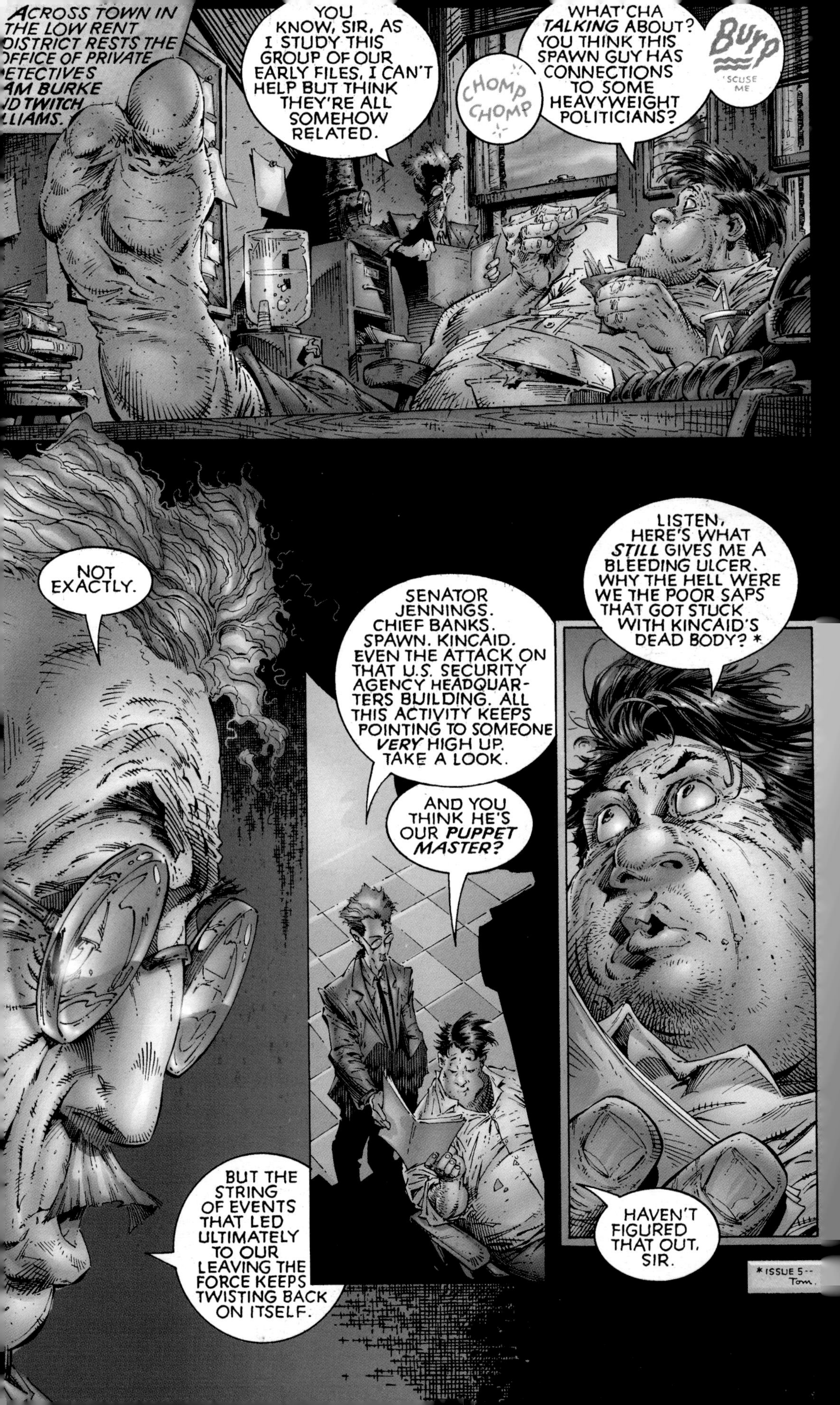

ACROSS TOWN IN THE LOW RENT DISTRICT RESTS THE OFFICE OF PRIVATE ETECTIVES AM BURKE ID TWITCH LLIAMS.
YOU KNOW, SIR, AS I STUDY THIS GROUP OF OUR EARLY FILES, I CAN'T HELP BUT THINK THEY'RE ALL SOMEHOW RELATED.
CHOMP CHOMP
WHAT'CHA TALKING ABOUT? YOU THINK THIS SPAWN GUY HAS CONNECTIONS TO SOME HEAVYWEIGHT POLITICIANS?
BURP
'SCUSE ME
NOT EXACTLY.
SENATOR JENNINGS. CHIEF BANKS. SPAWN. KINCAID. EVEN THE ATTACK ON THAT U.S. SECURITY AGENCY HEADQUARTERS BUILDING. ALL THIS ACTIVITY KEEPS POINTING TO SOMEONE VERY HIGH UP. TAKE A LOOK.
AND YOU THINK HE'S OUR PUPPET MASTER?
LISTEN, HERE'S WHAT STILL GIVES ME A BLEEDING ULCER. WHY THE HELL WERE WE THE POOR SAPS THAT GOT STUCK WITH KINCAID'S DEAD BODY? *
BUT THE STRING OF EVENTS THAT LED ULTIMATELY TO OUR LEAVING THE FORCE KEEPS TWISTING BACK ON ITSELF.
HAVEN'T FIGURED THAT OUT, SIR.
* ISSUE 5 -- Tom.

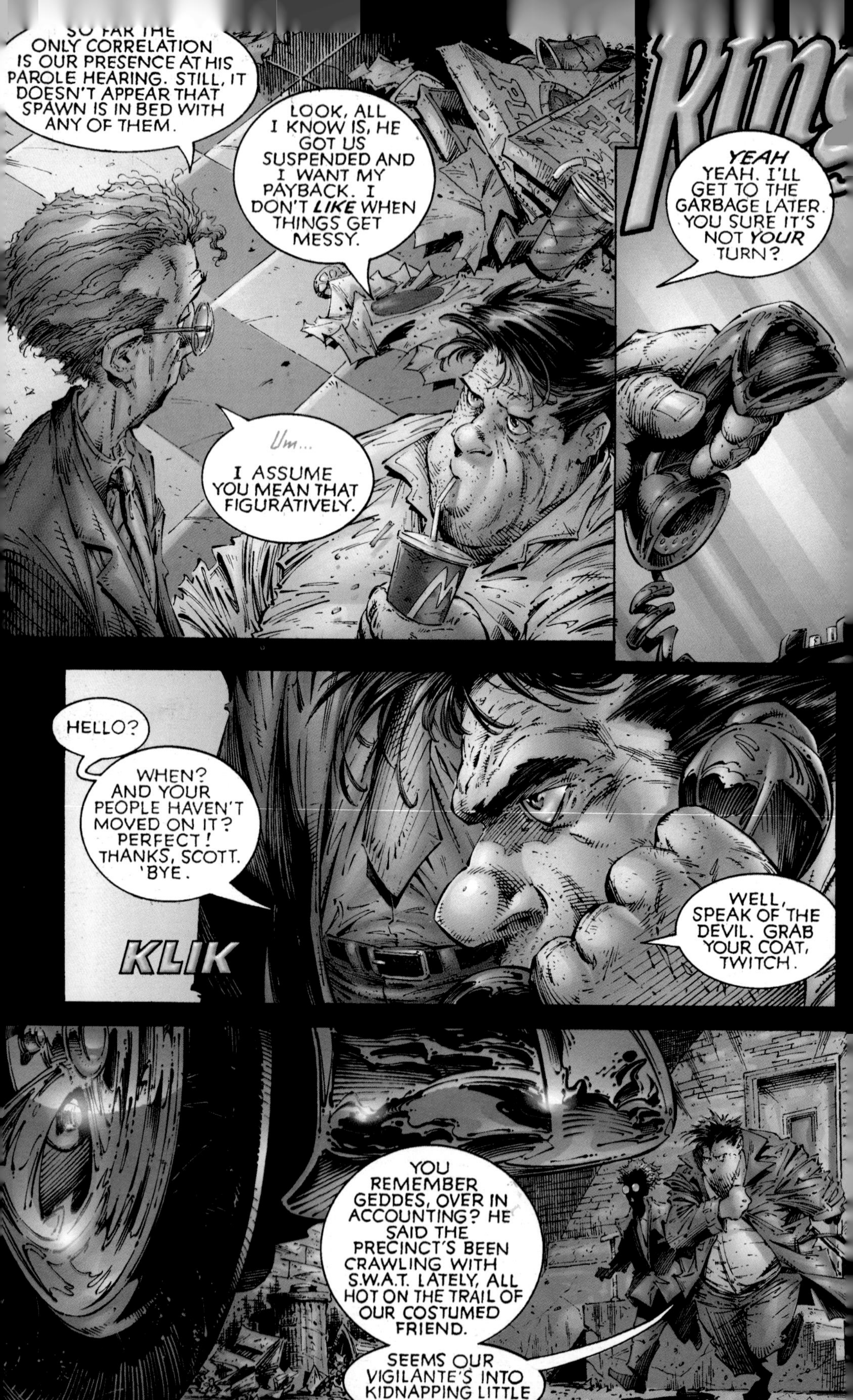
SO FAR THE ONLY CORRELATION IS OUR PRESENCE AT HIS PAROLE HEARING. STILL, IT DOESN'T APPEAR THAT SPAWN IS IN BED WITH ANY OF THEM.
LOOK, ALL I KNOW IS, HE GOT US SUSPENDED AND I WANT MY PAYBACK. I DON'T LIKE WHEN THINGS GET MESSY.
Um...
I ASSUME YOU MEAN THAT FIGURATIVELY.
YEAH YEAH. I'LL GET TO THE GARBAGE LATER. YOU SURE IT'S NOT YOUR TURN?
HELLO?
WHEN? AND YOUR PEOPLE HAVEN'T MOVED ON IT? PERFECT! THANKS, SCOTT. 'BYE.
KLIK
WELL, SPEAK OF THE DEVIL. GRAB YOUR COAT, TWITCH.
YOU REMEMBER GEDDES, OVER IN ACCOUNTING? HE SAID THE PRECINCT'S BEEN CRAWLING WITH S.W.A.T. LATELY, ALL HOT ON THE TRAIL OF OUR COSTUMED FRIEND.
SEEMS OUR VIGILANTE'S INTO KIDNAPPING LITTLE GIRLS.

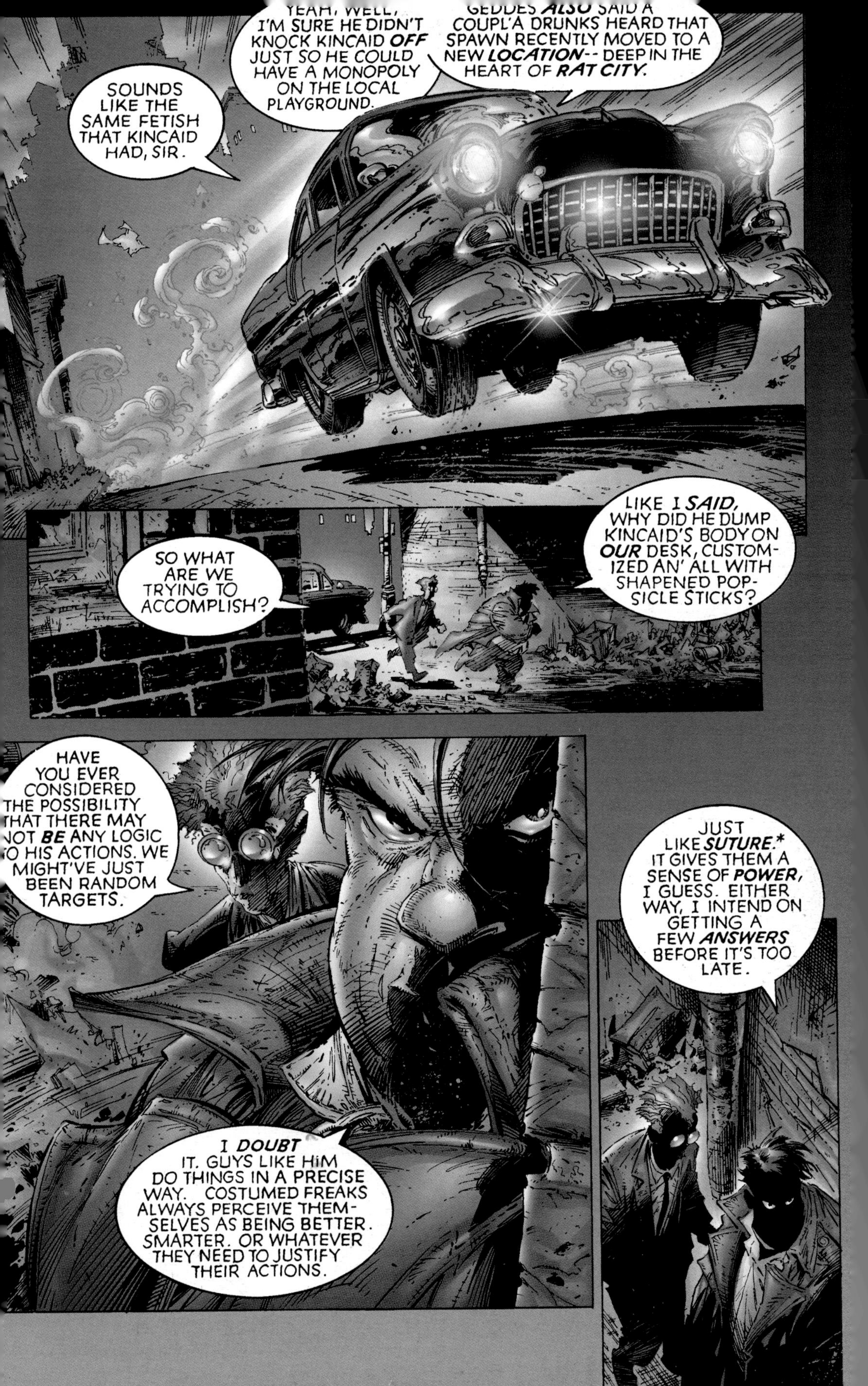
SOUNDS LIKE THE SAME FETISH THAT KINCAID HAD, SIR.
YEAH, WELL, I'M SURE HE DIDN'T KNOCK KINCAID OFF JUST SO HE COULD HAVE A MONOPOLY ON THE LOCAL PLAYGROUND.
GEDDES ALSO SAID A COUPL'A DRUNKS HEARD THAT SPAWN RECENTLY MOVED TO A NEW LOCATION-- DEEP IN THE HEART OF RAT CITY.
SO WHAT ARE WE TRYING TO ACCOMPLISH?
LIKE I SAID, WHY DID HE DUMP KINCAID'S BODY ON OUR DESK, CUSTOMIZED AN' ALL WITH SHAPENED POPSICLE STICKS?
HAVE YOU EVER CONSIDERED THE POSSIBILITY THAT THERE MAY NOT BE ANY LOGIC TO HIS ACTIONS. WE MIGHT'VE JUST BEEN RANDOM TARGETS.
I DOUBT IT. GUYS LIKE HIM DO THINGS IN A PRECISE WAY. COSTUMED FREAKS ALWAYS PERCEIVE THEMSELVES AS BEING BETTER. SMARTER. OR WHATEVER THEY NEED TO JUSTIFY THEIR ACTIONS.
JUST LIKE SUTURE.* IT GIVES THEM A SENSE OF POWER, I GUESS. EITHER WAY, I INTEND ON GETTING A FEW ANSWERS BEFORE IT'S TOO LATE.
*SEE CURSE OF THE SPAWN 5 THROUGH 8 -- Tom.

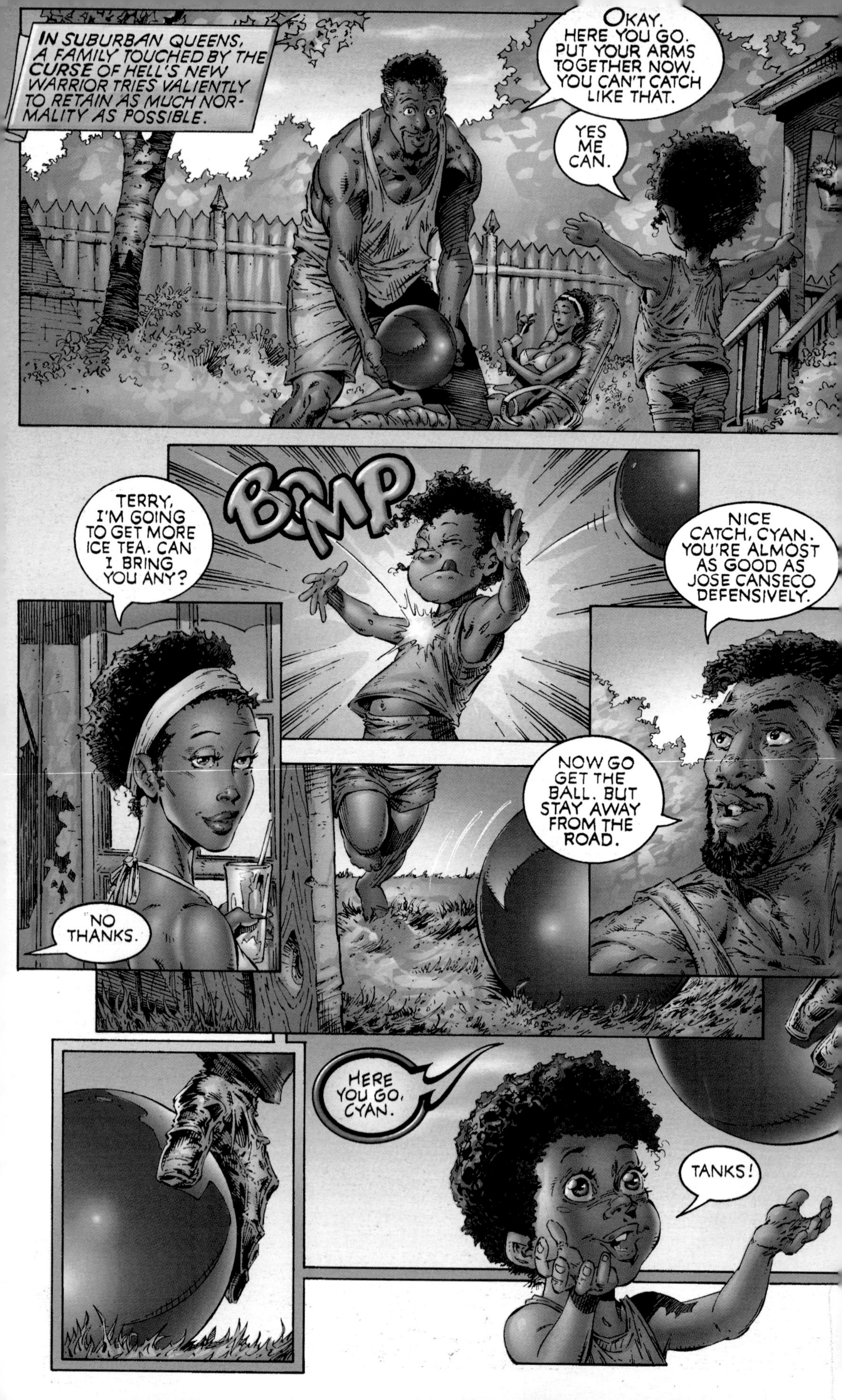

IN SUBURBAN QUEENS, A FAMILY TOUCHED BY THE CURSE OF HELL'S NEW WARRIOR TRIES VALIENTLY TO RETAIN AS MUCH NORMALITY AS POSSIBLE.
OKAY. HERE YOU GO. PUT YOUR ARMS TOGETHER NOW. YOU CAN'T CATCH LIKE THAT.
YES ME CAN.
BOMP
TERRY, I'M GOING TO GET MORE ICE TEA. CAN I BRING YOU ANY?
NICE CATCH, CYAN. YOU'RE ALMOST AS GOOD AS JOSE CANSECO DEFENSIVELY.
NO THANKS.
NOW GO GET THE BALL. BUT STAY AWAY FROM THE ROAD.
HERE YOU GO, CYAN.
TANKS!

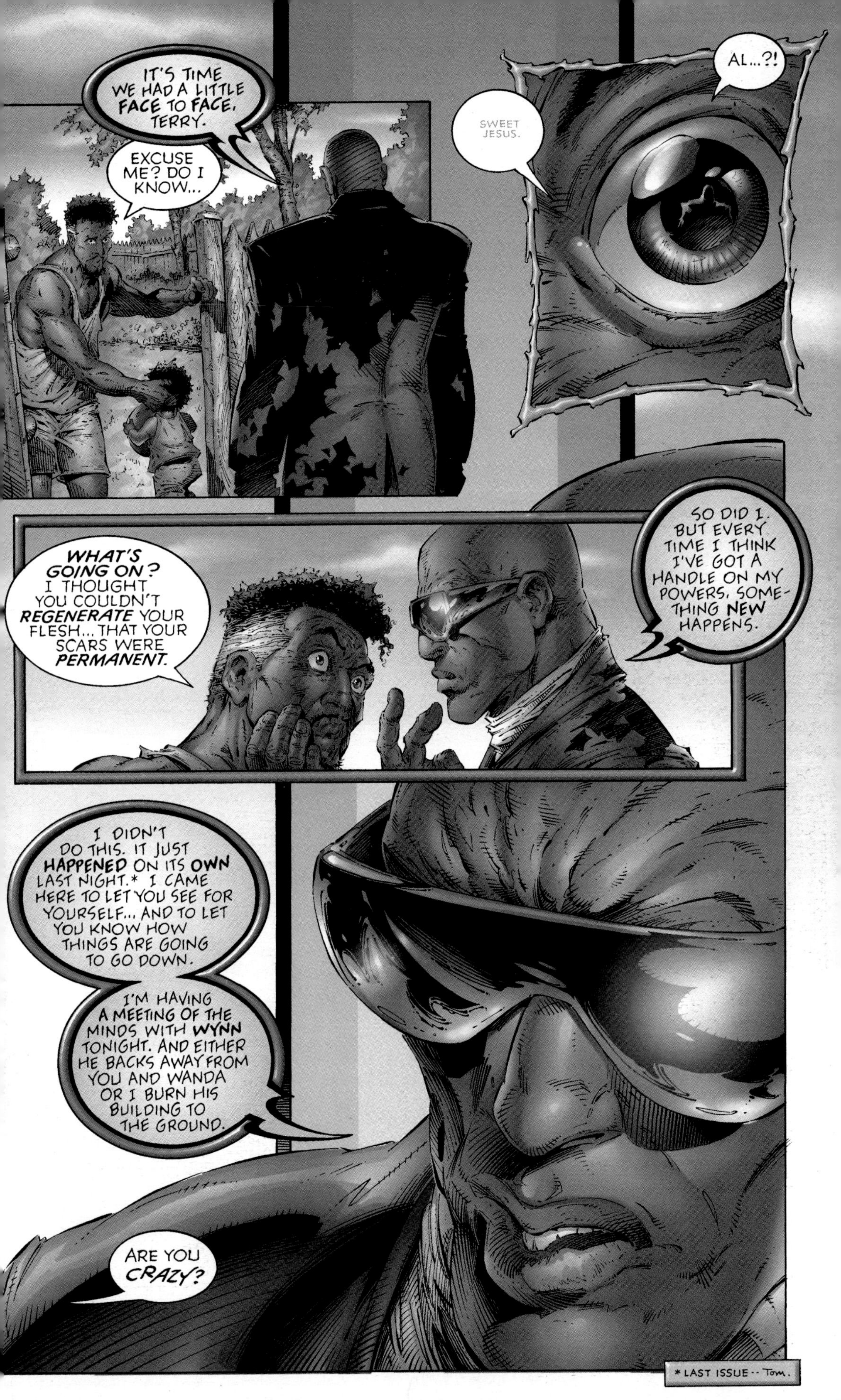
IT'S TIME WE HAD A LITTLE FACE TO FACE, TERRY.
EXCUSE ME? DO I KNOW...
SWEET JESUS.
AL...?!
WHAT'S GOING ON? I THOUGHT YOU COULDN'T REGENERATE YOUR FLESH... THAT YOUR SCARS WERE PERMANENT.
SO DID I. BUT EVERY TIME I THINK I'VE GOT A HANDLE ON MY POWERS, SOMETHING NEW HAPPENS.
I DIDN'T DO THIS. IT JUST HAPPENED ON ITS OWN LAST NIGHT.* I CAME HERE TO LET YOU SEE FOR YOURSELF... AND TO LET YOU KNOW HOW THINGS ARE GOING TO GO DOWN.
I'M HAVING A MEETING OF THE MINDS WITH WYNN TONIGHT. AND EITHER HE BACKS AWAY FROM YOU AND WANDA OR I BURN HIS BUILDING TO THE GROUND.
ARE YOU CRAZY?
*LAST ISSUE -- Tom.

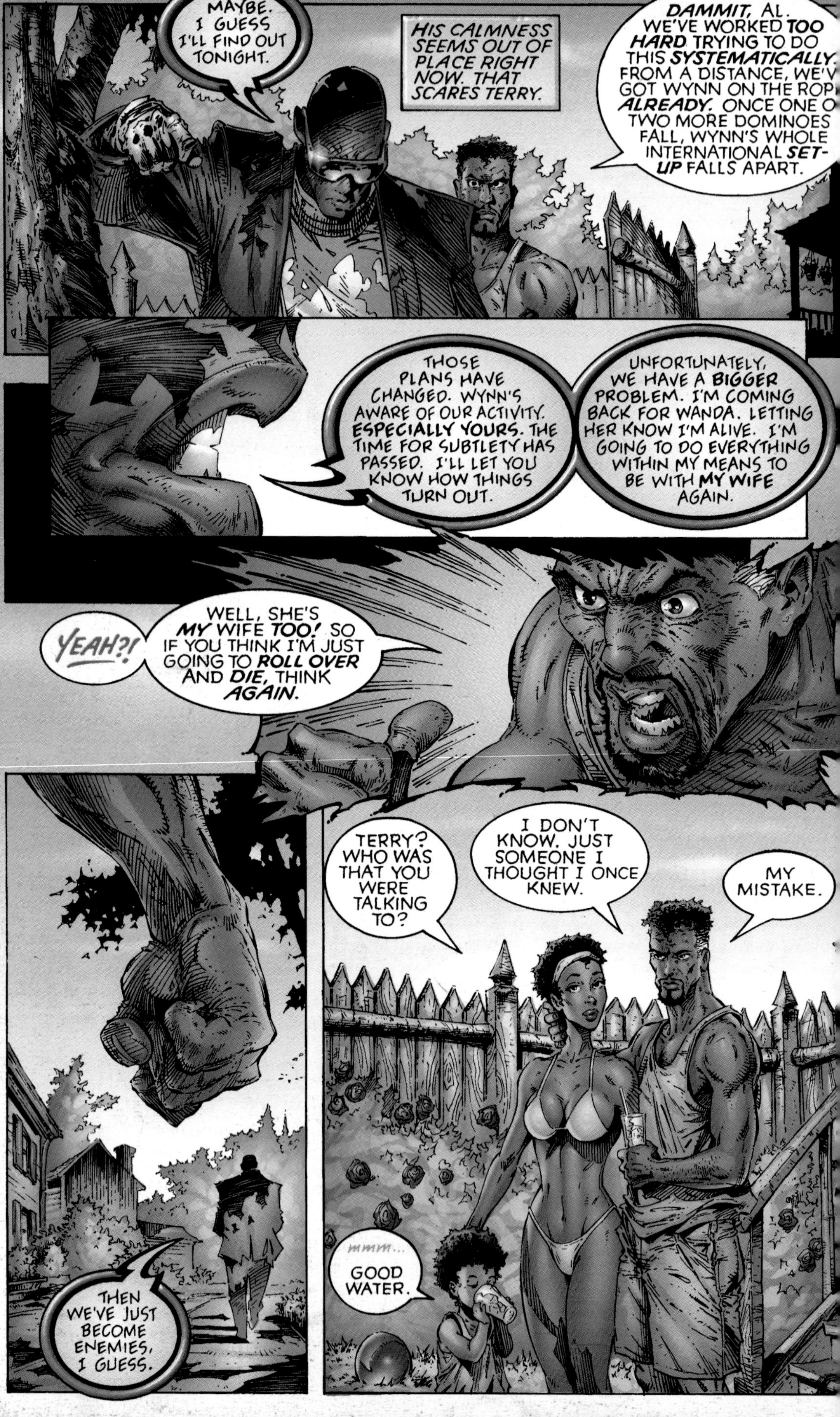
MAYBE. I GUESS I'LL FIND OUT TONIGHT.
HIS CALMNESS SEEMS OUT OF PLACE RIGHT NOW. THAT SCARES TERRY.
DAMMIT, AL. WE'VE WORKED TOO HARD TRYING TO DO THIS SYSTEMATICALLY. FROM A DISTANCE, WE'V GOT WYNN ON THE ROP ALREADY. ONCE ONE O TWO MORE DOMINOES FALL, WYNN'S WHOLE INTERNATIONAL SET-UP FALLS APART.
THOSE PLANS HAVE CHANGED. WYNN'S AWARE OF OUR ACTIVITY. ESPECIALLY YOURS. THE TIME FOR SUBTLETY HAS PASSED. I'LL LET YOU KNOW HOW THINGS TURN OUT.
UNFORTUNATELY, WE HAVE A BIGGER PROBLEM. I'M COMING BACK FOR WANDA. LETTING HER KNOW I'M ALIVE. I'M GOING TO DO EVERYTHING WITHIN MY MEANS TO BE WITH MY WIFE AGAIN.
YEAH?!
WELL, SHE'S MY WIFE TOO! SO IF YOU THINK I'M JUST GOING TO ROLL OVER AND DIE, THINK AGAIN.
THEN WE'VE JUST BECOME ENEMIES, I GUESS.
TERRY? WHO WAS THAT YOU WERE TALKING TO?
I DON'T KNOW. JUST SOMEONE I THOUGHT I ONCE KNEW.
MY MISTAKE.
MMM...
GOOD WATER.

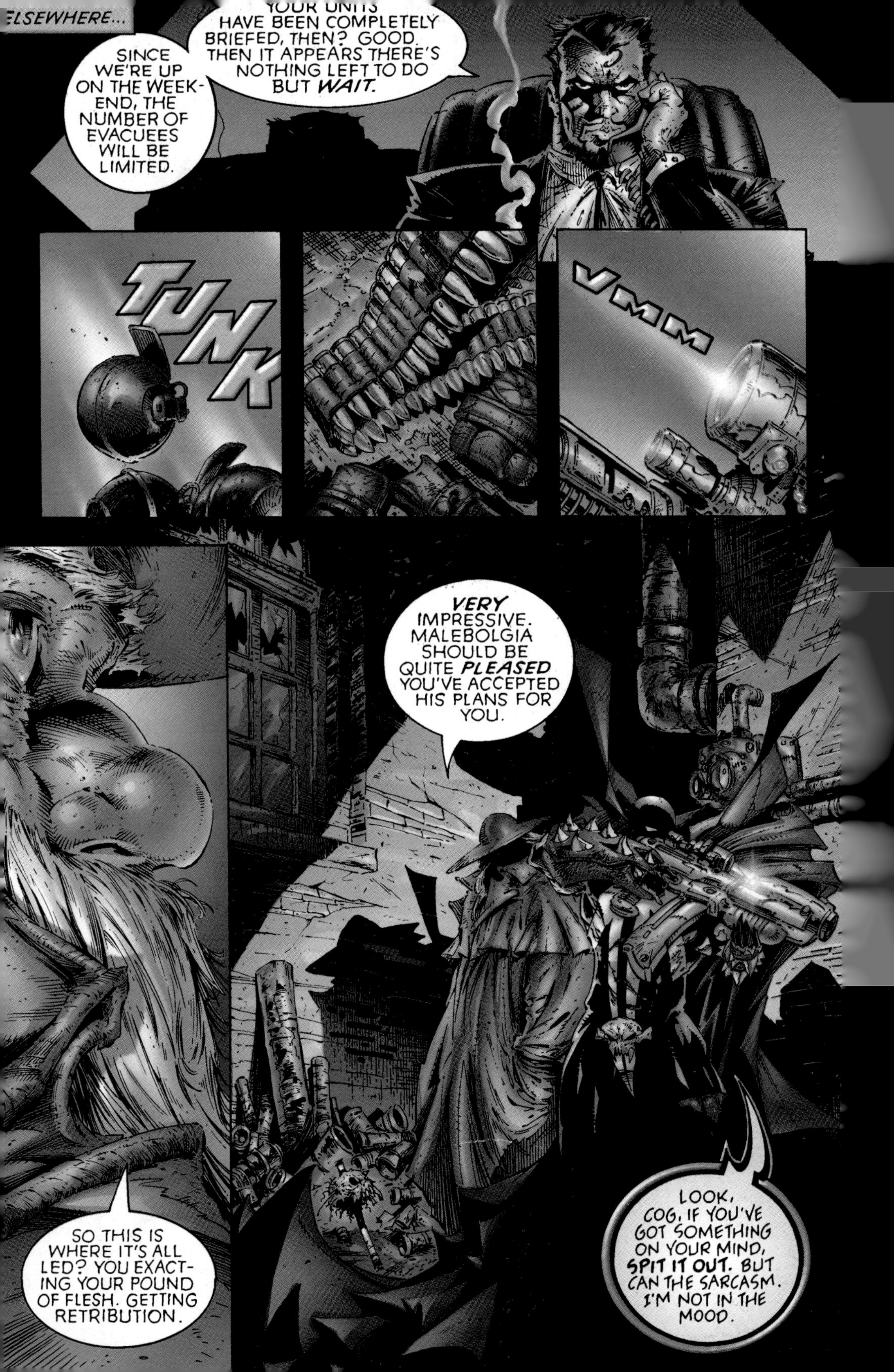
ELSEWHERE...
SINCE WE'RE UP ON THE WEEK-END, THE NUMBER OF EVACUEES WILL BE LIMITED.
YOUR UNITS HAVE BEEN COMPLETELY BRIEFED, THEN? GOOD. THEN IT APPEARS THERE'S NOTHING LEFT TO DO BUT WAIT.
TUNK
VMM
VERY IMPRESSIVE. MALEBOLGIA SHOULD BE QUITE PLEASED YOU'VE ACCEPTED HIS PLANS FOR YOU.
SO THIS IS WHERE IT'S ALL LED? YOU EXACT-ING YOUR POUND OF FLESH. GETTING RETRIBUTION.
LOOK, COG, IF YOU'VE GOT SOMETHING ON YOUR MIND, SPIT IT OUT. BUT CAN THE SARCASM. I'M NOT IN THE MOOD.

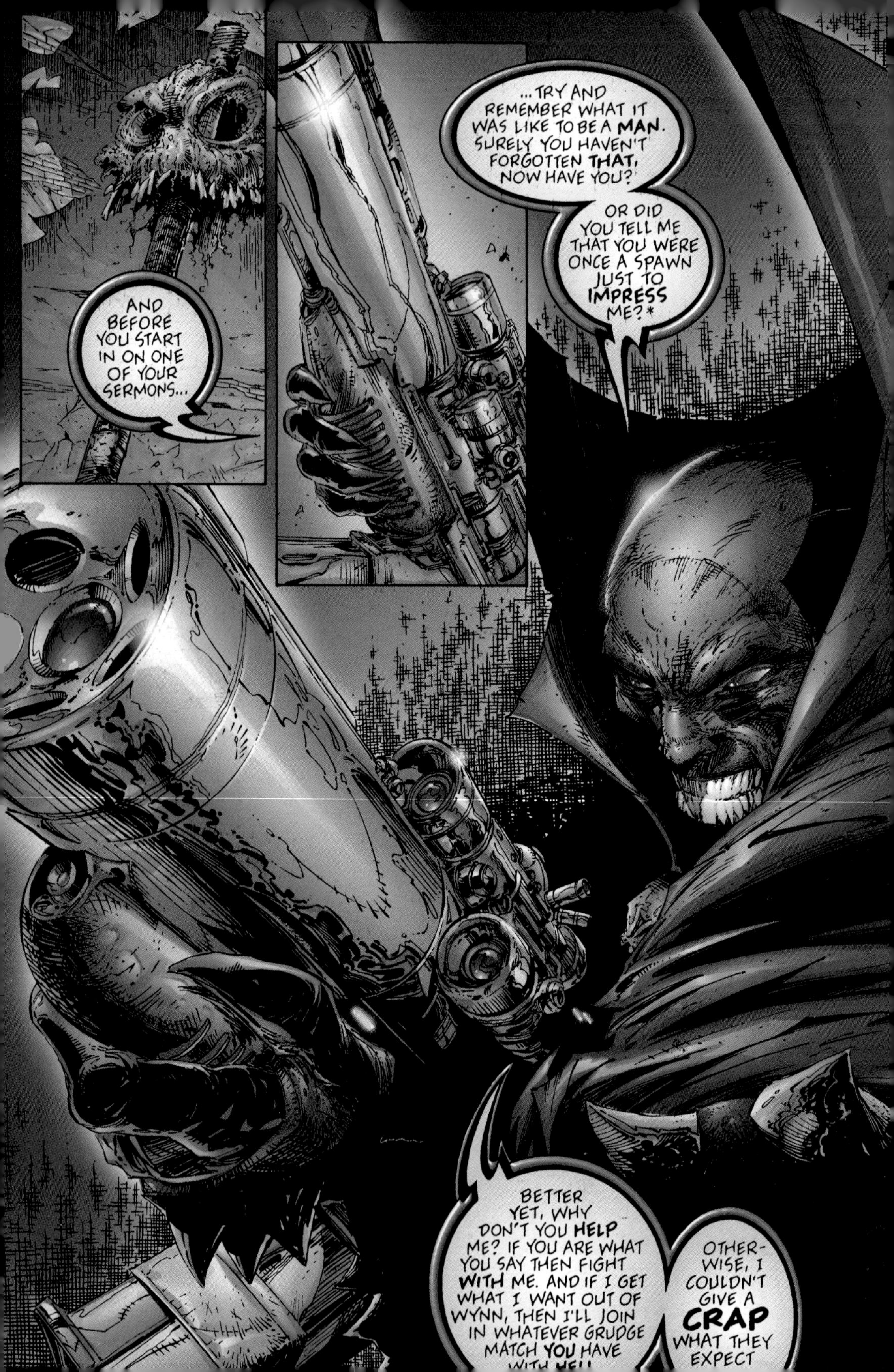
AND BEFORE YOU START IN ON ONE OF YOUR SERMONS...
...TRY AND REMEMBER WHAT IT WAS LIKE TO BE A **MAN**. SURELY YOU HAVEN'T FORGOTTEN **THAT**, NOW HAVE YOU?
OR DID YOU TELL ME THAT YOU WERE ONCE A SPAWN JUST TO **IMPRESS** ME?*
BETTER YET, WHY DON'T YOU **HELP** ME? IF YOU ARE WHAT YOU SAY THEN FIGHT **WITH** ME. AND IF I GET WHAT I WANT OUT OF WYNN, THEN I'LL JOIN IN WHATEVER GRUDGE MATCH **YOU** HAVE
OTHER-WISE, I COULDN'T GIVE A **CRAP** WHAT THEY EXPECT

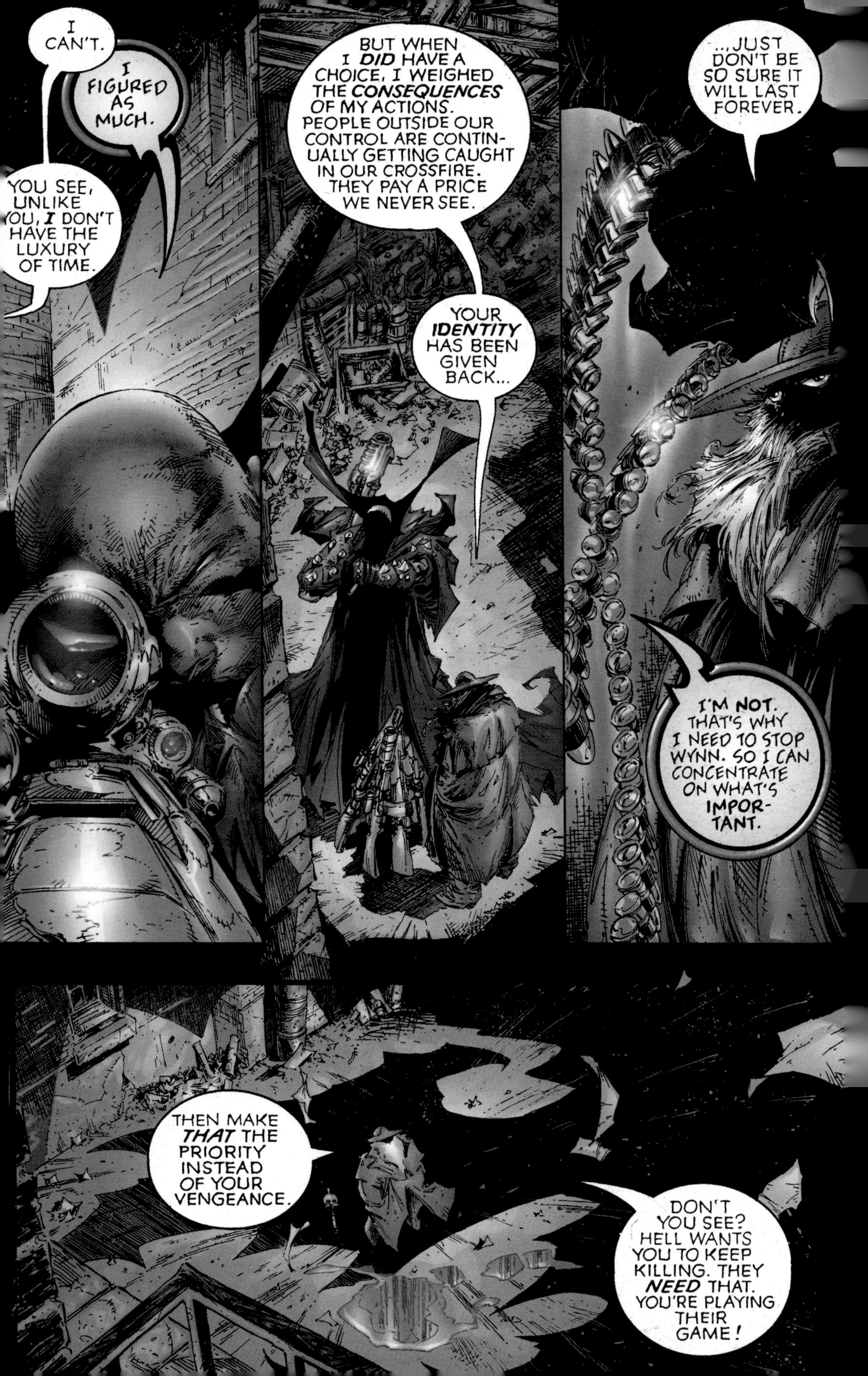

I CAN'T.
I FIGURED AS MUCH.
YOU SEE, UNLIKE YOU, I DON'T HAVE THE LUXURY OF TIME.
BUT WHEN I DID HAVE A CHOICE, I WEIGHED THE CONSEQUENCES OF MY ACTIONS. PEOPLE OUTSIDE OUR CONTROL ARE CONTINUALLY GETTING CAUGHT IN OUR CROSSFIRE. THEY PAY A PRICE WE NEVER SEE.
YOUR IDENTITY HAS BEEN GIVEN BACK...
...JUST DON'T BE SO SURE IT WILL LAST FOREVER.
I'M NOT. THAT'S WHY I NEED TO STOP WYNN. SO I CAN CONCENTRATE ON WHAT'S IMPORTANT.
THEN MAKE THAT THE PRIORITY INSTEAD OF YOUR VENGEANCE.
DON'T YOU SEE? HELL WANTS YOU TO KEEP KILLING. THEY NEED THAT. YOU'RE PLAYING THEIR GAME!

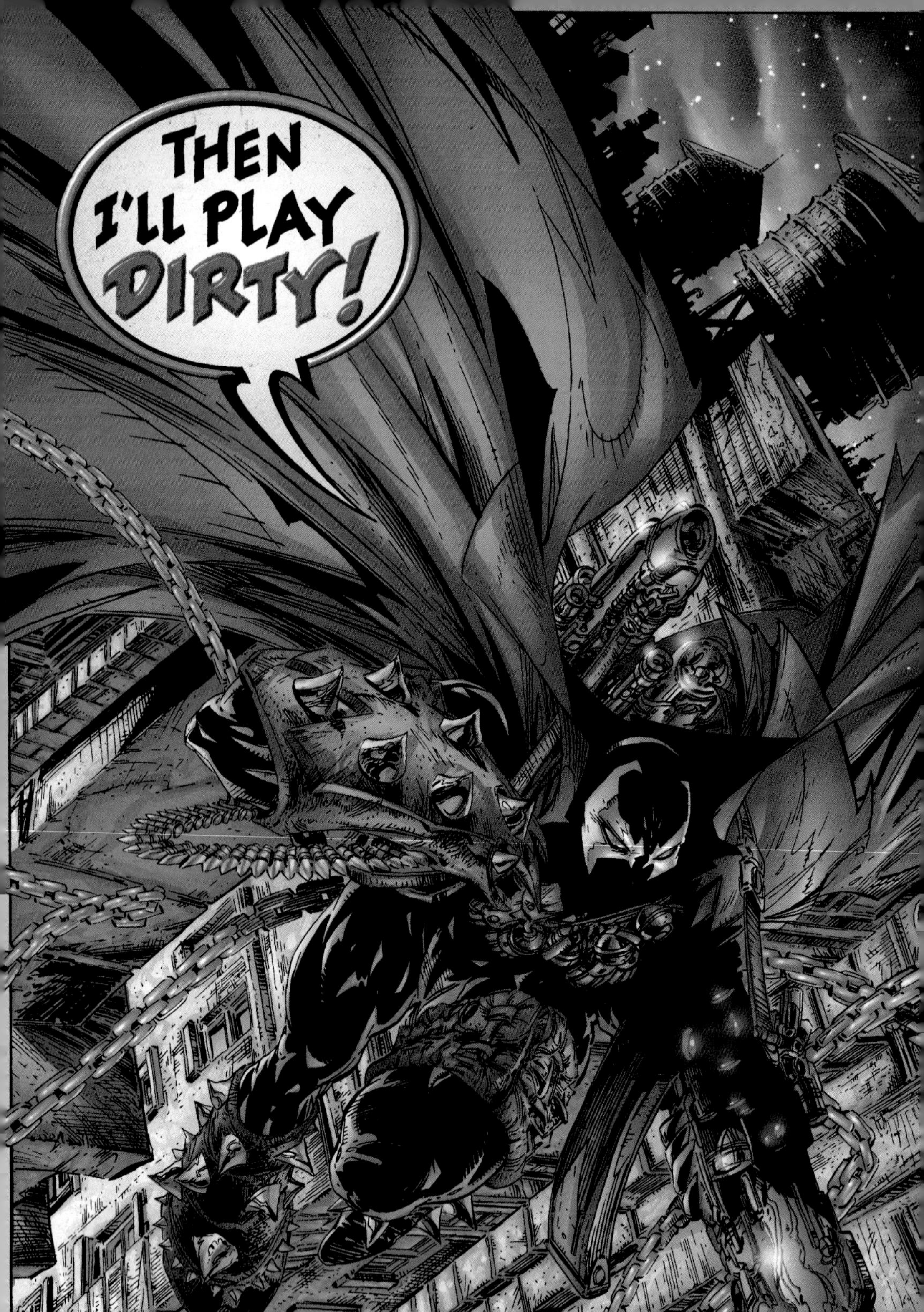
THEN I'LL PLAY DIRTY!

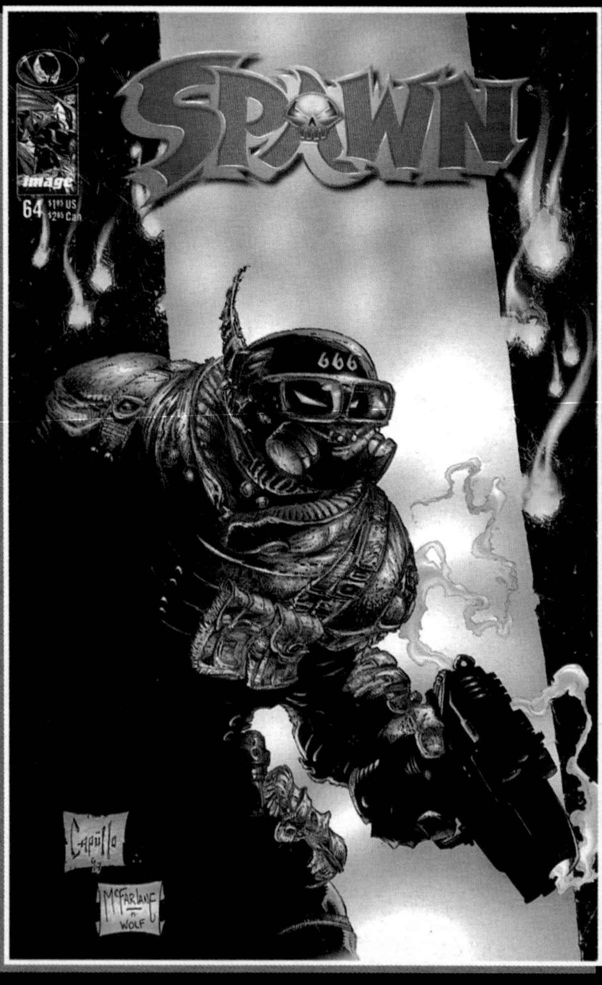
SPAWN
image
64 $1.95 US $2.65 Can
666
Capullo
McFarlane n Wolf

H E C K M A T E

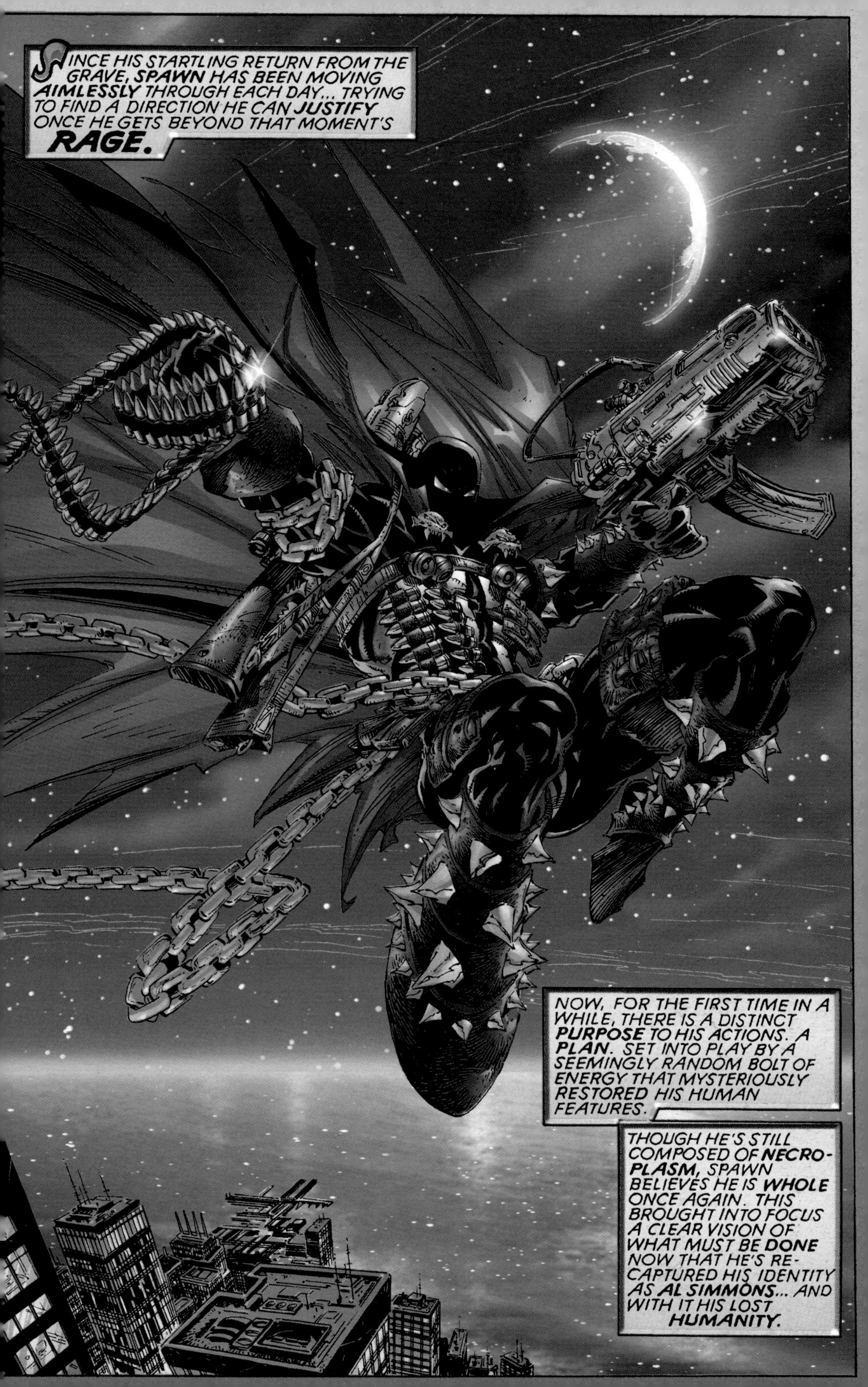
SINCE HIS STARTLING RETURN FROM THE GRAVE, SPAWN HAS BEEN MOVING AIMLESSLY THROUGH EACH DAY... TRYING TO FIND A DIRECTION HE CAN JUSTIFY ONCE HE GETS BEYOND THAT MOMENT'S RAGE.
NOW, FOR THE FIRST TIME IN A WHILE, THERE IS A DISTINCT PURPOSE TO HIS ACTIONS. A PLAN. SET INTO PLAY BY A SEEMINGLY RANDOM BOLT OF ENERGY THAT MYSTERIOUSLY RESTORED HIS HUMAN FEATURES.
THOUGH HE'S STILL COMPOSED OF NECRO-PLASM, SPAWN BELIEVES HE IS WHOLE ONCE AGAIN. THIS BROUGHT INTO FOCUS A CLEAR VISION OF WHAT MUST BE DONE NOW THAT HE'S RE-CAPTURED HIS IDENTITY AS AL SIMMONS... AND WITH IT HIS LOST HUMANITY.

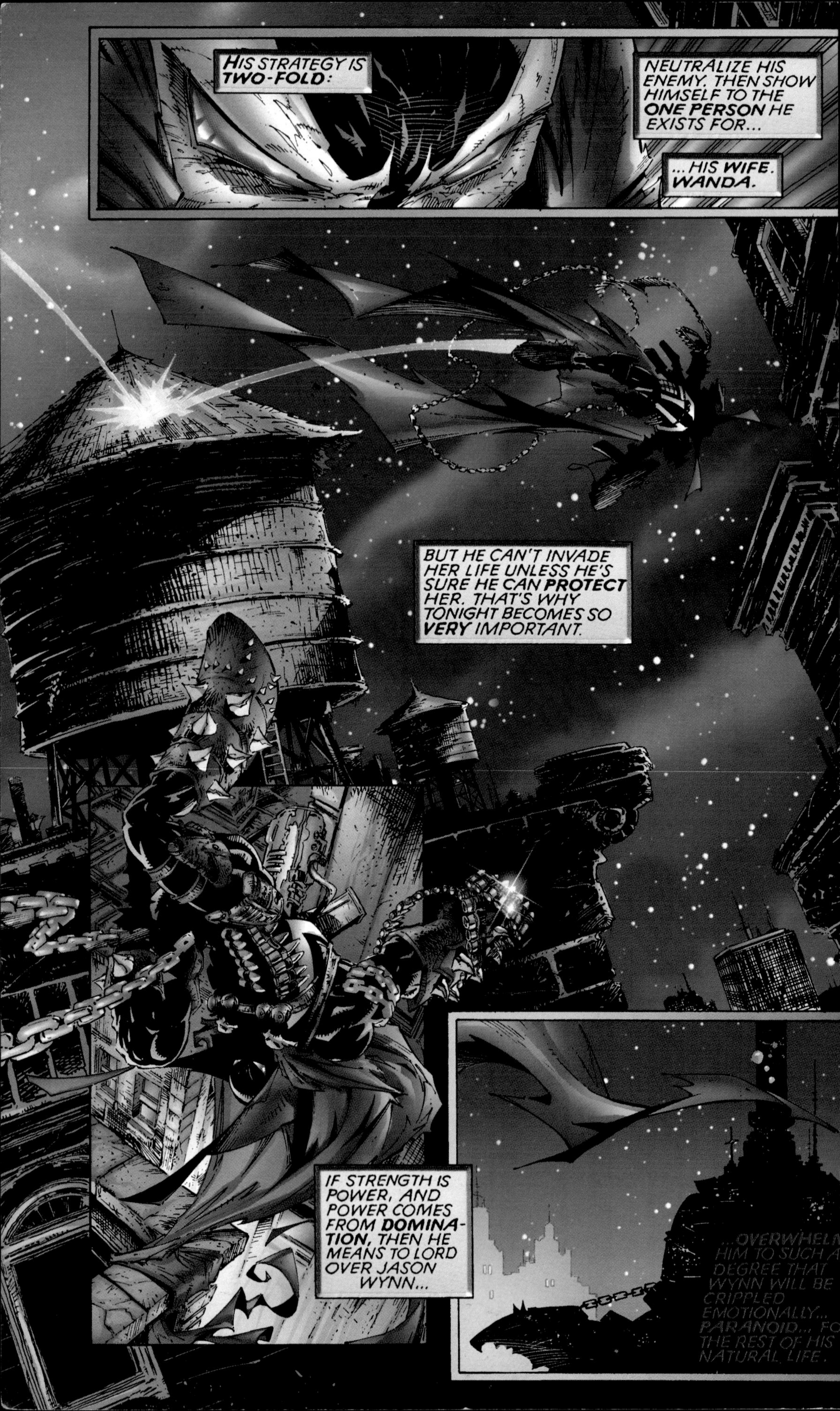

HIS STRATEGY IS TWO-FOLD:
NEUTRALIZE HIS ENEMY. THEN SHOW HIMSELF TO THE ONE PERSON HE EXISTS FOR...
...HIS WIFE. WANDA.
BUT HE CAN'T INVADE HER LIFE UNLESS HE'S SURE HE CAN PROTECT HER. THAT'S WHY TONIGHT BECOMES SO VERY IMPORTANT.
IF STRENGTH IS POWER, AND POWER COMES FROM DOMINATION, THEN HE MEANS TO LORD OVER JASON WYNN...
...OVERWHEL
HIM TO SUCH A
DEGREE THAT
WYNN WILL BE
CRIPPLED
EMOTIONALLY...
PARANOID... FO
THE REST OF HIS
NATURAL LIFE.

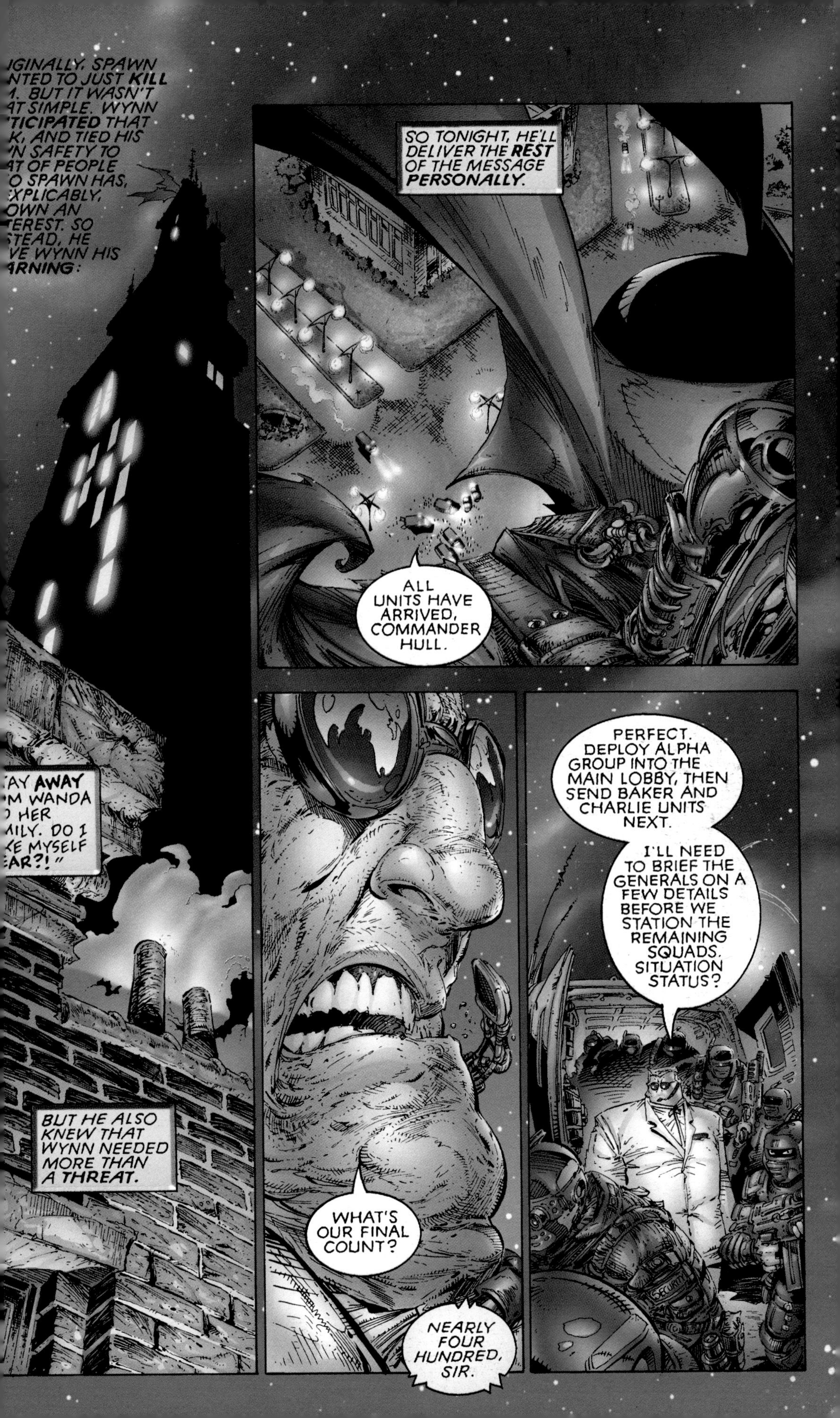
IGINALLY, SPAWN NTED TO JUST KILL 1. BUT IT WASN'T AT SIMPLE. WYNN TICIPATED THAT K, AND TIED HIS N SAFETY TO AT OF PEOPLE O SPAWN HAS, EXPLICABLY, OWN AN TEREST. SO STEAD, HE VE WYNN HIS ARNING:
TAY AWAY M WANDA D HER MILY. DO I KE MYSELF EAR?!"
SO TONIGHT, HE'LL DELIVER THE REST OF THE MESSAGE PERSONALLY.
ALL UNITS HAVE ARRIVED, COMMANDER HULL.
BUT HE ALSO KNEW THAT WYNN NEEDED MORE THAN A THREAT.
WHAT'S OUR FINAL COUNT?
NEARLY FOUR HUNDRED, SIR.
PERFECT. DEPLOY ALPHA GROUP INTO THE MAIN LOBBY, THEN SEND BAKER AND CHARLIE UNITS NEXT.
I'LL NEED TO BRIEF THE GENERALS ON A FEW DETAILS BEFORE WE STATION THE REMAINING SQUADS. SITUATION STATUS?

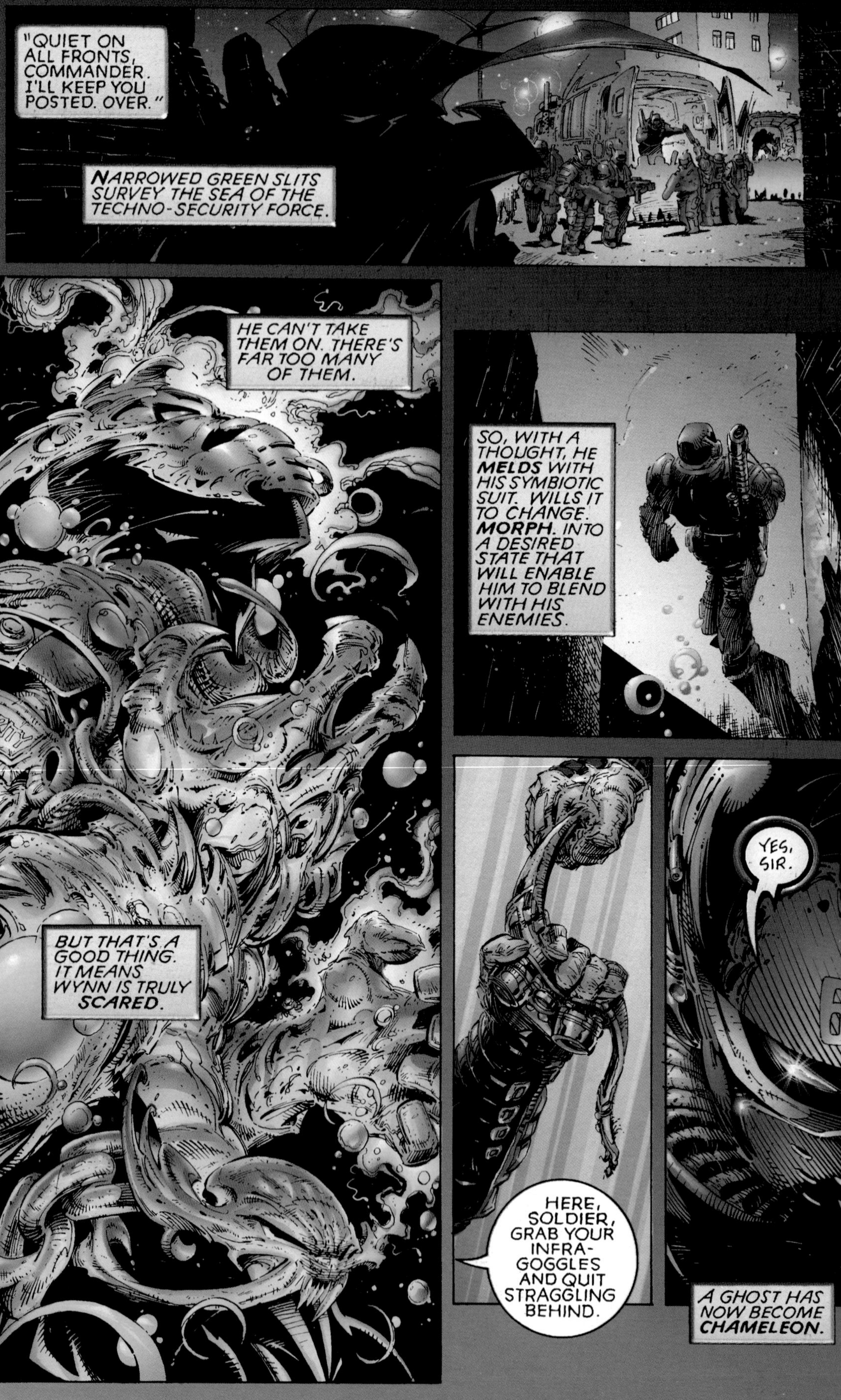
"QUIET ON ALL FRONTS, COMMANDER. I'LL KEEP YOU POSTED. OVER."
NARROWED GREEN SLITS SURVEY THE SEA OF THE TECHNO-SECURITY FORCE.
HE CAN'T TAKE THEM ON. THERE'S FAR TOO MANY OF THEM.
BUT THAT'S A GOOD THING. IT MEANS WYNN IS TRULY SCARED.
SO, WITH A THOUGHT, HE MELDS WITH HIS SYMBIOTIC SUIT. WILLS IT TO CHANGE. MORPH. INTO A DESIRED STATE THAT WILL ENABLE HIM TO BLEND WITH HIS ENEMIES.
HERE, SOLDIER, GRAB YOUR INFRA-GOGGLES AND QUIT STRAGGLING BEHIND.
YES, SIR.
A GHOST HAS NOW BECOME CHAMELEON.

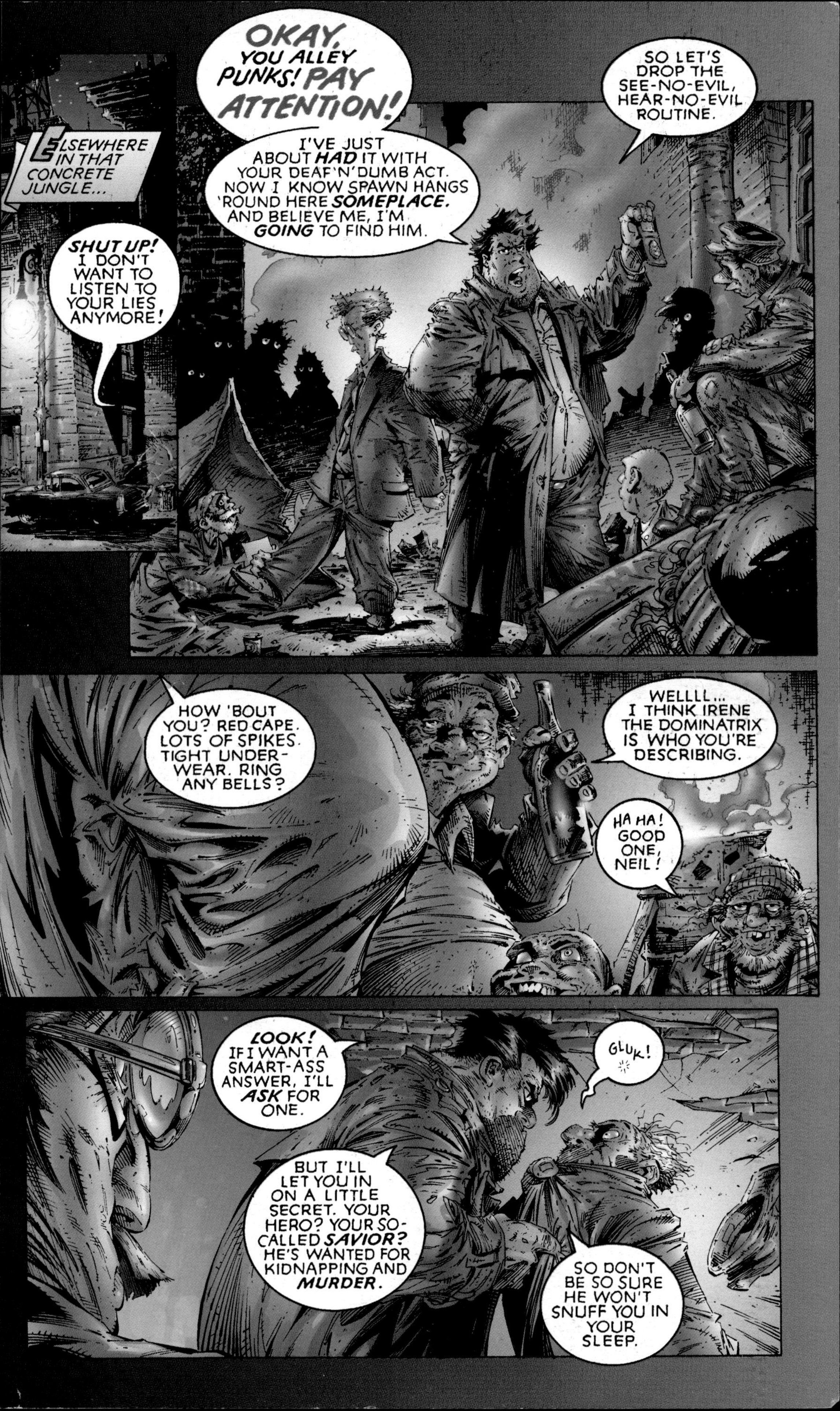

ELSEWHERE IN THAT CONCRETE JUNGLE...
OKAY, YOU ALLEY PUNKS! PAY ATTENTION!
I'VE JUST ABOUT HAD IT WITH YOUR DEAF'N'DUMB ACT. NOW I KNOW SPAWN HANGS 'ROUND HERE SOMEPLACE. AND BELIEVE ME, I'M GOING TO FIND HIM.
SO LET'S DROP THE SEE-NO-EVIL, HEAR-NO-EVIL ROUTINE.
SHUT UP! I DON'T WANT TO LISTEN TO YOUR LIES ANYMORE!
HOW 'BOUT YOU? RED CAPE. LOTS OF SPIKES. TIGHT UNDER-WEAR. RING ANY BELLS?
WELLLL... I THINK IRENE THE DOMINATRIX IS WHO YOU'RE DESCRIBING.
HA HA! GOOD ONE, NEIL!
LOOK! IF I WANT A SMART-ASS ANSWER, I'LL ASK FOR ONE.
GLUK!
BUT I'LL LET YOU IN ON A LITTLE SECRET. YOUR HERO? YOUR SO-CALLED SAVIOR? HE'S WANTED FOR KIDNAPPING AND MURDER.
SO DON'T BE SO SURE HE WON'T SNUFF YOU IN YOUR SLEEP.

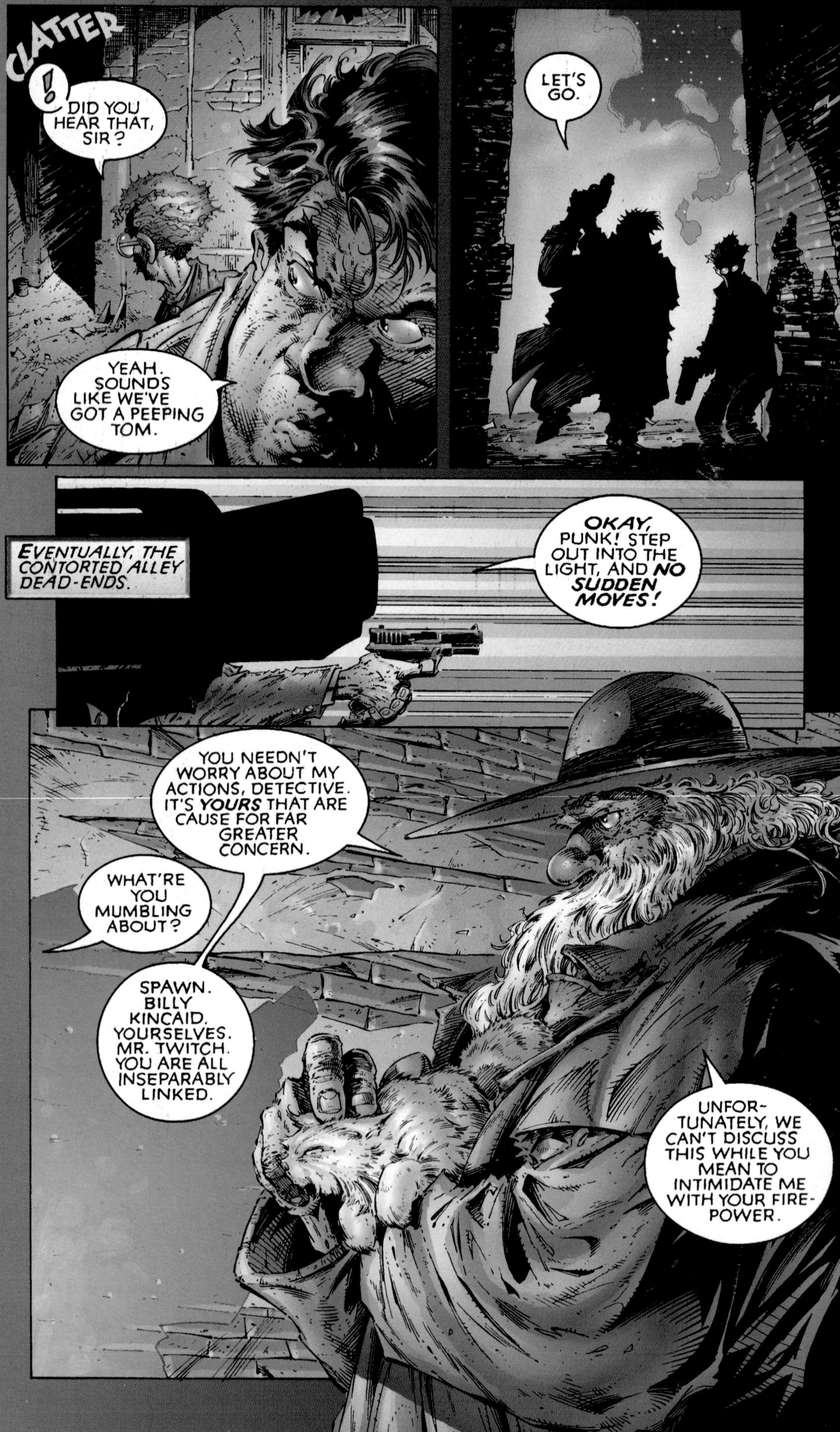
CLATTER
!
DID YOU HEAR THAT, SIR?
YEAH. SOUNDS LIKE WE'VE GOT A PEEPING TOM.
LET'S GO.
EVENTUALLY, THE CONTORTED ALLEY DEAD-ENDS.
OKAY, PUNK! STEP OUT INTO THE LIGHT, AND NO SUDDEN MOVES!
YOU NEEDN'T WORRY ABOUT MY ACTIONS, DETECTIVE. IT'S YOURS THAT ARE CAUSE FOR FAR GREATER CONCERN.
WHAT'RE YOU MUMBLING ABOUT?
SPAWN. BILLY KINCAID. YOURSELVES. MR. TWITCH. YOU ARE ALL INSEPARABLY LINKED.
UNFOR-TUNATELY, WE CAN'T DISCUSS THIS WHILE YOU MEAN TO INTIMIDATE ME WITH YOUR FIRE-POWER.

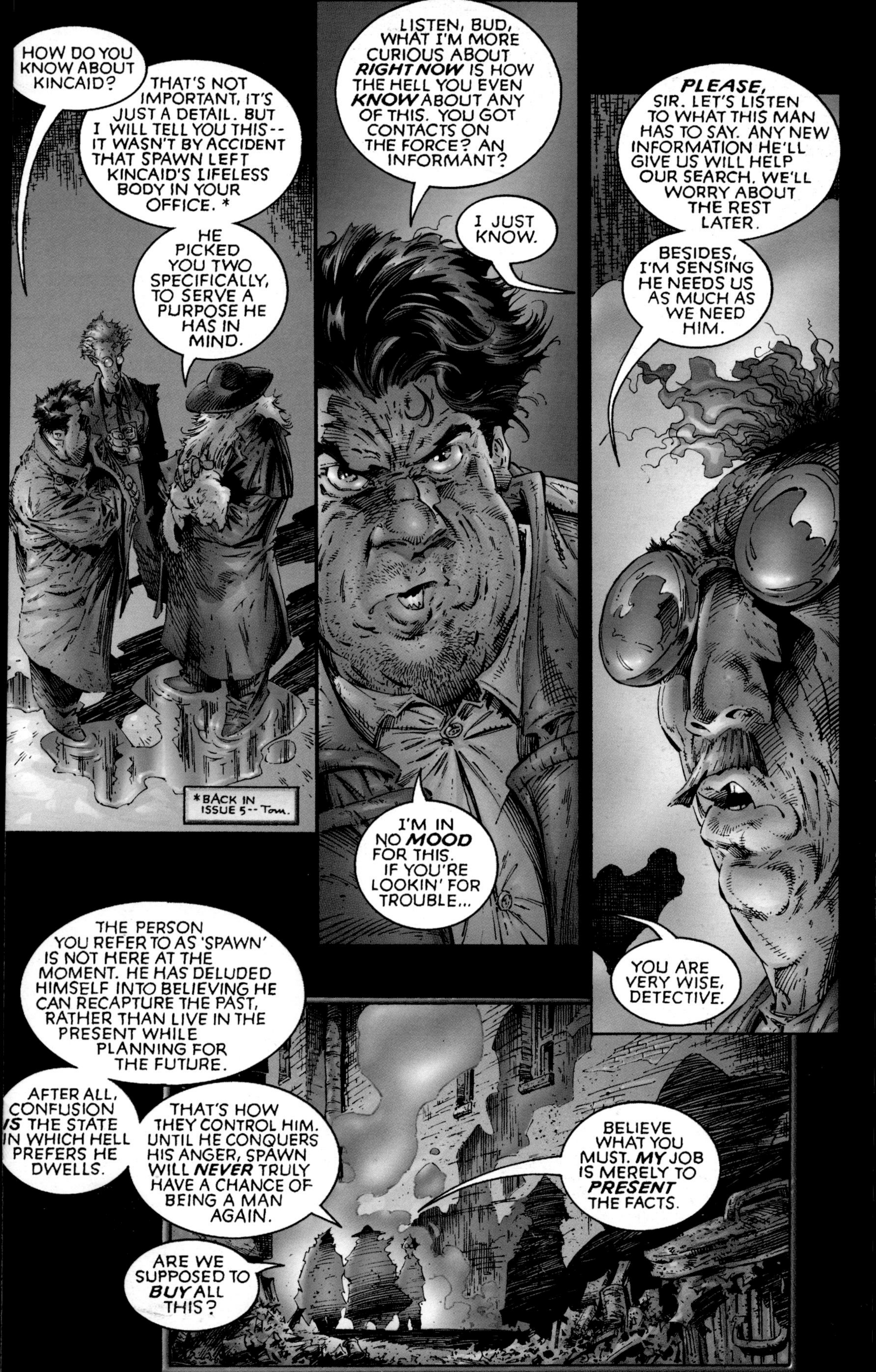
HOW DO YOU KNOW ABOUT KINCAID?
THAT'S NOT IMPORTANT, IT'S JUST A DETAIL. BUT I WILL TELL YOU THIS-- IT WASN'T BY ACCIDENT THAT SPAWN LEFT KINCAID'S LIFELESS BODY IN YOUR OFFICE. *
HE PICKED YOU TWO SPECIFICALLY, TO SERVE A PURPOSE HE HAS IN MIND.
*BACK IN ISSUE 5-- Tom.
LISTEN, BUD, WHAT I'M MORE CURIOUS ABOUT **RIGHT NOW** IS HOW THE HELL YOU EVEN **KNOW** ABOUT ANY OF THIS. YOU GOT CONTACTS ON THE FORCE? AN INFORMANT?
I JUST KNOW.
I'M IN NO **MOOD** FOR THIS. IF YOU'RE LOOKIN' FOR TROUBLE...
**PLEASE,** SIR. LET'S LISTEN TO WHAT THIS MAN HAS TO SAY. ANY NEW INFORMATION HE'LL GIVE US WILL HELP OUR SEARCH. WE'LL WORRY ABOUT THE REST LATER.
BESIDES, I'M SENSING HE NEEDS US AS MUCH AS WE NEED HIM.
YOU ARE VERY WISE, DETECTIVE.
THE PERSON YOU REFER TO AS 'SPAWN' IS NOT HERE AT THE MOMENT. HE HAS DELUDED HIMSELF INTO BELIEVING HE CAN RECAPTURE THE PAST, RATHER THAN LIVE IN THE PRESENT WHILE PLANNING FOR THE FUTURE.
AFTER ALL, CONFUSION **IS** THE STATE IN WHICH HELL PREFERS HE DWELLS.
THAT'S HOW THEY CONTROL HIM. UNTIL HE CONQUERS HIS ANGER, SPAWN WILL **NEVER** TRULY HAVE A CHANCE OF BEING A MAN AGAIN.
ARE WE SUPPOSED TO **BUY** ALL THIS?
BELIEVE WHAT YOU MUST. **MY** JOB IS MERELY TO **PRESENT** THE FACTS.

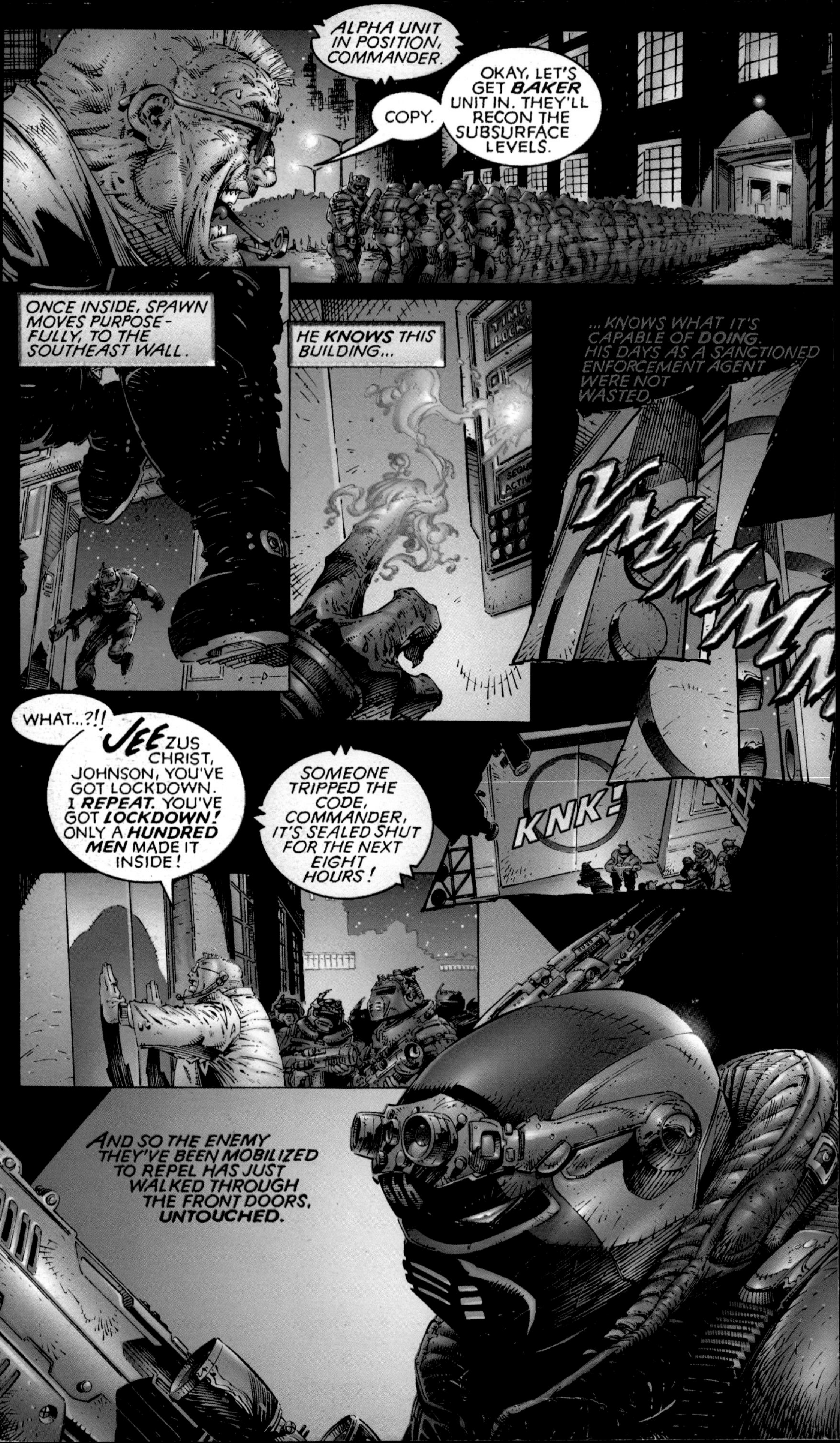

ALPHA UNIT IN POSITION, COMMANDER.
COPY.
OKAY, LET'S GET BAKER UNIT IN. THEY'LL RECON THE SUBSURFACE LEVELS.
ONCE INSIDE, SPAWN MOVES PURPOSE-FULLY, TO THE SOUTHEAST WALL.
HE KNOWS THIS BUILDING...
...KNOWS WHAT IT'S CAPABLE OF DOING. HIS DAYS AS A SANCTIONED ENFORCEMENT AGENT WERE NOT WASTED.
VMMMM
KNK!
WHAT...?!!
JEEZUS CHRIST, JOHNSON, YOU'VE GOT LOCKDOWN. I REPEAT. YOU'VE GOT LOCKDOWN! ONLY A HUNDRED MEN MADE IT INSIDE!
SOMEONE TRIPPED THE CODE, COMMANDER, IT'S SEALED SHUT FOR THE NEXT EIGHT HOURS!
AND SO THE ENEMY THEY'VE BEEN MOBILIZED TO REPEL HAS JUST WALKED THROUGH THE FRONT DOORS, UNTOUCHED.

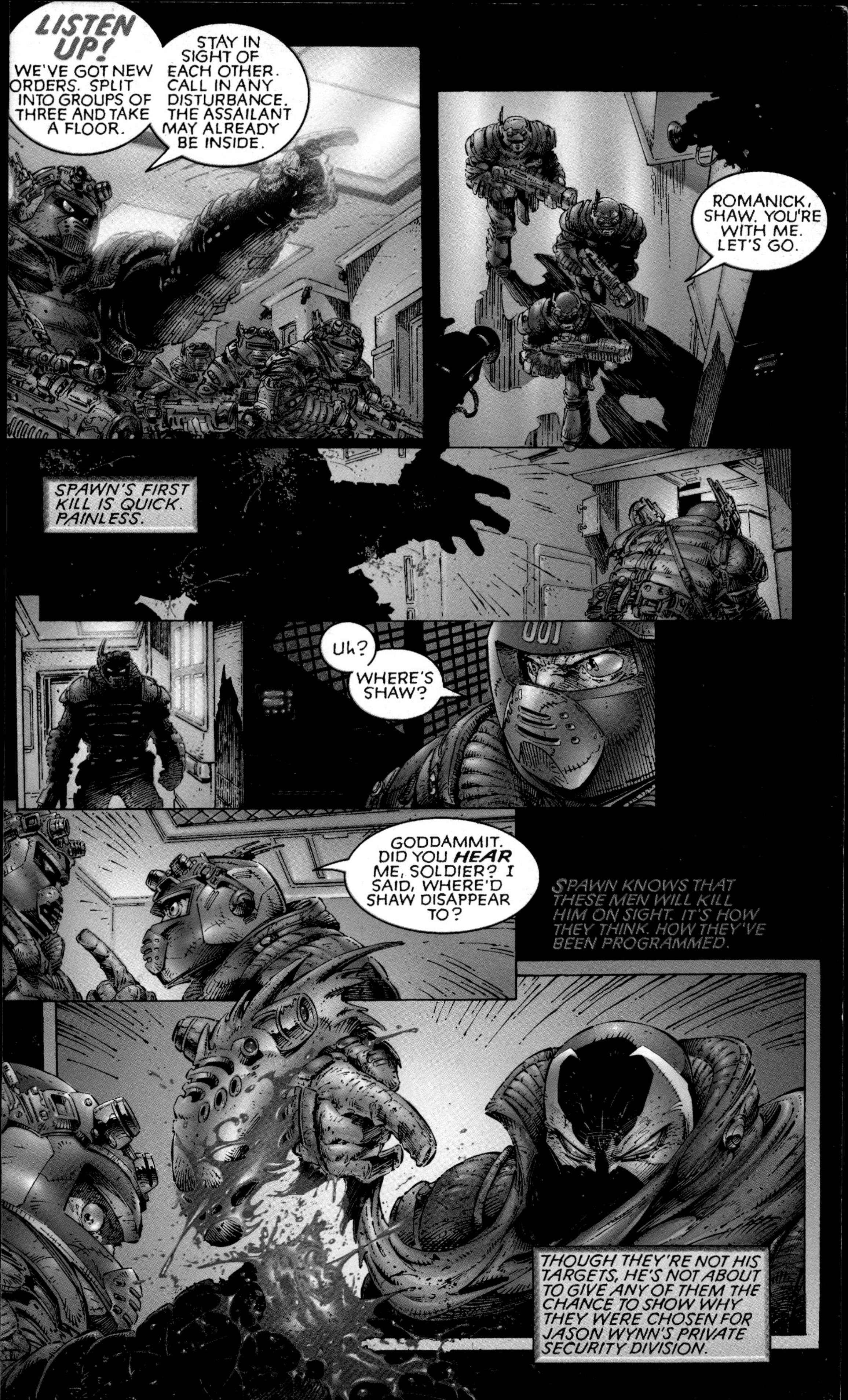
LISTEN UP! WE'VE GOT NEW ORDERS. SPLIT INTO GROUPS OF THREE AND TAKE A FLOOR.
STAY IN SIGHT OF EACH OTHER. CALL IN ANY DISTURBANCE. THE ASSAILANT MAY ALREADY BE INSIDE.
ROMANICK, SHAW. YOU'RE WITH ME. LET'S GO.
SPAWN'S FIRST KILL IS QUICK. PAINLESS.
Uh?
WHERE'S SHAW?
GODDAMMIT. DID YOU HEAR ME, SOLDIER? I SAID, WHERE'D SHAW DISAPPEAR TO?
SPAWN KNOWS THAT THESE MEN WILL KILL HIM ON SIGHT. IT'S HOW THEY THINK. HOW THEY'VE BEEN PROGRAMMED.
THOUGH THEY'RE NOT HIS TARGETS, HE'S NOT ABOUT TO GIVE ANY OF THEM THE CHANCE TO SHOW WHY THEY WERE CHOSEN FOR JASON WYNN'S PRIVATE SECURITY DIVISION.

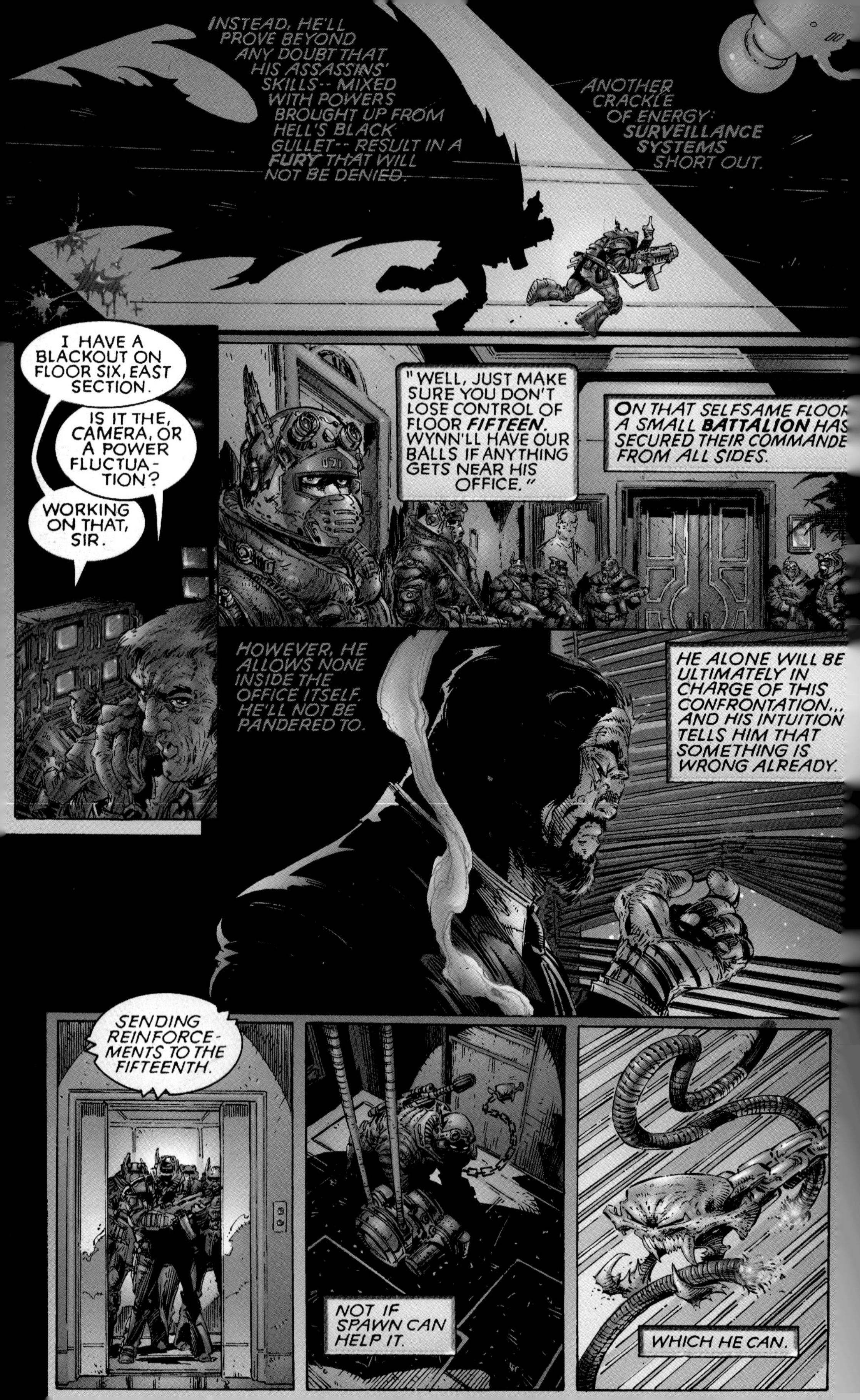
INSTEAD, HE'LL PROVE BEYOND ANY DOUBT THAT HIS ASSASSINS' SKILLS-- MIXED WITH POWERS BROUGHT UP FROM HELL'S BLACK GULLET-- RESULT IN A FURY THAT WILL NOT BE DENIED.
ANOTHER CRACKLE OF ENERGY: SURVEILLANCE SYSTEMS SHORT OUT.
I HAVE A BLACKOUT ON FLOOR SIX, EAST SECTION.
IS IT THE CAMERA, OR A POWER FLUCTUATION?
WORKING ON THAT, SIR.
"WELL, JUST MAKE SURE YOU DON'T LOSE CONTROL OF FLOOR FIFTEEN. WYNN'LL HAVE OUR BALLS IF ANYTHING GETS NEAR HIS OFFICE."
ON THAT SELFSAME FLOOR A SMALL BATTALION HAS SECURED THEIR COMMANDE FROM ALL SIDES.
HOWEVER, HE ALLOWS NONE INSIDE THE OFFICE ITSELF. HE'LL NOT BE PANDERED TO.
HE ALONE WILL BE ULTIMATELY IN CHARGE OF THIS CONFRONTATION... AND HIS INTUITION TELLS HIM THAT SOMETHING IS WRONG ALREADY.
SENDING REINFORCEMENTS TO THE FIFTEENTH.
NOT IF SPAWN CAN HELP IT.
WHICH HE CAN.

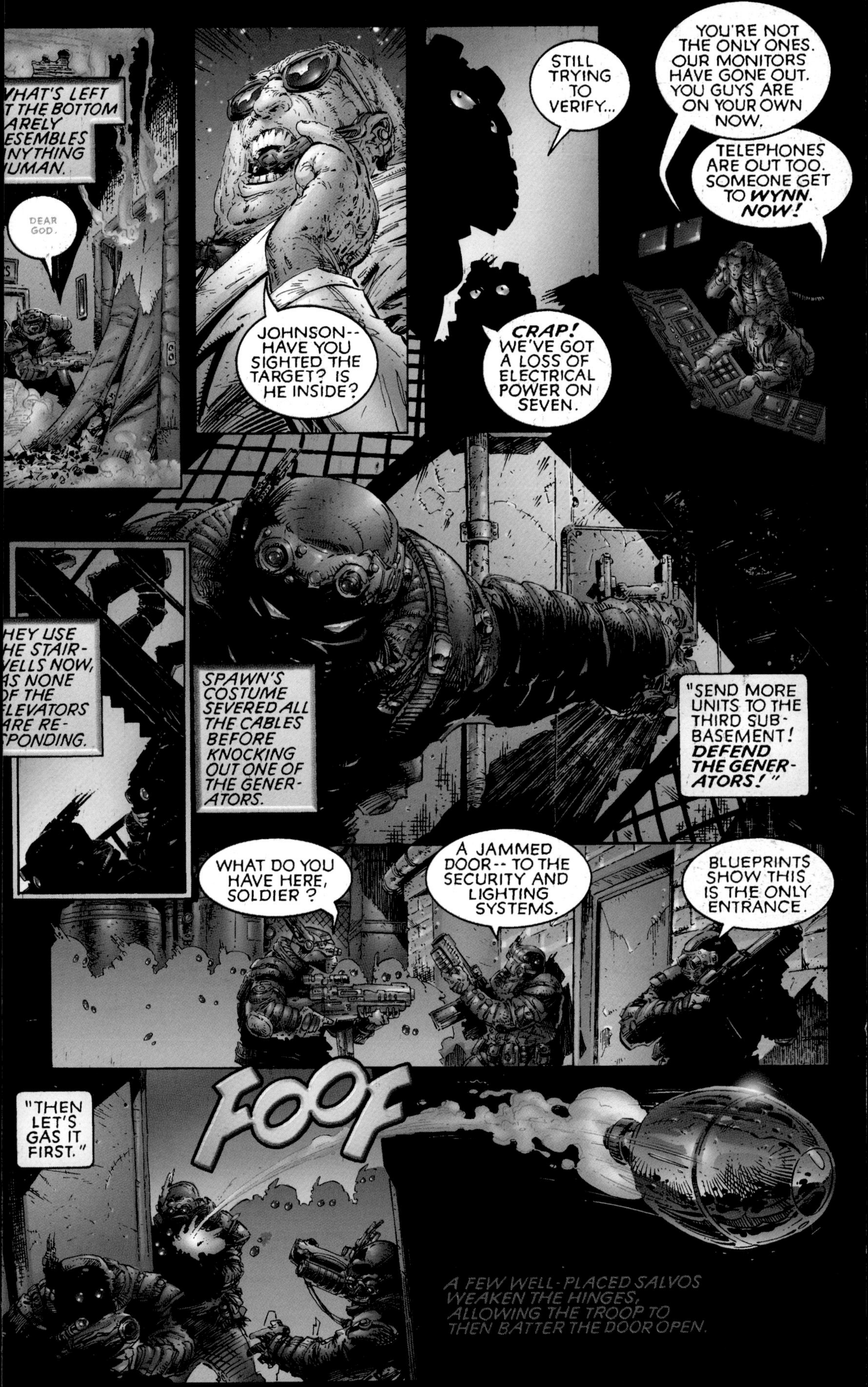
WHAT'S LEFT AT THE BOTTOM BARELY RESEMBLES ANYTHING HUMAN.
DEAR GOD.
JOHNSON-- HAVE YOU SIGHTED THE TARGET? IS HE INSIDE?
STILL TRYING TO VERIFY...
CRAP! WE'VE GOT A LOSS OF ELECTRICAL POWER ON SEVEN.
YOU'RE NOT THE ONLY ONES. OUR MONITORS HAVE GONE OUT. YOU GUYS ARE ON YOUR OWN NOW.
TELEPHONES ARE OUT TOO. SOMEONE GET TO WYNN. NOW!
THEY USE THE STAIR-WELLS NOW, AS NONE OF THE ELEVATORS ARE RE-SPONDING.
SPAWN'S COSTUME SEVERED ALL THE CABLES BEFORE KNOCKING OUT ONE OF THE GENER-ATORS.
"SEND MORE UNITS TO THE THIRD SUB-BASEMENT! DEFEND THE GENER-ATORS!"
WHAT DO YOU HAVE HERE, SOLDIER?
A JAMMED DOOR-- TO THE SECURITY AND LIGHTING SYSTEMS.
BLUEPRINTS SHOW THIS IS THE ONLY ENTRANCE.
"THEN LET'S GAS IT FIRST."
FOOF
A FEW WELL-PLACED SALVOS WEAKEN THE HINGES, ALLOWING THE TROOP TO THEN BATTER THE DOOR OPEN.

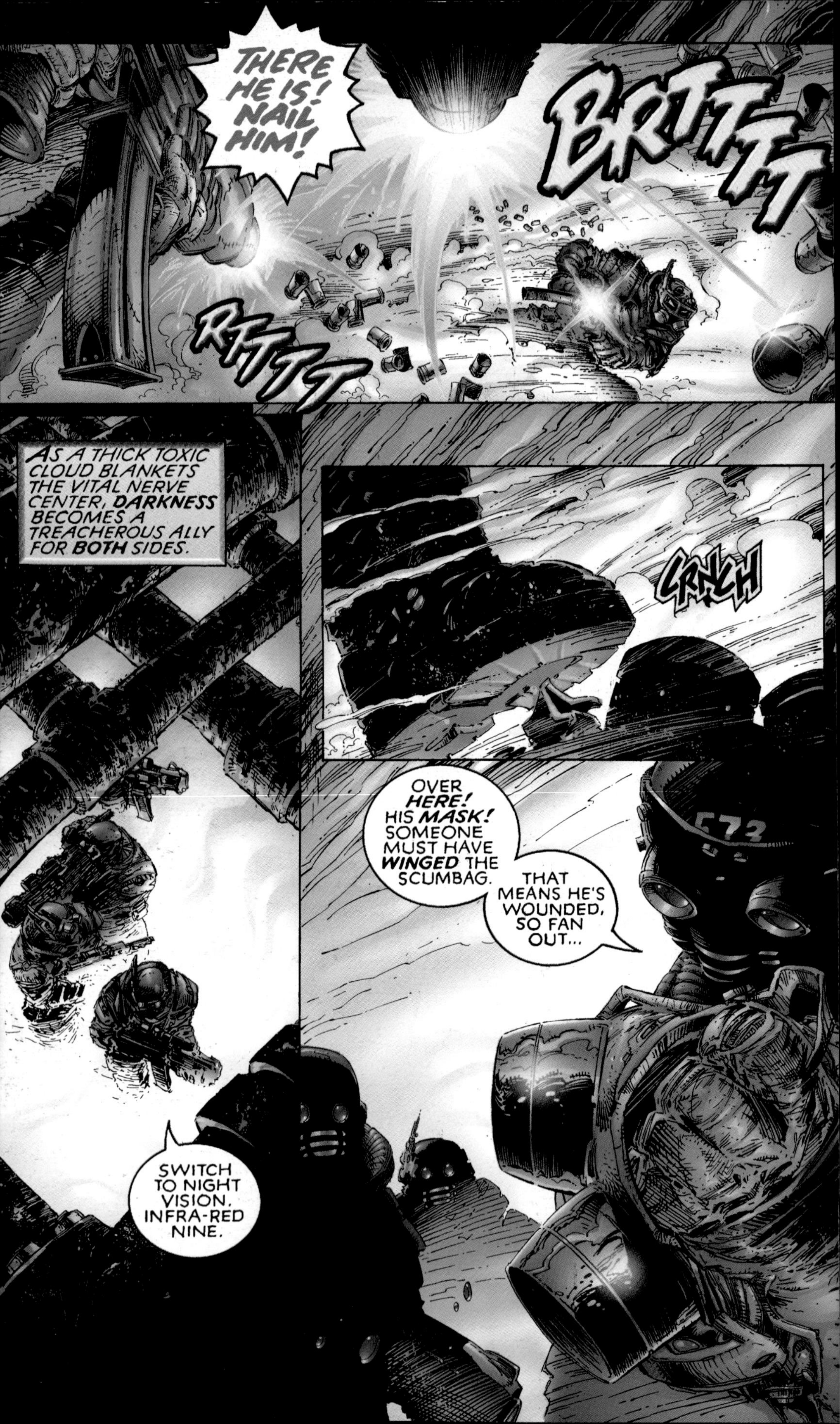
THERE HE IS! NAIL HIM!
BRTTTT
RTTTT
AS A THICK TOXIC CLOUD BLANKETS THE VITAL NERVE CENTER, DARKNESS BECOMES A TREACHEROUS ALLY FOR BOTH SIDES.
CRNCH
OVER HERE! HIS MASK! SOMEONE MUST HAVE WINGED THE SCUMBAG.
THAT MEANS HE'S WOUNDED, SO FAN OUT...
SWITCH TO NIGHT VISION. INFRA-RED NINE.

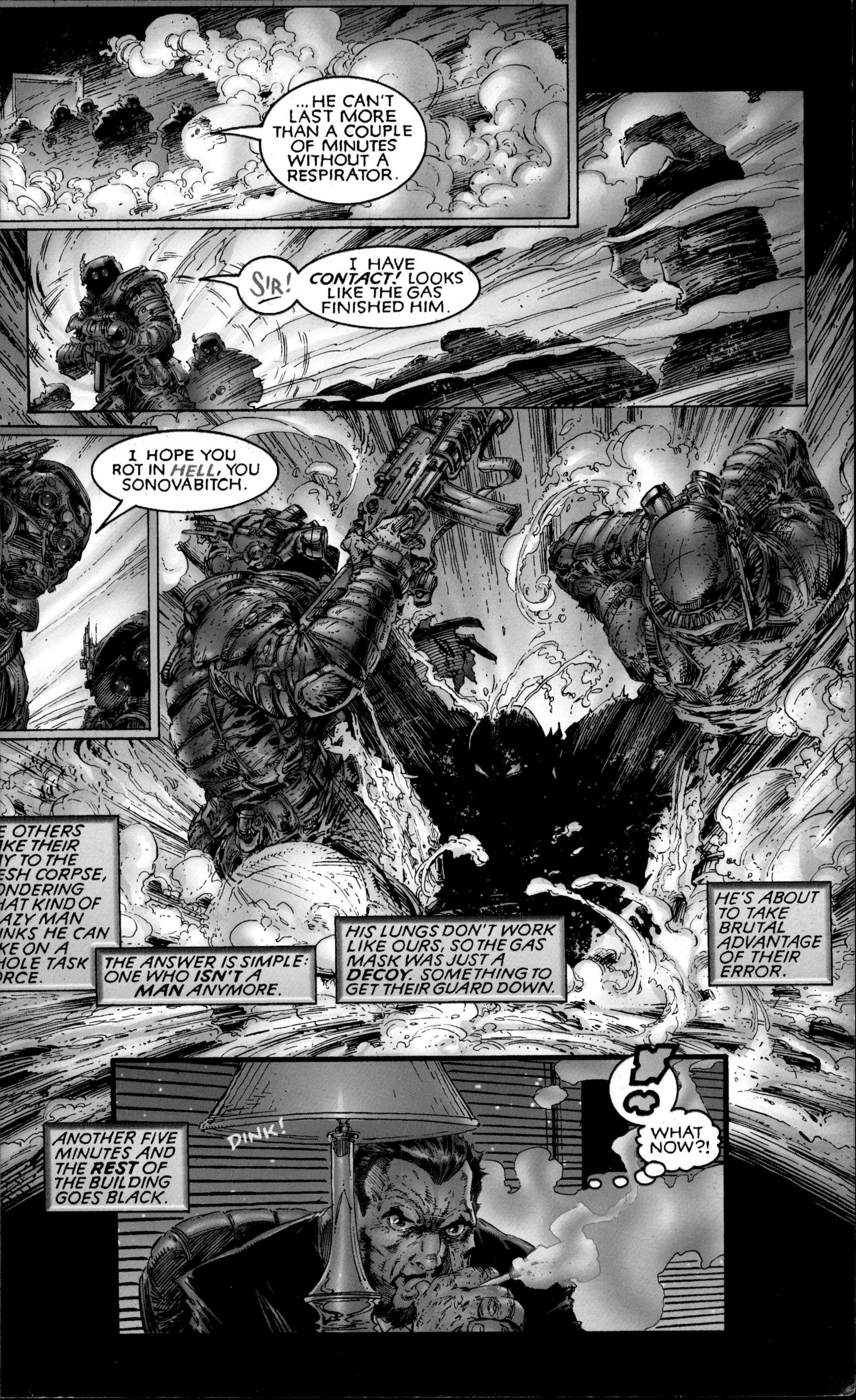

...HE CAN'T LAST MORE THAN A COUPLE OF MINUTES WITHOUT A RESPIRATOR.
SIR!
I HAVE CONTACT! LOOKS LIKE THE GAS FINISHED HIM.
I HOPE YOU ROT IN HELL, YOU SONOVABITCH.
E OTHERS IKE THEIR Y TO THE ESH CORPSE, ONDERING HAT KIND OF AZY MAN INKS HE CAN KE ON A HOLE TASK ORCE.
THE ANSWER IS SIMPLE: ONE WHO ISN'T A MAN ANYMORE.
HIS LUNGS DON'T WORK LIKE OURS, SO THE GAS MASK WAS JUST A DECOY. SOMETHING TO GET THEIR GUARD DOWN.
HE'S ABOUT TO TAKE BRUTAL ADVANTAGE OF THEIR ERROR.
ANOTHER FIVE MINUTES AND THE REST OF THE BUILDING GOES BLACK.
DINK!
WHAT NOW?!

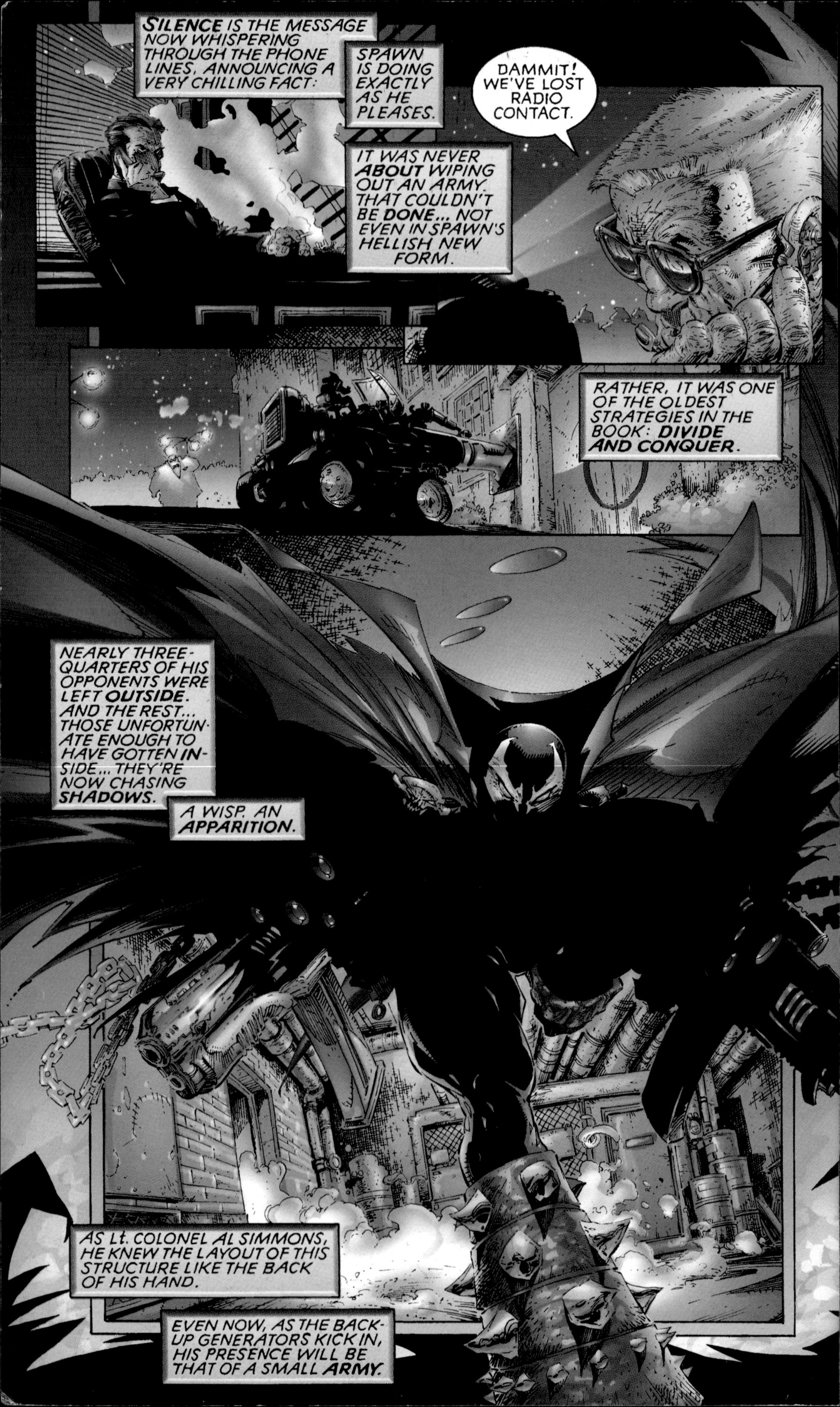

SILENCE IS THE MESSAGE NOW WHISPERING THROUGH THE PHONE LINES, ANNOUNCING A VERY CHILLING FACT:
SPAWN IS DOING EXACTLY AS HE PLEASES.
DAMMIT! WE'VE LOST RADIO CONTACT.
IT WAS NEVER ABOUT WIPING OUT AN ARMY. THAT COULDN'T BE DONE... NOT EVEN IN SPAWN'S HELLISH NEW FORM.
RATHER, IT WAS ONE OF THE OLDEST STRATEGIES IN THE BOOK: DIVIDE AND CONQUER.
NEARLY THREE-QUARTERS OF HIS OPPONENTS WERE LEFT OUTSIDE. AND THE REST... THOSE UNFORTUNATE ENOUGH TO HAVE GOTTEN INSIDE... THEY'RE NOW CHASING SHADOWS.
A WISP. AN APPARITION.
AS Lt. COLONEL AL SIMMONS, HE KNEW THE LAYOUT OF THIS STRUCTURE LIKE THE BACK OF HIS HAND.
EVEN NOW, AS THE BACK-UP GENERATORS KICK IN, HIS PRESENCE WILL BE THAT OF A SMALL ARMY.

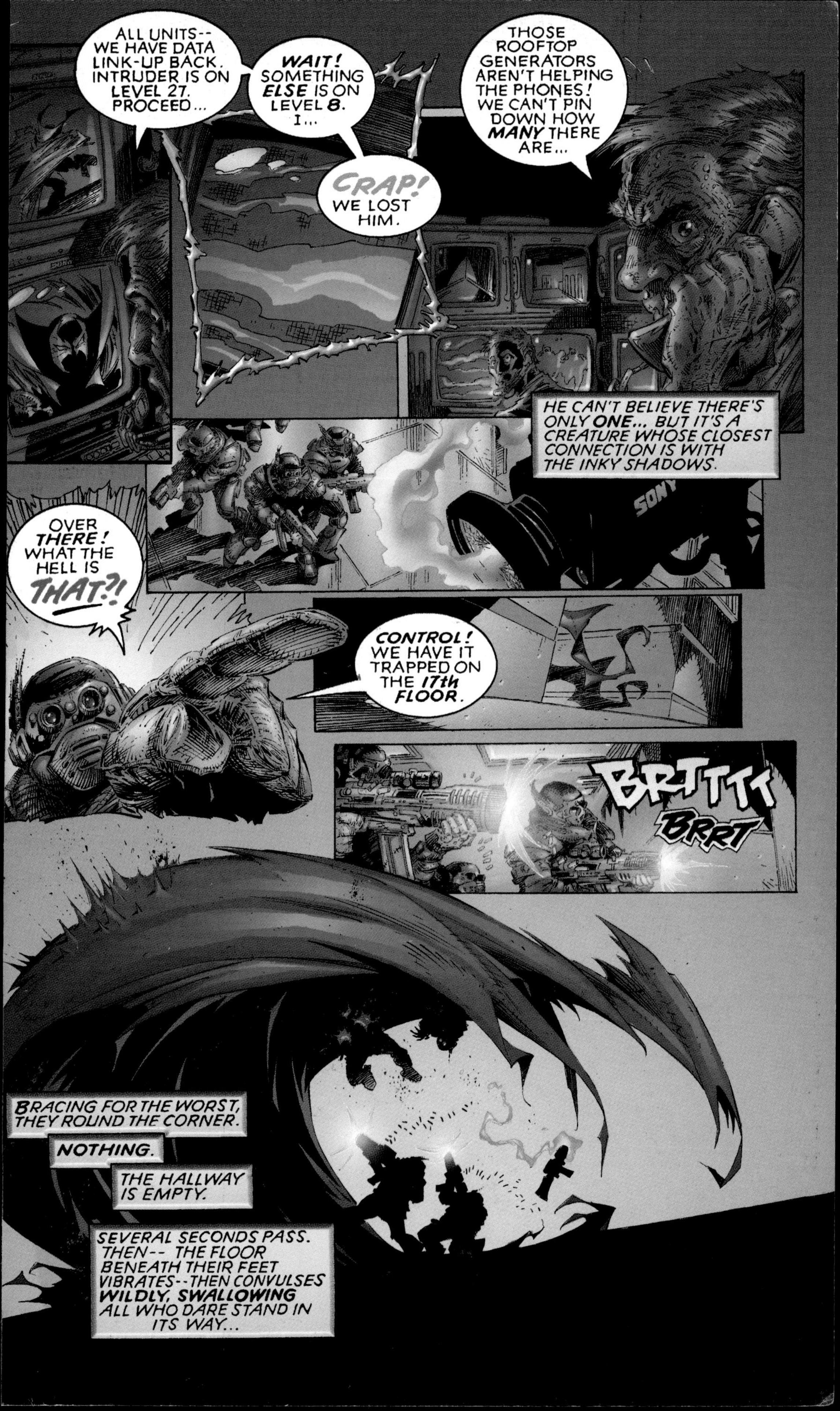

ALL UNITS-- WE HAVE DATA LINK-UP BACK. INTRUDER IS ON LEVEL 27. PROCEED...
WAIT! SOMETHING ELSE IS ON LEVEL 8. I...
CRAP! WE LOST HIM.
THOSE ROOFTOP GENERATORS AREN'T HELPING THE PHONES! WE CAN'T PIN DOWN HOW MANY THERE ARE...
HE CAN'T BELIEVE THERE'S ONLY ONE... BUT IT'S A CREATURE WHOSE CLOSEST CONNECTION IS WITH THE INKY SHADOWS.
SONY
OVER THERE! WHAT THE HELL IS THAT?!
CONTROL! WE HAVE IT TRAPPED ON THE 17th FLOOR.
BRTTTT
BRRT
BRACING FOR THE WORST, THEY ROUND THE CORNER.
NOTHING.
THE HALLWAY IS EMPTY.
SEVERAL SECONDS PASS. THEN-- THE FLOOR BENEATH THEIR FEET VIBRATES--THEN CONVULSES WILDLY, SWALLOWING ALL WHO DARE STAND IN ITS WAY...

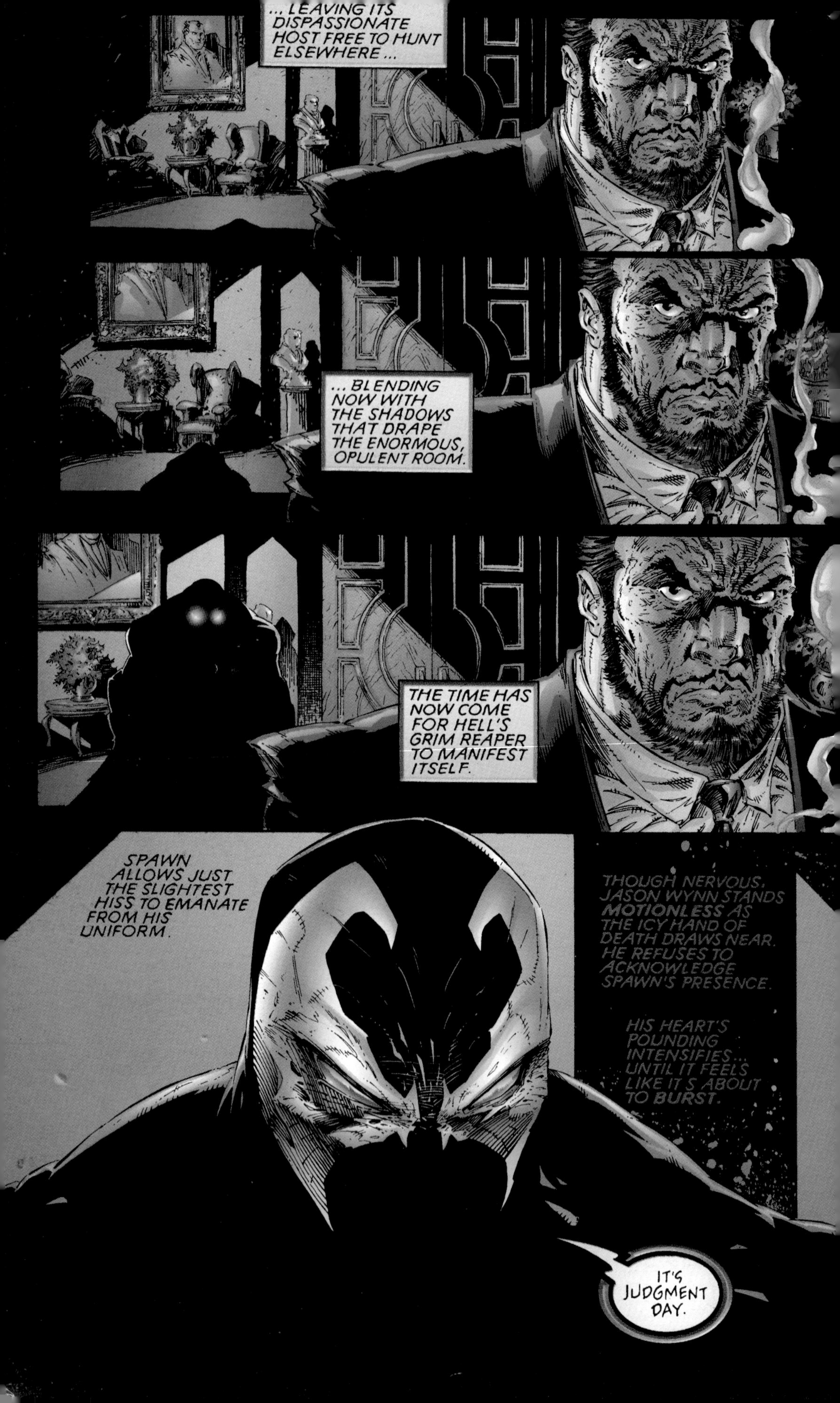

... LEAVING ITS DISPASSIONATE HOST FREE TO HUNT ELSEWHERE ...
... BLENDING NOW WITH THE SHADOWS THAT DRAPE THE ENORMOUS, OPULENT ROOM.
THE TIME HAS NOW COME FOR HELL'S GRIM REAPER TO MANIFEST ITSELF.
SPAWN ALLOWS JUST THE SLIGHTEST HISS TO EMANATE FROM HIS UNIFORM.
THOUGH NERVOUS, JASON WYNN STANDS MOTIONLESS AS THE ICY HAND OF DEATH DRAWS NEAR. HE REFUSES TO ACKNOWLEDGE SPAWN'S PRESENCE.
HIS HEART'S POUNDING INTENSIFIES... UNTIL IT FEELS LIKE IT'S ABOUT TO BURST.
IT'S JUDGMENT DAY.

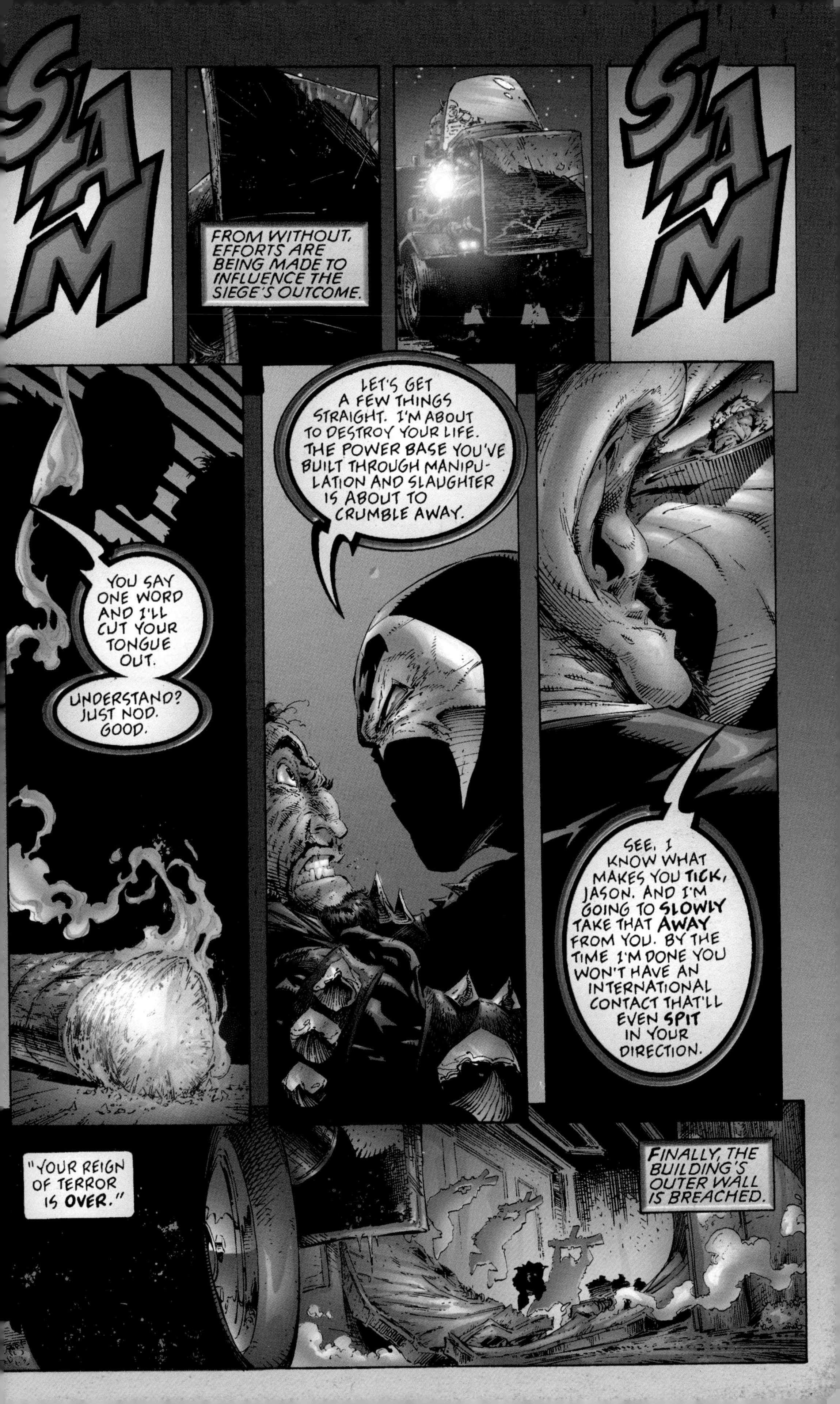
SLAM
FROM WITHOUT, EFFORTS ARE BEING MADE TO INFLUENCE THE SIEGE'S OUTCOME.
SLAM
YOU SAY ONE WORD AND I'LL CUT YOUR TONGUE OUT.
UNDERSTAND? JUST NOD. GOOD.
LET'S GET A FEW THINGS STRAIGHT. I'M ABOUT TO DESTROY YOUR LIFE. THE POWER BASE YOU'VE BUILT THROUGH MANIPULATION AND SLAUGHTER IS ABOUT TO CRUMBLE AWAY.
SEE, I KNOW WHAT MAKES YOU TICK, JASON. AND I'M GOING TO SLOWLY TAKE THAT AWAY FROM YOU. BY THE TIME I'M DONE YOU WON'T HAVE AN INTERNATIONAL CONTACT THAT'LL EVEN SPIT IN YOUR DIRECTION.
"YOUR REIGN OF TERROR IS OVER."
FINALLY, THE BUILDING'S OUTER WALL IS BREACHED.

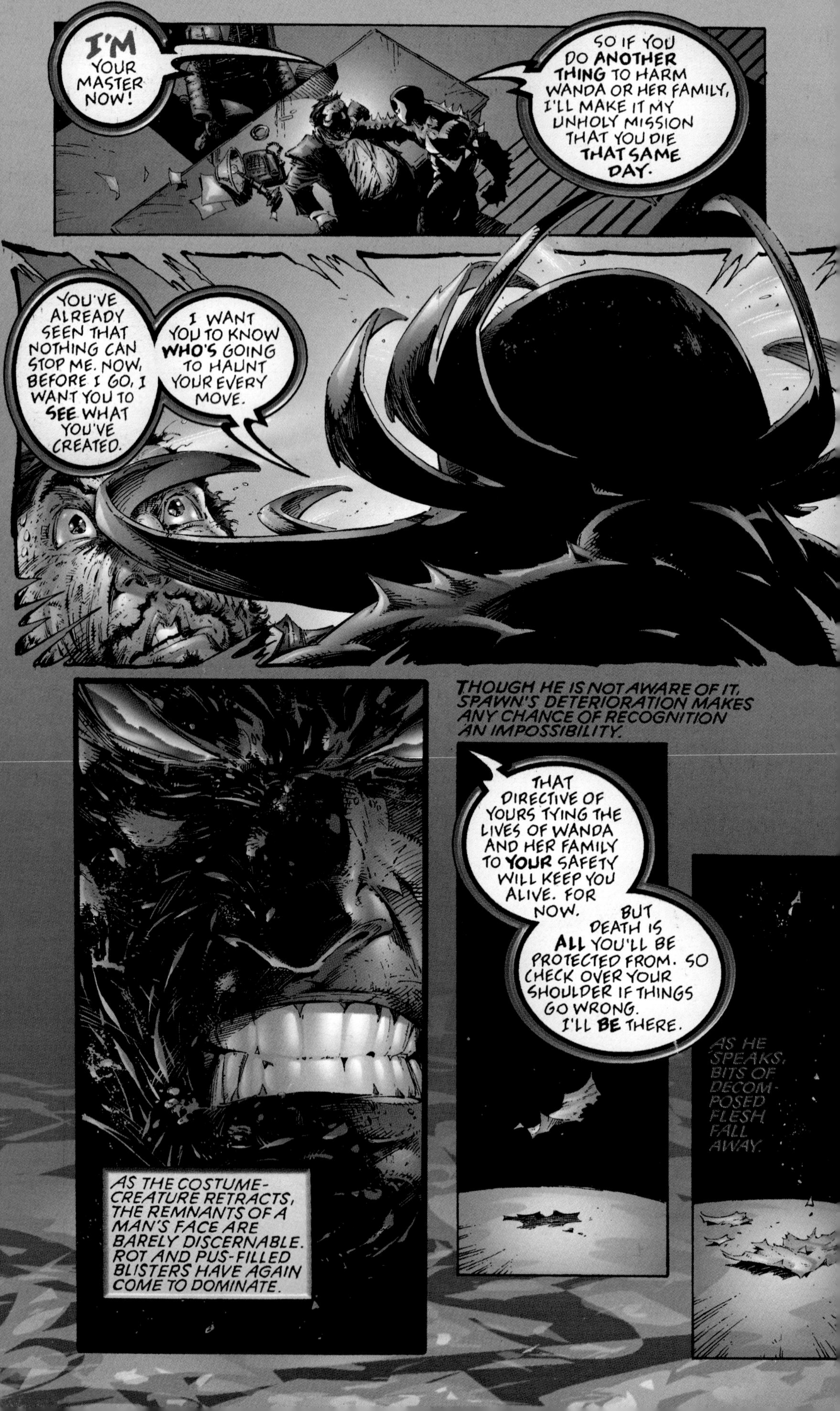
I'M YOUR MASTER NOW!
SO IF YOU DO ANOTHER THING TO HARM WANDA OR HER FAMILY, I'LL MAKE IT MY UNHOLY MISSION THAT YOU DIE THAT SAME DAY.
YOU'VE ALREADY SEEN THAT NOTHING CAN STOP ME. NOW, BEFORE I GO, I WANT YOU TO SEE WHAT YOU'VE CREATED.
I WANT YOU TO KNOW WHO'S GOING TO HAUNT YOUR EVERY MOVE.
THOUGH HE IS NOT AWARE OF IT, SPAWN'S DETERIORATION MAKES ANY CHANCE OF RECOGNITION AN IMPOSSIBILITY.
AS THE COSTUME-CREATURE RETRACTS, THE REMNANTS OF A MAN'S FACE ARE BARELY DISCERNABLE. ROT AND PUS-FILLED BLISTERS HAVE AGAIN COME TO DOMINATE.
THAT DIRECTIVE OF YOURS TYING THE LIVES OF WANDA AND HER FAMILY TO YOUR SAFETY WILL KEEP YOU ALIVE. FOR NOW.
BUT DEATH IS ALL YOU'LL BE PROTECTED FROM. SO CHECK OVER YOUR SHOULDER IF THINGS GO WRONG. I'LL BE THERE.
AS HE SPEAKS, BITS OF DECOM-POSED FLESH FALL AWAY.

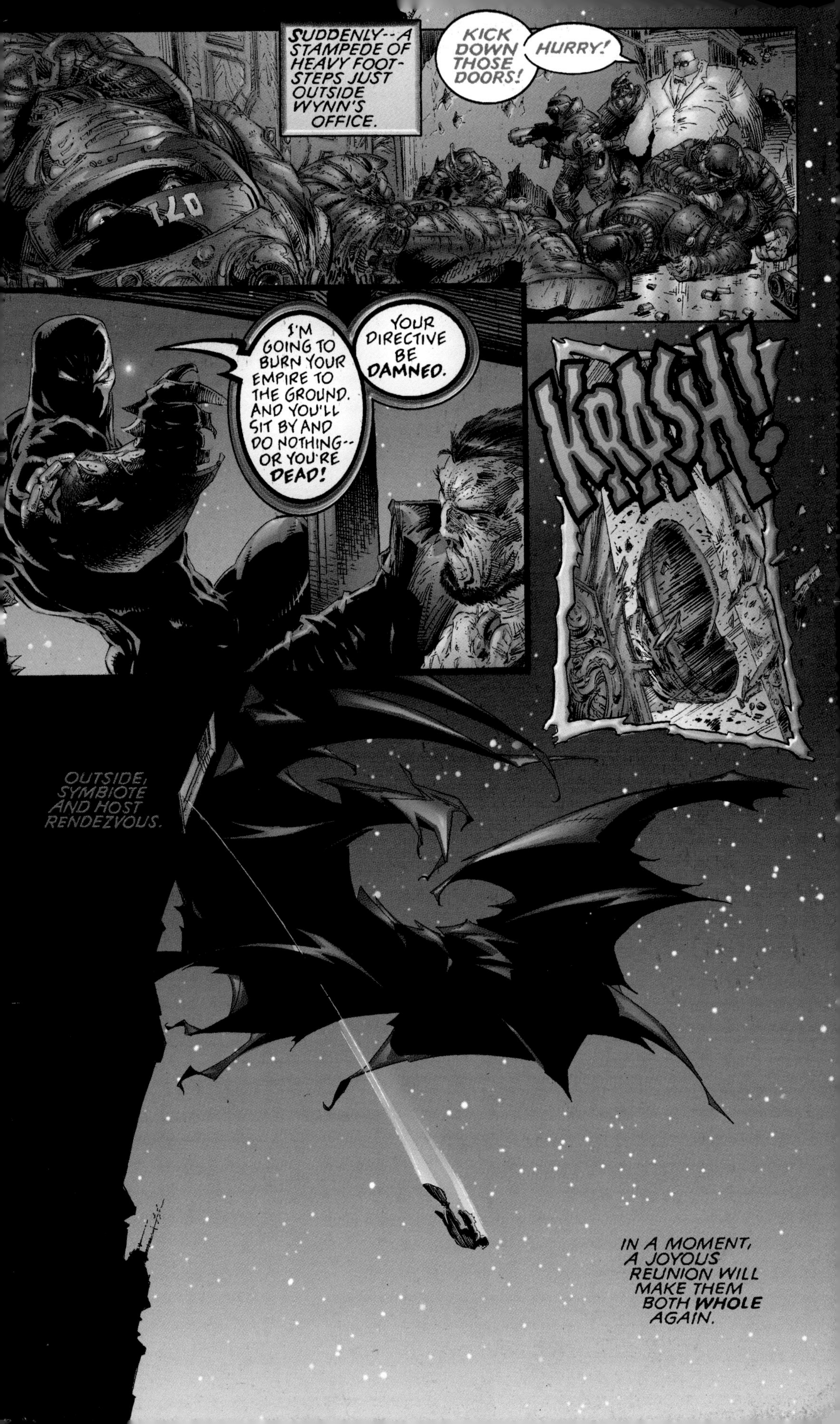
SUDDENLY--A STAMPEDE OF HEAVY FOOT-STEPS JUST OUTSIDE WYNN'S OFFICE.
KICK DOWN THOSE DOORS!
HURRY!
I'M GOING TO BURN YOUR EMPIRE TO THE GROUND. AND YOU'LL SIT BY AND DO NOTHING--OR YOU'RE DEAD!
YOUR DIRECTIVE BE DAMNED.
KRASH!
OUTSIDE, SYMBIOTE AND HOST RENDEZVOUS.
IN A MOMENT, A JOYOUS REUNION WILL MAKE THEM BOTH WHOLE AGAIN.

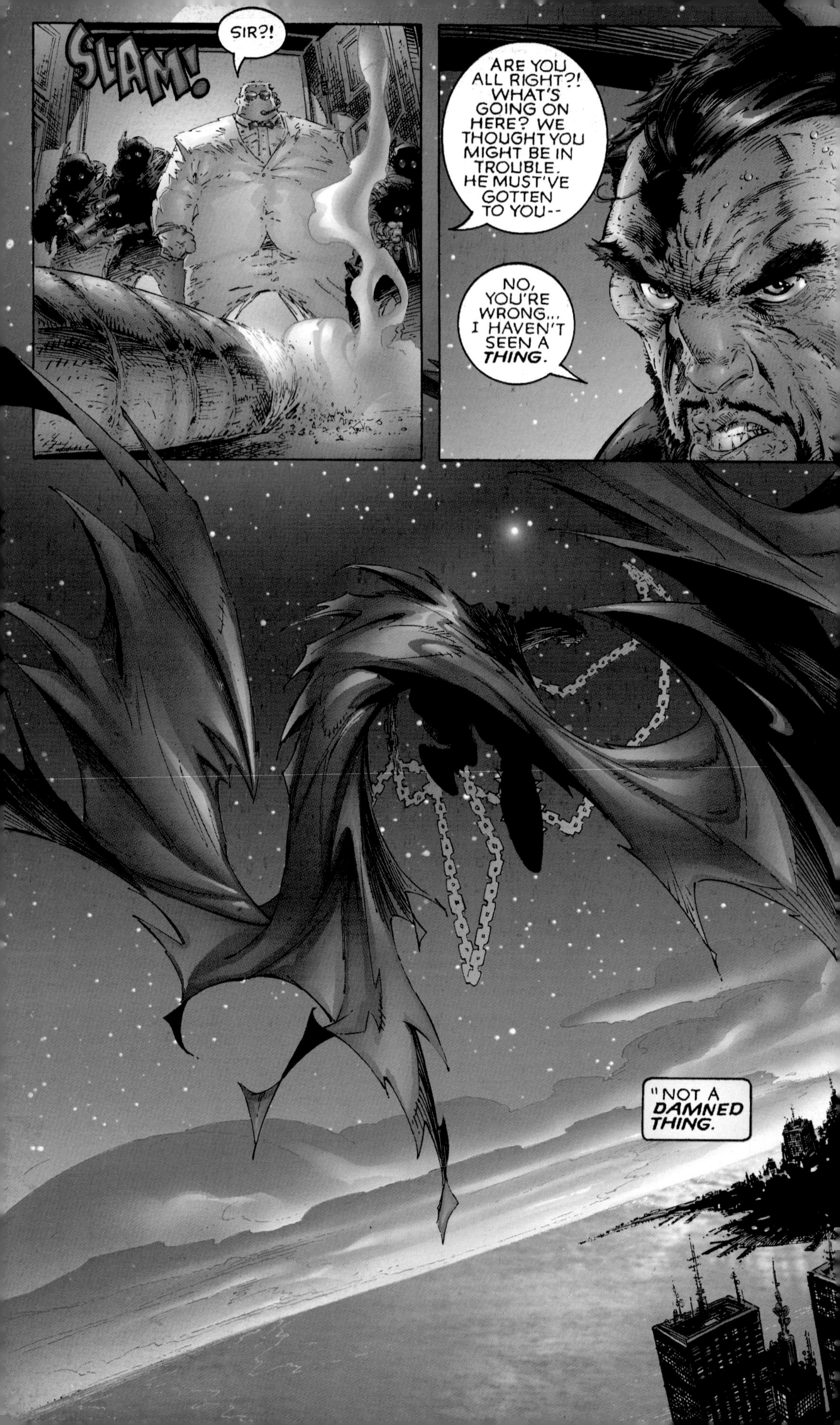
SLAM!
SIR?!
ARE YOU ALL RIGHT?! WHAT'S GOING ON HERE? WE THOUGHT YOU MIGHT BE IN TROUBLE. HE MUST'VE GOTTEN TO YOU--
NO, YOU'RE WRONG... I HAVEN'T SEEN A THING.
"NOT A DAMNED THING.

## VANISHED"

Todd McFarlane – *story*
Greg Capullo – *pencils*
Todd McFarlane, Chance Wolf & Danni Miki – *inks*
Tom Orzechowski – *copy editor & letters*
Brian Haberlin & Dan Kemp – *colour*

## DWARFED"

Todd McFarlane – *story*
Greg Capullo – *pencils*
Todd McFarlane & Chance Wolf – *inks*
Tom Orzechowski – *copy editor & letters*
Brian Haberlin & Dan Kemp – *colour*

*child's art by Cyan McFarlane*

## SANCTUARY"

Todd McFarlane – *story*
Greg Capullo – *pencils*
Todd McFarlane & Chance Wolf – *inks*
Tom Orzechowski – *copy editor & letters*
Brian Haberlin & Dan Kemp – *colour*

## RETURN"

Todd McFarlane – *story*
Greg Capullo – *pencils*
Todd McFarlane & Chance Wolf – *inks*
Tom Orzechowski – *copy editor & letters*
Brian Haberlin & Dan Kemp – *colour*

## IDENTITY"

Todd McFarlane – *story*
Greg Capullo – *pencils*
Todd McFarlane & Chance Wolf – *inks*
Tom Orzechowski – *copy editor & letters*
Brian Haberlin & Dan Kemp – *colour*

## CHECKMATE"

Todd McFarlane – *story*
Greg Capullo – *pencils*
Todd McFarlane & Chance Wolf – *inks*
Tom Orzechowski – *copy editor & letters*
Brian Haberlin & Dan Kemp – *colour*

COLLECTIONS FROM
TITAN BOOKS

NOW AVAILABLE...

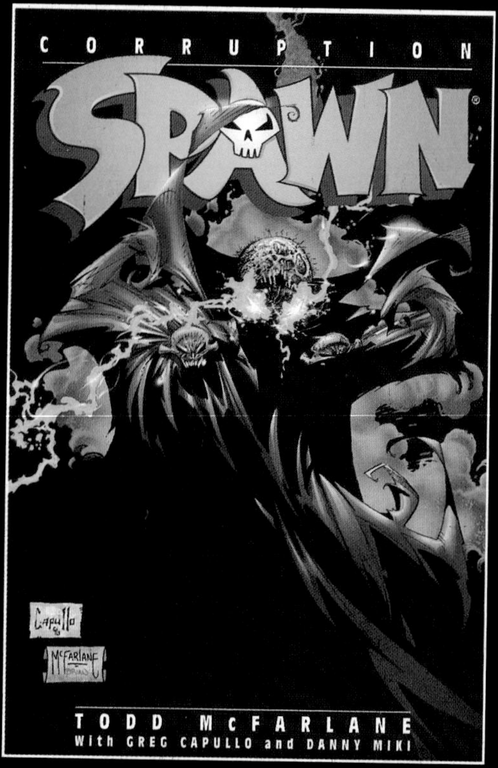
CORRUPTION
SPAWN
TODD McFARLANE
With GREG CAPULLO and DANNY MIKI

**SPAWN®: Corruption**
ISBN 1 84023 031 2

Spawn submits to the will of Malebolgia, and forms a new alliance with

# S P A W N ®
# C O L L E C T I O N S   F R O M
# T I T A N   B O O K S

## C O M I N G   S O O N . . .

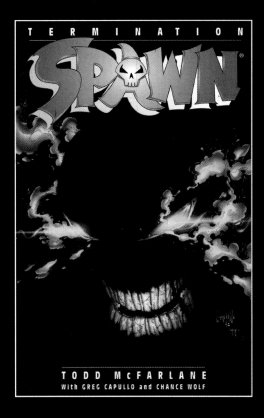

## SPAWN®: Termination
### ISBN 1 84023 161 0

Even a Hellspawn can die... and the Freak knows exactly how
to go about it!
To order telephone 01858 433169.